A Theory of Fields

A Theory of Fields

NEIL FLIGSTEIN
DOUG McADAM

OXFORD
UNIVERSITY PRESS

OXFORD
UNIVERSITY PRESS

Oxford University Press is a department of the University of Oxford.
It furthers the University's objective of excellence in research, scholarship,
and education by publishing worldwide.

Oxford   New York

Auckland   Cape Town   Dar es Salaam   Hong Kong   Karachi
Kuala Lumpur   Madrid   Melbourne   Mexico City   Nairobi
New Delhi   Shanghai   Taipei   Toronto

With offices in

Argentina   Austria   Brazil   Chile   Czech Republic   France   Greece
Guatemala   Hungary   Italy   Japan   Poland   Portugal   Singapore
South Korea   Switzerland   Thailand   Turkey   Ukraine   Vietnam

Oxford is a registered trade mark of Oxford University Press
in the UK and certain other countries.

Published in the United States of America by
Oxford University Press
198 Madison Avenue, New York, NY 10016

Library of Congress Cataloging-in-Publication Data
Fligstein, Neil.
A theory of fields / Neil Fligstein, Doug McAdam.
p.   cm.
Includes bibliographical references and index.
ISBN 978-0-19-985994-8 (hardback : alk. paper); 978-0-19-024145-2 (paperback : alk. paper)
1. Change. 2. Stability. 3. Social movements. I. McAdam, Doug. II. Title.
BD373.F57   2012
303.4—dc23   2011037122

For Heather and Tracy
&
Kylie, Molly, and Taylor

TABLE OF CONTENTS

ACKNOWLEDGMENTS

This book marks the end of a very long journey. We began talking about this book in the late 1980s when we were both newly tenured faculty members at the University of Arizona. At the time, Doug was working on his book *Freedom Summer*, and Neil was working on *The Transformation of Corporate Control*. Our conversations about our respective projects and past work led us to a startling conclusion: we came to see that, in many ways, we were working on the same generic sociological problem. At the most general level, both of us were interested in understanding strategic action and stability and change in emerging or established "fields." In the case of the civil rights movement, we were struck by how a combination of international and domestic change processes in the middle decades of the twentieth century had undermined a host of established fields—including the international system of nation-states, U.S. constitutional law, and the Democratic Party—granting civil rights forces the leverage to press for significant racial change. Eventually, these changes would grant civil rights activists—such as those responsible for planning and carrying out the Freedom Summer project—the opportunity to successfully challenge the system of racial politics in the United States.

In much the same way, we came to see that the emergence of large corporations in the United States was a result of a series of severe economic crises, crises whereby the owners of large corporations sought out ways to create a new kind of market world. They invented the modern corporation and its identities, tactics, and strategies to stabilize their world. The twentieth century continued to provide shocks to corporations, and they responded by finding new ways to innovate and create new worlds (and markets).

Based on what we saw as the common features of our cases, we began a series of discussions that ranged over several years. We talked about writing a book together but burdened with many other projects, never quite got around to it.

Finally, in the spring of 1990, when Neil accepted a position at Berkeley we were moved to act. In hopes of getting our basic ideas down on paper, we spent the summer and fall of 1990 writing feverishly, ultimately producing some 150 pages of text. That manuscript forms the basis of this one. To be sure, our thinking has evolved in a host of significant ways since 1990, but still this book remains remarkably similar in substance and spirit to the original document.

Armed with our 150 pages, we tried several times to return to the manuscript, but living in two different places made it hard to do. It was also the case that each of us took turns working on one or another major project that prevented us from devoting our full attention to the book. So, the 1990s passed and the manuscript continued to reside mainly on our word processors. In 2003 we tried again to finish the book but only got as far as rewriting the first two chapters. But some of the ideas that animated the original manuscript started to enter intellectual circulation. There were several versions of a general article we had written titled "A Political–Cultural Approach to the Problem of Strategic Action" that circulated widely. We presented that article in several venues, including the Asolimar Conference sponsored by the Stanford Center for Organizational Research; gave joint talks at the American Sociological Association meetings (several times); and gave individual talks in various departments around the country. All the while the core ideas of the project continued to enrich and inform the work we did individually. Both of us gave pieces of the original manuscript to graduate students, who used it to shape their dissertation projects. Then, too, countless other graduate students were exposed to the core ideas of the project through our classes. And eventually some of those ideas did find their way into print. Neil published the core of the theory of strategic action—the theory of social skill—in two pieces, one that appeared in the *American Behavioral Scientist* in 1989 and the other in *Sociological Theory* in 2001. Many of our core insights also found their way into various pieces that Doug wrote, including the extended introduction to the 1999 edition of his book, *Political Process and the Development of Black Insurgency, 1930–1970*. And we finally did collaborate on a 2011 article in *Sociological Theory* that presented the theory in summary form.

In our substantive fields of social movements, political sociology, organizations, and economic sociology, other scholars began to address the problem of the creation of mesolevel social orders. In the early 1990s, rational choice institutionalists, sociological institutionalists, and historical institutionalists began to recognize that we were all engaged in a similar theoretical project. While those efforts never yielded a systematic theory, important insights were being generated by scholars in a range of subfields in sociology and political science. In the social movements literature, the concepts of political opportunities, cultural framing, and episodes of contention, among others, came to be important foci of the literature. Increasingly, social movement scholars and organizational theorists found themselves in dialogue—a dialogue in which we both played active roles—and this fruitful exchange has focused attention on a number of questions we take up here. At roughly the same time, some network analysts began to edge toward and attempt to model a more dynamic view of mesolevel social order.

During this same general period (i.e., the early 1990s) we also first encountered the work of Pierre Bourdieu. We are intensely sympathetic to the Bourdieusian project. We realized that we had been thinking about many of the same issues with which Bourdieu had been concerned. Not surprisingly, one will find in the book considerable affinity between our work and his. We drew insights from these various lines of work, but just as important, we found the central thrust of these literatures powerfully affirming of some of our own core insights. It was that affirmation as much as anything that encouraged us to work intensively on the book over the past three years.

We believe the reason that all of these scholars across so many disciplines, subfields, and methodological and theoretical persuasions have come to find one another is because we have all inadvertently discerned a set of foundational truths about social life. The problem of mesolevel social order and the creation of strategic action fields is the central problem of a social science interested in how people engage in collective action, how they construct the opportunity to do so, the skills they bring to the enterprise, how they sometimes succeed, and if they do succeed, how they seek to stabilize and maintain the resulting order. These issues are central to an understanding of how people make political change, build a new product to take to market, challenge existing laws by lobbying governments, as well as how actors maintain a stable hierarchical order in popular music, haute cuisine, or any other cultural field. It is this deep sociological problem that is at the core of what we are writing about. As such, we are happy to acknowledge our interest in and relation to the wide and voluminous literature that has developed on these topics in recent years. We have learned from these various literatures, borrowed from them, and tried to contribute to them. We have returned to this manuscript in order to clarify some of the literatures' critical insights and to finally consolidate and elaborate the various strands of our own thinking.

Given the book's exceptionally long gestation period, we have accumulated a massive number of debts to both individuals and institutions. The Department of Sociology at the University of Arizona offered us both an amazing opportunity to grow and take chances. Our colleagues there—among them Mike Hout, Stan Lieberson, Al Bergesen, Bill Sewell, Lis Clemens, Woody Powell, Debra Friedman, Michael Hechter, David Snow, Roberto Fernandez, Mark Schneiberg, Cal Morrill, and Harrison White—shaped our thinking on these topics. At Berkeley, Neil would like to acknowledge Chris Ansell, Steve Weber, Ernie Haas,

Loic Wacquant, Elizabeth Armstrong, Sean Stryker, Jason McNichol, Doug Guthrie, Richard Arum, Taekjin Shin, Basak Kus, Frederic Merand, Darren Noy, Stephanie Mudge, Adam Goldstein, Jacob Habinek, and Steve Vaisey for many conversations over the years. Neil has had the great fortune to organize and run a seminar/workshop based at the Center for Culture, Organization, and Politics for the past thirteen years. The many participants in that seminar have both affected and been affected by the perspective developed in this book. He has also profited from discussions over the years with John Meyer, Dick Scott, Alec Stone Sweet, Wayne Sandholtz, Wolfgang Streeck, Paul Pierson, Woody Powell (once again), and Kathy Thelen. During the course of the book's long germination, Doug was lucky enough to collaborate with a host of others, including Chuck Tilly, Sid Tarrow, Dave Snow, Sarah Soule, Laurie Edelman, Jack Goldstone, John McCarthy, Mayer Zald, Dick Scott, Bill Sewell, and Jerry Davis, who significantly shaped his thinking on these topics. The ongoing Political Sociology Workshop at Stanford—under the leadership of Susan Olzak and Andy Walder—has served as a consistent source of intellectual stimulation since Doug joined the faculty in 1998.

We also owe a deep debt of gratitude both to our editor at Oxford, James Cook, who believed in the project from the outset, and to the four anonymous reviewers who read and commented on an earlier draft of the manuscript for Oxford and one other press. All four reviews were extraordinary, broadly affirming, incredibly constructive and, most important, seriously challenging, pushing us on a host of issues and in general urging us to clarify the most original elements of the theory. We have spent the better part of a year revising the manuscript in response to those reviews. We are convinced that the manuscript is significantly stronger for the effort. If that is so, the reviewers deserve the lion's share of the credit for the upgrade. We don't know who they are, but we are hoping they will read these acknowledgements and realize how much we are indebted to them.

Finally, the length of this journey corresponds almost exactly to the period of time in which we both raised families. Indeed, the demands of those families probably contributed to the long delay in bringing the project to fruition. We wouldn't have had it any other way. Our families have been, and continue to be, by a wide margin, the richest, most important part of our lives. It is to those families that we dedicate the book.

A Theory of Fields

1

The Gist of It

Accounting for social change and social order is one of the enduring problems of social science. The central goal of this book is to explicate an integrated theory that explains how stability and change are achieved by social actors in circumscribed social arenas. In constructing this perspective we draw upon the rich body of integrative scholarship produced in recent years by economic sociologists, institutional theorists in both sociology and political science, and social movement scholars. To this foundational corpus we add several distinctive elements of our own. Later in the chapter we sketch the basic features of the perspective in some detail, differentiating the new elements from the old. Here, however, we begin by highlighting three main components of the theory. First, the theory rests on a view that sees *strategic action fields,* which can be defined as mesolevel social orders, as the basic structural building block of modern political/organizational life in the economy, civil society, and the state. A concern with stability and change in field-level dynamics is central to the work of a number of theorists including Bourdieu and Wacquant (1992), DiMaggio and Powell (1983), Fligstein (1996, 2001b), Martin (2003), and Scott and Meyer (1983).

Second, we see any given field as embedded in a broader environment consisting of countless *proximate* or *distal fields* as well as states, which are themselves organized as intricate systems of strategic action fields. The source of many of the opportunities and challenges a given field faces stems from its relations with this broader environment. Crises and opportunities for the construction of new fields or the transformation of existing strategic action fields normally arise as a result of destabilizing change processes that develop within proximate state or nonstate fields. Finally, at the core of the theory is an account of how embedded social actors seek to fashion and maintain order in a given field. While most such theories stress the central importance of interests and power, we insist that strategic action in fields turns on a complicated blend of material and "existential" considerations. We posit an underlying microfoundation—rooted in an understanding of what we term the "existential functions of the social"—that helps account for the essence of human sociability and a related capacity for strategic action. In turn, this microfoundation informs our conception of "social skill," which we define as the capacity for inter-subjective thought and action that shapes the provision of meaning, interests, and identity in the service of collective ends.

In fashioning this perspective we draw heavily on research and theory generated by scholars in the fields of social movement studies, organizational theory, economic sociology, and historical institutionalism in political science. The volume of work at the intersection of organizational theory and social movement studies has grown especially rapidly in the past decade and a half (for some examples, see Armstrong 2002; Binder 2002; Brown and Fox 1998; Campbell 2005; Clemens 1997; Clemens and Minkoff 2004; Creed 2003; Cress 1997; Davis et al. 2005; Davis and McAdam 2000; Davis and Thompson 1994; Dobbin and Sutton 1998; Fligstein 1990, 1996; Haveman and Rao 1997; Jenkins and Ekert 1986; Kurzman 1998; Lounsbury, Ventresca, and Hirsch 2003; McAdam and Scott 2005; McCammon 2001; Minkoff 1995; Moore and Hala 2002; Morrill, Zald, and Rao 2003; Rao 2009; Rao, Morrill, and Zald 2000; Schneiberg and Soule 2005; Smith 2002; Strang and Soule 1998; Stryker 1994; Swaminathan and Wade 2001; Weber, Rao, and Thomas 2009). Social movement scholars, organizational theorists, economic sociologists, and institutionalists in political science are all concerned with how organizations can control and effect change in their environments. All are interested in how "the rules of the game" are set up and how this creates winners and losers. At the core of these concerns is the foundational problem of collective strategic action. All of these scholars are interested in how it is that actors cooperate with one another, even when there is conflict and competition and how this cooperation can work to create larger arenas of action. All have discovered that in times of dramatic change, new ways of organizing "cultural frames" or "logics of action" come into existence. These are wielded by skilled social actors, sometimes called "institutional entrepreneurs," who come to innovate, propagate, and organize strategic action fields.

In spite of the attention to, and cross-referencing of, different literatures, the increasing tendency toward disciplinary and even subfield specialization acts to balkanize thought and discourage synthesis and broader integrative theorizing. Speaking only of sociology, the subfield division of labor within the discipline has tended to make empirical specialists of most of us and for the most part the vocabularies, ideas, and even methods of the various subfields constrain broader, integrative discourse. This empirical specialization has proven fruitful to a certain degree. But it has its limits. We think it is useful to explore the commonalities across these subfields. We are convinced that most of the concepts employed in this book can be traced back to scholarship on social movements, organizations, economic sociology, and institutional analysis within political science. We are also convinced that this is so because scholars in all of these areas have discovered a foundational social reality at work, a generic theory of social action, one that provides the building blocks for the theory on offer here.

It is useful to consider what these fields have in common. All are focused on the emergence, stabilization/institutionalization, and transformation of socially constructed arenas in which embedded actors compete for material and status rewards. Political sociology focuses centrally on change and stability in the institutions and agencies of the state and their relation to civil society. Much energy has been spent trying to show how the state is a set of organizations and how powerful nonstate actors take their grievances to the state (for example, Evans, Rueschemeyer, and Skocpol 1985; Laumann and Knoke 1987). For their part, social movement scholars have been centrally interested in how perceived "threats and opportunities" catalyze the mobilization of new actors who, in turn, have the capacity to destabilize established institutions and fields in society (Goldstone 2004; McAdam 1999; Tarrow 2011; Tilly 1978). Organizational theory has been traditionally concerned with the emergence and spread of formal organizations and the role of the environment, key actors, and the state in this process (Scott 2001). Economic sociology has focused on the formation of markets and the role of firms and states in their construction (Fligstein 2001b). Historical institutionalists in political science have sought to understand how institutions emerge as answers to recurring problems of conflict and coordination and how they are reproduced—or not—over time (Mahoney and Thelen 2009; Pierson 2004; Steinmo, Thelen, and Longstreth 1992).

Scholars in all of these fields are concerned with the ability of actors to engage in successful collective strategic action within constructed social orders. We call the terrain of action within which all of these collective actors operate a strategic action field when it is well defined and unorganized social space when it is not.

Scholars in all of these subfields are also centrally concerned with the state. For political sociologists and scientists and social movement scholars, this interest makes intuitive sense. For their part, organizational theorists and economic sociologists have conceived of the state mostly as an exogenous force that provides rules for what constitutes an organization, an enforcer of those rules, and the creator of organizational environments (Dobbin 1994; Fligstein 1990). After favoring structural accounts of action for an extended period of time, a renewed interest in culture is another emphasis these subfields share in common. Culture, as a concept, has crept back into political sociology and political science (particularly historical institutionalism) in recent years. It is also central to institutional theory in organizational study (Powell and DiMaggio 1991). The "cultural turn" has been very much in evidence in the study of social movements since the mid-1980s, with much of this interest focused on the role of "framing processes" in collective action (Snow et al. 1986). But just as we will argue that sociologists have not gone very far in conceptualizing social space, we likewise see the notions of culture that inform current work in these subfields as generally impoverished. We will have much more to say about this issue later in the chapter.

The problem is that these elements—collective action, social space, culture, organization, the state, and mobilization—which are present in all of these literatures, have not been integrated into a systematic theory in any of the subfields. Indeed, authors tend to focus not only on a specific empirical phenomenon but often also on a theoretical view that only emphasizes a few of these elements. This is understandable in light of the fact that the subfield concerns often require focus on fairly narrow empirical phenomena. But this means that authors rarely engage in theory building with an eye to fashioning a more general perspective that incorporates all of these elements in a systematic fashion. This is very much our goal here.

We are also interested in rethinking the problems of the relationship between agency and structure (Giddens 1984; Sewell 1992) and the links between macrosocial processes and microinteractions (Alexander et al. 1987; Coleman 1986). Much of sociology posits that people are enmeshed in social structures that are out of their control and operating at a level that is above or outside of them. This gives people little leeway to act autonomously and makes them entirely subject to the control of social forces. Examples of such structures include the class system and patriarchy. Those concerned with the issues of micro/macro linkages and especially the structure/agent problem have struggled to understand how it is that individuals act in spite of these macro processes and/or structural constraints. Scholars in this area are also interested in the conditions under which actors are either the direct beneficiaries or the victims of structures and the conditions under which it may be possible for actors to resist structures and create alternative worlds.

While this debate has been useful in clarifying some issues, it has generally been highly abstract in orientation. For example, the debate has successfully highlighted the fact that structural accounts underestimate the role of actors in reproducing everyday life (Giddens 1984). Every time we go to work, for instance, we reproduce the part we play in the system of labor relations. If even a fraction of us stopped going to work, much of social life would quickly bog down. The debate, however, has proven less useful in other ways. It has been carried out at such an abstract level and generally outside of empirical subfields that it has not informed actual research in sociology. As a result the central concepts of both structure and action remain empirically underspecified. In spite of much concern with the idea of actors' resistance to structure, there is very little elaboration of a genuinely sociological view of how actors enact structure in the first place and the role they play in sustaining or changing these structures over time. We have only begun to theorize the complex dynamics of emergence and institutionalization, stability and change, and rupture and settlement in constructed social worlds. While scholars have invoked the idea of institutional entrepreneurs as agents of change, there has been little concern with thinking about what kind of specific social processes and skills helps these actors get what they want or successfully resist other actors' power. There has also been a decided lack of attention to how the opportunities and constraints that shape the prospects for strategic action within fields depend critically on the complex latticework of relations that tie the strategic action field to a host of other state and nonstate fields.

The literatures on organizations, historical institutionalism, economic sociology, and social movements have been directly concerned with dealing with these questions. They are concerned with how some actors work to set up stable mesolevel social worlds. Scholars in these fields have had to think long and hard about how such orders are built, held together, and destroyed. Scholars have discovered that the most useful way to push forward the discussion about agents and structures is by creating a mesolevel theory of action that involves asking what a sociological theory of actors should look like. A mesolevel theory of action implies that action takes place between and within organized groups. By understanding more clearly the role of social actors in producing, reproducing, and transforming their local fields of action, we think we can gain a great deal of leverage on many foundational issues in social life.

Finally, much of the concern in these subfields has been with trying to understand the problem of social change. On the one hand, many aspects of social life appear extremely stable across the life course and even across generations. On the other hand, it often feels as if change is ubiquitous in social life. We do not necessarily see a contradiction between these perspectives. We argue that stability is relative and even when achieved is the result of actors working very hard to reproduce their local social order. That is, even under generally stable conditions, actors are engaged in a constant set of adjustments that introduce incremental change into constructed social worlds. Skilled social actors work to improve their position in an existing strategic action field or defend their privilege. To a degree, change is always going on.

Even more difficult is the question of the emergence of genuinely new social arenas or fields. There are two related problems here. The first is to specify the conditions under which this happens. The second is to theorize the agency involved in these processes. *How* are new fields created and by whom and for what purposes? The fields of political science, political sociology, organizations, social movements, and economic sociology have been searching for the answers to these kinds of questions since at least 1960. In recent years, scholars in a number of these fields have begun to emphasize the role of framing and entrepreneurship in such efforts. It is interesting that the researchers in these subfields have ended up focusing on these few elements as central to their particular micro/macro, agent/structure problems somewhat *independently* of one another.

It is this convergence that leads us to believe that a unified theoretical view of field-based strategic collective action is possible.

In this book, we mean to offer a general theory of social change and stability rooted in a view of social life as dominated by a complex web of strategic action fields. In proposing this theory we hope to fill a significant conceptual void in contemporary social theory. Theory in sociology has become a subfield almost entirely divorced from empirical research. Within this subfield, as Abend (2008) points out, there are at least seven distinct views of what theory means. As research subfields have proliferated, so too have specialized perspectives designed to explain the specific empirical phenomenon central to the area of study. Reflecting this trend, we now have distinct "theories" (or, perhaps more accurately, orienting perspectives) for social movements, organizations, religion, culture, and so on. But increasingly these seem "thin" to us, insufficiently general to tell us much about the overall structure of contemporary society and the forms of action that shape that structure. That is what we hope to come closer to describing in the perspective on offer here.

To be sure, there *is* a handful of theories that we see as legitimate alternatives to our perspective. These include new institutional theory in organizational studies, Anthony Giddens's theory of "structuration," and, closest to our perspective, Bourdieu's account of the role of habitus, field, and capital in social and political life. We have borrowed elements from each of these perspectives and admire the ambition inherent in all of them. At the same time, however, we see all of these alternatives as, in one way or another, inadequate to the task at hand, which we take to be explaining the underlying structure of, and sources of change and stability in, institutional life in modern society.

We begin by sketching the basic elements of the theory. We then use these elements to think about the dynamics of field emergence, stability, and change. We end by critiquing some of the alternative theories on offer in contemporary sociology.

The Central Elements of the Theory

In this section we identify and briefly describe what we see as the key components of the theory. We will elaborate these ideas in subsequent chapters. We stress the following seven key elements of the perspective:

1. strategic action fields
2. incumbents, challengers, and governance units
3. social skill and the existential functions of the social

4. the broader field environment
5. exogenous shocks, mobilization, and the onset of contention
6. episodes of contention
7. settlement

We take up each of these elements in turn.

1. Strategic Action Fields—We hold the view that strategic action fields are the fundamental units of collective action in society. A strategic action field is a constructed mesolevel social order in which actors (who can be individual or collective) are attuned to and interact with one another on the basis of shared (which is not to say consensual) understandings about the purposes of the field, relationships to others in the field (including who has power and why), and the rules governing legitimate action in the field. A stable field is one in which the main actors are able to reproduce themselves and the field over a fairly long period of time.

All collective actors (e.g., organizations, clans, supply chains, social movements, and governmental systems) are themselves made up of strategic action fields. When these fields are organized in a formal bureaucratic hierarchy, with fields essentially embedded within other fields, the resulting vertical system looks a lot like a traditional Russian doll: with any number of smaller fields nested inside larger ones. So, for example, an office in a firm can be a strategic action field. It is itself located in a larger structure within a firm, say a division. That division vies for resources in a firm structure. The firm interacts in a larger field with its competitors and challengers. They are embedded in an international division of labor. Each of these strategic action fields constitutes a mesolevel social order in the sense that it can be fruitfully analyzed as containing all of the elements of an order from the perspective we outline here. In general, the ties between fields highlight the interdependence of strategic action fields and their very real potential to effect change in one another. Indeed, we will argue that these links constitute one of the main sources of change and stability in all fields.

This first element of the theory is the insight that action takes place in constructed mesolevel social orders, which is implied in various versions of institutional theory. These orders have been variously called *sectors* (Scott and Meyer 1983), *organizational fields* (DiMaggio and Powell 1983), *games* (Scharpf 1997), *fields* (Bourdieu and Wacquant 1992), *networks* (Powell et al. 2005), and, in the case of government, *policy domains* (Laumann and Knoke 1987) and *policy systems/subsystems* (Sabatier 2007). In the economic realm, *markets* can be thought of as a specific kind of constructed order (Fligstein 1996, 2001b). For their part, social movement scholars conceive of movements as emergent orders composed, in the most successful cases, of collections of formal social movement organizations and more informal groups of activists. McCarthy and Zald

(1973, 1977) refer to these emergent orders as *social movement industries*. Movements also have the potential to spawn *conflict arenas* composed of movement groups, state actors, the media, and countermovement groups, among others (McAdam 1999: chapter 5).

If, however, many analysts have come to focus on mesolevel orders as central to institutional life, their conceptions of these fields are quite varied. Bourdieu sees "social power" as the underlying key to both the structure and logic of any given field. Institutional theorists such as Jepperson (1991) tend toward a more culturally constructionist view of fields, stressing the unifying force of shared understandings among a set of mutually attuned actors resulting in a "taken for granted" everyday reality.

Our view attempts to combine the social constructionist aspects of institutional theory with a central interest in understanding the sources of stability and change in strategic action fields. We see strategic action fields as socially constructed arenas within which actors with varying resource endowments vie for advantage (Bourdieu and Wacquant 1992; Emirbayer and Johnson 2008; Martin 2003). Strategic action fields are socially constructed in three important respects. First, membership in these fields is based far more on subjective "standing" than on objective criteria. So, for example, while there are some 2,500 four-year colleges and universities in the United States, they do not, ordinarily, constitute a single strategic action field. Instead subsets of these schools have come to regard themselves as comparator institutions. It is within these more narrowly constructed educational fields that schools compete and cooperate with each other.

The boundaries of strategic action fields are not fixed but shift depending on the definition of the situation and the issues at stake. So, for instance, imagine if Congress was to take up a sweeping reform bill that threatened to change the tax status of all institutions of higher education. For the duration of the conflict, the narrow comparator strategic action fields described above would cease to be all that relevant. Instead the conflict would define a new field, composed of all 2,500 colleges and universities, which would probably unite and oppose such legislation. So fields are constructed on a situational basis, as shifting collections of actors come to define new issues and concerns as salient.

Finally, and most important, fields are constructed in the sense that they turn on a set of understandings fashioned over time by members of the field. The term "institutional logics" has often been used to characterize these shared understandings (Friedland and Alford 1991; Scott 2001). We think this concept is too broad and too amorphous to really capture the set of shared meanings that structure field dynamics. We want to distinguish between four categories of shared understandings that are critical to field-level interaction. First, there is a general, shared understanding of what is going on in the field, that is, what is at stake (Bourdieu and Wacquant 1992). Here, we would expect that actors in a settled strategic action field would share a consensus as to what is going on. Such a consensus does not imply that the division of spoils in the field is viewed as legitimate, only that the overall account of the terrain of the field is shared by most field actors.

Second, there is a set of actors in the field who can be generally viewed as possessing more or less power. Here, we have in mind that actors occupy a general position within the field and further that they share a generalized sense of how their position relates to that of others in the strategic action field. One way of thinking about this is that actors know who their friends, their enemies, and their competitors are because they know who occupies those roles in the field.

Third, there is a set of shared understandings about the nature of the "rules" in the field. By this, we mean that actors understand what tactics are possible, legitimate, and interpretable for each of the roles in the field. This is different from knowing what is generally at stake. This is the cultural understanding of what forms of action and organization are viewed as legitimate and meaningful within the context of the field.

Finally, there is the broad interpretive frame that individual and collective strategic actors bring to make sense of what others within the strategic action field are doing. And here, rather than positing a consensual frame that holds for all actors, which is implied by the idea of "logics," we expect instead to see different interpretative frames reflecting the relative positions of actors within the strategic action field. We expect that actors will tend to see the moves of others from their own perspective in the field. In most fields, for example, we expect that dominant or incumbent actors will embrace a frame of reference that encapsulates their self-serving view of the field, while dominated or challenger actors will adopt/ fashion an "oppositional" perspective. The reactions of more and less powerful actors to the actions of others thus reflect their social position in the field.

All of these aspects of strategic action field structure are lumped together in the conventional view of institutional logics. This leads to a number of problems. The use of the term "institutional logic" tends to imply way too much consensus in the field about what is going on and why and way too little concern over actors' positions, the creation of rules in the field that favor the more powerful over the less powerful, and the general use of power in strategic action fields. In short, the relative and potentially oppositional positions of actors within the field are not well captured by the concept of institutional logic. The term fails to capture the ways in which different actors in different positions in the strategic action field will vary in their interpretation of events and respond to them from their own point of view.

One of the key differences between our perspective and most versions of institutional theory is that we see fields as only rarely organized around a truly consensual "taken for granted" reality. The general image for most institutionalists is one of routine social order and reproduction. In most versions of institutional theory, the routine reproduction of that field is assured because all actors share the same perceptions of their opportunities and constraints and act accordingly. To the extent that change occurs at all, it is relatively rare and almost never intentional. In contrast, for us, there is constant jockeying going on in fields as a result of their contentious nature. Actors make moves and other actors have to interpret them, consider their options, and act in response. Actors who are both more and less powerful are constantly making adjustments to the conditions in the field given their position and the actions of others. This leaves substantial latitude for routine jockeying and piecemeal change in the positions that actors occupy. Even in "settled times," less powerful actors can learn how to take what the system will give them and are always looking to marginally improve their positions in the field. Constant low-level contention and incremental change are the norm in fields rather than the image of routine reproduction that tends to define most versions of institutional theory.

We can extend this view even more. In place of the simplistic distinction between settled and unsettled fields, we argue that even settled fields exhibit enormous variation in the extent to which there is consensus. Settled fields should, we argue, be arrayed along a continuum, anchored on one end by those exceedingly rare strategic action fields that exhibit very high consensus on all of the subjective dimensions touched on above and on the other by those fields that, despite widespread dissent and open conflict, nonetheless exhibit a stable structure over time. Indeed, if one studies a particular strategic action field over time, one could observe it moving back and forth on such a continuum as crisis undermines existing relationships and meanings and order becomes reestablished with a new set of relationships and groups. If the field is more oriented toward the pole of settlement, conflict will be lessened and the positions of actors more easily reproduced.

But if there are more unsettled conditions or the relative power of actors is equalized, then there is a possibility for a good deal of jockeying for advantage. All of the meanings in a field can break down including what the purpose of the field is, what positions the actors occupy, what the rules of the game are, and how actors come to understand what others are doing. Indeed, at this extreme, we have left the continuum and entered the realm of open conflict in which the very existence and structure of a strategic action field is up for grabs. It is possible for a whole new order to appear with a redefinition of the positions of the players, the rules of the game, and the overriding ends of the strategic action field. The purpose of our theorization is to understand better where such orders come from and how they are continuously contested and constantly oscillating between greater or lesser stability and order. In short, we expect strategic action fields to always be in some sort of flux, as the process of contention is ongoing and the threats to an order always present to some degree. This stress on the essential contentious character of fields and the constancy of change pressures within strategic action fields is one of the distinctive new elements that we bring to this theoretical project.

Our view has a great deal of implication for how to think about change and stability in fields. We think it is useful to separate out the dramatic changes that occur in the formation and transformation of a field from the more piecemeal changes that result from contention in fields on an ongoing basis. The more radical moments of change can be characterized through a more social movement–like process that we will describe shortly. The more continuous sources of change will be the result of the period to period jockeying for position within the field. We expect that as the arrangements in the field are challenged successfully by various groups, the possibility for change is ongoing. We will discuss this issue more thoroughly in chapter 4.

2. Incumbents, Challengers, and Governance Units—Our interest in the dynamics of both conflict/change and stability/order is reflected in our general characterization of the composition of strategic action fields. We see fields as composed of *incumbents, challengers,* and very often *governance units.* First introduced by Gamson (1975), the incumbent/challenger distinction has long been a conceptual staple of social movement theory. Incumbents are those actors who wield disproportionate influence within a field and whose interests and views tend to be heavily reflected in the dominant organization of the strategic action field.[1] Thus, the purposes and structure of the field are adapted to their interests, and the positions in the field are defined by their claim on the lion's share of material and status rewards. In addition, the rules of the field tend to favor them, and shared meanings tend to legitimate and support their privileged position within the strategic action field.

Challengers, on the other hand, occupy less privileged niches within the field and ordinarily wield little influence over its operation. While they recognize the nature of the field and the dominant logic of incumbent actors, they can usually articulate an alternative vision of the field and their position in it. This does not, however, mean that challengers are normally in open revolt against the inequities of the field or aggressive purveyors of oppositional logics. On the contrary, most of the time challengers can be expected to conform to the prevailing order, although they often do so grudgingly, taking what the system gives them and awaiting new opportunities to challenge the structure and logic of the system.

In addition to incumbents and challengers, many strategic action fields have *internal governance units* that are charged with overseeing compliance with field

---

[1] Gamson's actual distinction was between challengers and *members,* but "incumbents" has come to be the preferred alternative term.

rules and, in general, facilitating the overall smooth functioning and reproduction of the system. It is important to note that these units are *internal* to the field and distinct from *external* state structures that hold jurisdiction over all, or some aspect of, the strategic action field. Virtually every industry has its trade association. The system of higher education in the United States has various accrediting bodies, police departments have internal affairs divisions, and bond markets have their rating agencies. It is important to note that virtually all such governance units bear the imprint of the influence of the most powerful incumbents in the field and the ideas that are used to justify their dominance. Regardless of the legitimating rhetoric that motivates the creation of such units, the units are generally there *not* to serve as neutral arbiters of conflicts between incumbents and challengers but to reinforce the dominant perspective and guard the interests of the incumbents.

The presence of these governance units aids the incumbents in at least three ways. First, in overseeing the smooth functioning of the system, they free incumbents from the kind of overall field management and leadership that they necessarily exercised during the emergence of the strategic action field. Second, the very presence of these units serves to legitimate and "naturalize" the logic and rules of the field. They do this in a variety of ways. They often collect and provide information about the field to both incumbents and challengers. They also produce standardized versions of this information that can serve to inform the actions of all parties. Finally, besides their "internal" functions, such units typically serve as the liaison between the strategic action field and important external fields. So trade associations typically cultivate powerful allies in various state fields that exercise nominal control over the strategic action field in question. They are in a position to call on these allies for help should a crisis begin to develop within the field. In short, governance units can be expected to serve as defenders of the status quo and are a generally conservative force during periods of conflict within the strategic action field. While the incumbent/challenger distinction draws on a long line of theorizing by social movement scholars, the concept of the *internal governance unit* is one of the unique elements we bring to the proposed theory.

Field stability is generally achieved in one of two ways: through the imposition of hierarchical power by a single dominant group or the creation of some kind of political coalition based on the cooperation of a number of groups. At the core of the problem is whether or not the strategic action field will be built on coercion, competition, or cooperation. In practice, it should be noted that fields contain elements of all three, but it is useful to consider these as ideal types. Coercion implies the threat or actual use of physical force or the withholding of valued resources. Competition occurs when different groups vie for advantage without resorting to violence. The outcome of the competition is expected to turn on some combination of initial resource endowments, the strength of internal and external allies, and variable social skill. The eventual winners will command subsequent resource flows and the opportunities to exploit them. The losers may get less but may manage to remain in the field.

Cooperation involves building a political coalition to keep the strategic action field together. The purpose of a given cooperative project is to provide resources—both material and "existential"—to members. (We will have more to say about these "existential" rewards in the next section and even more in the next chapter.) A political coalition reflects an alliance between two or more groups in relation to other groups. Our ideal typical view of political coalitions is that they are based on cooperation. This cooperation is generally rooted in a combination of shared interests and a common collective identity. People join groups and cooperate for narrow material rewards but also for the existential benefits that a sense of meaning and membership affords. In practice, a stable strategic action field can be built on any of these three bases or some combination of them (Wagner-Pacifici 2000).

Forging political coalitions is a tricky task that requires social skill. Actors have to convince other groups that if they join together, their collective interests will in fact be served. If groups are of different size and purpose, then the larger groups obviously have advantages. Strategic actors use cooperative coalitions and enforced hierarchies as alternative means to organize fields. They can form coalitions with some groups in a strategic action field to build a larger group and then use that larger group to coerce or compete with other groups.

Depending on the evenness of the distribution of resources and position, political coalitions at one extreme are clearly based on cooperation between social groups, but at the other, where one group has more power, political coalitions may come to resemble a hierarchy. Equally sized incumbent groups can share power in one kind of political coalition, making it look "flat" rather than hierarchical. But we can also imagine a situation in which a dominant incumbent group controls a strategic action field in coalition with a number of much smaller partners. The latter closely resembles a hierarchical field even though the relationship between coalition members is nominally cooperative. Over time, the relative power of individuals or social groups can change, thereby moving the strategic action field toward either more hierarchy or more coalition.

The structure of incumbents and challengers depends on the nature of the strategic action field. So, for example, the number of incumbent groups will reflect the relative power of those groups and the underlying basis of that power. Incumbent groups may fashion an informal agreement to share the field. The result might be separate spheres of influence within the field, allowing these groups to cooperate without stepping on one another's toes. They might even ritualize this agreement even as they periodically test its limits. For their part, challengers can use their resource dependence within a strategic action field to their advantage. If groups are dependent upon other groups, this can create a stable situation in which "contracts" are made. There will always be tension in these kinds of relations because they define the roles of unequal partners.

In our ideal types, we have associated hierarchies with coercion and competition and political coalitions with cooperation. In reality, hierarchies are not just held in place by coercive or competitive advantage, and political coalitions do not rely entirely on cooperation. Hierarchies often depend on the tacit consent of challengers and can even provide some rewards for compliance with a hierarchical order. So, incumbents will keep the lion's share of resources for themselves but allow challengers to survive and share in the spoils, even if in a somewhat inequitable manner. In return, challengers will keep their opposition to incumbents generally in check. By the same token, political coalitions often experience some level of ongoing conflict and competition. Groups in the coalition will believe that they are not getting their fair share of rewards. They may also believe that their vision of the coalition is not being honored. They can try to remake the coalition by mobilizing a different collection of groups based on an emergent oppositional account of the field. Obviously, the changing size of groups and their resources can affect the ongoing politics of hierarchy and coalition. The idea that fields can be organized either in a hierarchical or coalitional fashion offers a more integrated view of the possibility of field order. This is also a new element in our perspective.

3. Social Skill and the Existential Function of the Social—The next new element in our perspective is a unique theory of "social skill" peculiar to humans and rooted in a fundamental understanding of what we term the "existential function of the social." So central to our perspective is this distinctive microfoundation that we will devote a good part of chapter 2 to its explication. For now, we content ourselves with only the most general introduction to this aspect of the theory.

How to think about the role that actors play in the construction of social life has been one of the core controversies in social theory in the past twenty years (Fraser 2003; Honneth 1995; Jasper 2004, 2006). On the one hand, sociologists tend to see overriding cultural or structural factors as facilitating or impeding the ability of individuals or organized groups to actively affect their life chances. On the other, it is hard to be a participant in social life without being impressed at how individuals and groups are able to affect what happens to them (Ganz 2000, 2009). Much of sociology contends it is interested in society's challengers, the downtrodden and the dispossessed. This concern, when combined with the view that there is little challengers can do about their position (at least according to many sociological perspectives), puts sociologists in an awkward position, intellectually and politically. Our approach tries to define a sociological view of strategic action and link it to the possibilities for change in strategic action fields at different moments in their evolution.

Following Fligstein (2001a), we define strategic action as the attempt by social actors to create and sustain social worlds by securing the cooperation of others. Strategic action is about control in a given context (Padgett and Ansell 1993; White 1992). The creation of identities, political coalitions, and interests may be motivated by a desire to control other actors. But the ability to fashion such agreements and enforce them requires that strategic actors be able to "get outside of their own heads," take the role of the other, and work to fashion shared worlds and identities (Jasper 2004, 2006).

Put another way, the concept of social skill highlights the way in which individuals or collective actors possess a highly developed cognitive capacity for reading people and environments, framing lines of action, and mobilizing people in the service of broader conceptions of the world and of themselves (Fligstein 2001a; Jasper 2004, 2006; Snow and Benford 1988; Snow, et al. 1986). To discover, articulate, or appropriate and propagate these "existential packages" is inherently a social skill, one that underscores the "cultural" or "constructed" dimension of social action. We view social skill as an individual capacity and assume that it is distributed (perhaps normally) across the population.

What socially skilled actors will do will depend on what role they occupy in a particular strategic action field. In stable social worlds, skilled strategic actors in incumbent groups help to produce and reproduce a status quo. They are aided by a collective set of meanings shared by other actors that defines those actors' identities and interests. It is also the case that in "institutionalized" social worlds, meanings can be "taken for granted" and actions are readily framed in relation to those meanings. In emergent or unsettled strategic action fields, the task for skilled strategic actors is somewhat different. In unsettled strategic action fields, it is possible for skilled social actors to assume the role of "institutional entrepreneur" (DiMaggio 1988). Here, their ability to help link groups based on appeals to common interests and identities comes to the fore. These skills are at the greatest premium in unorganized or unstable strategic action fields. Here, actors use their skill to mobilize others, either to help them build a political coalition able to organize the field or to use their superior resources to produce a hierarchical field (Ganz 2000, 2009).

By emphasizing the cognitive, empathetic, and communicative dimensions of social skill, we hope to underscore the central point that actors who undertake strategic action must be able to use whatever perspective they have developed in an intersubjective enough fashion to secure the cooperation—willing or otherwise—of others (Fligstein 2001a). This kind of skill enables actors to transcend their own individual and narrow group interests and to take the role of the other as a prerequisite for shaping a broader conception of the collective rooted in an emergent worldview and shared identity (Mead 1934).

We make one final, crucial point regarding the exercise of the social skills alluded to here. Virtually all past perspectives on strategic action have focused primarily on disparities in power and preferences. Much of what we have said to this point in the book could be interpreted in this narrow instrumental light as well. However, we see strategic action as inextricably linked to the distinctive human capacity and *need* to fashion shared meanings and identities to ensure a viable existential ground for existence. This is not to say that power and preferences do not matter but that our attempts to exercise the former and achieve the latter are always bound up with larger issues of meaning and identity. What is more, our preferences themselves are generally rooted in the central sources of meaning and identify in our lives. We discuss this complicated topic in the next chapter. For now, we simply assert that for us collective strategic action is rooted at least as much in Weber's stress on meaning making and Mead's focus on empathy as on the naked instrumental orientation of Marx.

4. Broader Field Environment—Many other theorists, as we have noted, have proffered descriptions of the kind of mesolevel orders that we are calling strategic action fields. Virtually all of the previous work on fields, however, focuses only on the internal workings of these orders, depicting them as largely self-contained, autonomous worlds. The next distinctive feature of our perspective derives from the central analytic importance we accord the broader environment within which any given strategic action field is embedded. More specifically, we conceive of all fields as embedded in complex webs of other fields. Three sets of binary distinctions will help us characterize the nature of these "other fields" and their relationships with any given strategic action field. The first distinction is between *distant* and *proximate* fields. Proximate fields are those strategic action fields with recurring ties to, and whose actions routinely affect, the field in question. Distant fields are those that lack ties and have virtually no capacity to influence a given strategic action field.

The second distinction is between *dependent* and *interdependent fields*. The distinction captures the extent and direction of influence that characterizes the relationship between any two fields. A field that is largely subject to the influence of another is said to be *dependent* on it. This dependence can stem from a variety of sources, including formal legal or bureaucratic authority, resource dependence, or physical/military force. Formal bureaucratic hierarchies of the Russian doll variety embody the first of these sources of dependence. Within these vertically organized systems, all lower level fields are nested in, and formally dependent upon, all higher level systems. When two linked fields exercise more or less equal influence over each other, we say that they stand in an *interdependent* relation to one another. It should go without saying that fields can also be *independent* of one another, that is, unaffected by the actions of the other. Indeed, the great majority of strategic action fields are independent of each other.

The final distinction is between *state* and *nonstate fields*. The distinction is an obvious but important one. In the modern world state actors alone have the formal authority to intervene in, set rules for, and generally pronounce on the legitimacy and viability of most nonstate fields. This grants to states considerable and generally unrivaled potential to affect the stability of most strategic action fields. But states for us are also dense collections of fields whose relations can be described as either distant or proximate and, if proximate, can be characterized as existing in either a *horizontal* or *vertical* relationship to one another. We therefore reject the all too common notion of a singular, hegemonic state. On closer inspection states are made up of myriad social orders whose dynamics are nearly indistinguishable from other fields. Indeed, we see this particular conception of the state, as a dense system of interdependent fields, as another of the original contributions of the theory. We discuss states as collections of fields in chapter 3.

Armed with these distinctions, it is now easier to appreciate just how complicated and potentially consequential are the ties that link any given strategic action field to its broader field environment. Consider a single product division within a large firm. The division constitutes a field in its own right, but it is also tied vertically to the larger field defined by the entire firm and to all other divisions within the firm with which it routinely competes for resources. But this only exhausts the intrafirm fields to which the division is tied. The division is simultaneously embedded in a complex web of proximate fields external to the firm: financiers, suppliers, customers, competitors, and state regulators. We use this example and offer these distinctions to make a simple point. For all the attention paid to mesolevel orders by other analysts, the failure to take seriously the constraints (and opportunities) imposed on those orders by the myriad ties they share to other fields significantly truncates our understanding of field dynamics and, in particular, the potential for conflict and change in any given field. The stability of any given field is largely a function of its relations to other fields. While fields can devolve into conflict as a result of internal processes, it is far more common for an "episode of contention" to develop as a result of change pressures emanating from proximate state and/or nonstate fields.

5. *Exogenous Shocks, Mobilization, and the Onset of Contention*—The main theoretical implication of the interdependence of fields is that the broader field environment is a source of routine, rolling turbulence in modern society. A significant change in any given strategic action field is like a stone thrown in a still pond sending ripples outward to all proximate fields. This does not mean that all or even most of the ripples will destabilize other fields. Like stones, changes come in all sizes. Only the most dramatic are apt to send ripples of sufficient intensity to pose a real threat to the stability of proximate fields.

While these continuous moments of turbulence will offer challengers opportunities to better their positions and even change the rules of the game, in already existing fields, most incumbents are generally well positioned and fortified to withstand these pressures. For starters, they typically enjoy significant resource advantages over field challengers. They also may not face a challenge even in the face of a significant destabilizing shock because of the perception by challengers that incumbents are secure in their power. Finally, incumbents can generally count on the support of loyal allies within governance units both internal to the field and embedded in proximate state and nonstate fields. Possessed of these material, cultural, and political resources, incumbents are positioned to survive.

Sometimes, however, these advantages may not be enough to forestall an "episode of contention." In rare instances, the sheer magnitude of the perturbation—for example, the recent subprime mortgage crisis to which we will devote considerable attention in chapter 5—may virtually impose crisis on many proximate fields, especially those that stand in a vertically dependent relationship to the strategic action field in question. More typically, however, the magnitude of the destabilizing change is not so great as to compel crisis. Exactly how much of a threat the change proves to be is determined by the highly contingent mobilization process depicted in figure 1.1. This process speaks to the capacity for social construction and strategic agency that is at the heart of our perspective.

The process—which will be familiar to many social movement scholars (McAdam 1999; McAdam, Tarrow, and Tilly 2001)—consists of three linked mechanisms. The first is the collective *attribution of threat/opportunity*. The simple question is how are the destabilizing change processes interpreted by incumbents and challengers? Unless they are defined as posing a serious threat to, or opportunity for, the realization of collective interests, there is no possibility that any serious field crisis, or "episode of contention," will develop.

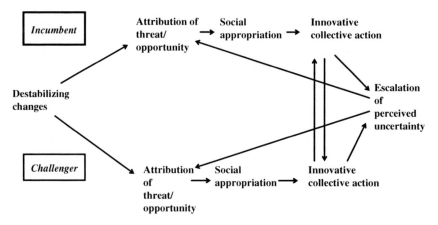

Figure 1.1

The collective *attribution of threat or/opportunity* is not, however, enough in and of itself to ensure the onset of contention. For that to take place, two other things must happen. First, those perceiving the threat/opportunity must command the organizational resources (e.g., *social appropriation*) needed to mobilize and sustain action. Second, the hallmark of a true episode of contention is heightened interaction involving the use of innovative and previously prohibited forms of collective action (e.g., *innovative action*). Should challengers, in the face of a shared sense of threat or opportunity, continue to hew to "proper channels" and established rules for pressing their claims, no crisis or sustained episode of contention is likely to develop.

An example may serve to make this more concrete. Rosa Parks's arrest in December 1955 for not giving up her seat to a white man on a Montgomery city bus hardly ordained the crisis that ensued. After all, countless blacks had been arrested for similar offenses in the past. But this time, perhaps because Parks was well connected to the city's civil rights establishment, the arrest was quickly defined as an opportunity to protest the injustices of the bus system (e.g., attribution of opportunity). But it was the next two steps in the process that transformed the arrest into the highly consequential episode of contention it became. By convincing the majority of black ministers in Montgomery to take to their pulpits on Sunday, December 4 to urge congregants to protest the arrest of Ms. Parks, civil rights leaders effectively "appropriated" the central institution of the black community—and for many the key source of meaning and identity in their lives—in the service of the incipient movement. Still, had the leaders sought to "protest" the arrest through traditional channels, there would have been no crisis. It was the decision to engage in innovative action by launching the one-day symbolic boycott of the buses that effectively triggered the episode of contention.

6. *Episodes of Contention*—An episode of contention "can be defined as a period of emergent, sustained contentious interaction between . . . [field] actors utilizing new and innovative forms of action vis-à-vis one another" (McAdam 2007: 253). Besides innovative action, contentious episodes contain a shared sense of uncertainty/crisis regarding the rules and power relations governing the field. In the case of fields already characterized by well-established incumbents and challengers, the mobilization of both groups can take on extraordinary intensity. An episode can be expected to last as long as the shared sense of uncertainty regarding the structure and dominant order of the field persists. Indeed, it is the pervading sense of uncertainty that reinforces the perceptions of threat and opportunity that more or less oblige all parties to the conflict to continue to struggle. In his book on the 1966–1968 Red Guard Movement in Beijing, Walder (2009a) offers an extraordinary description of just such an episode. He convincingly argues that it was not prior or even emergent interests that

motivated the conflict so much as the generalized sense of chaos and uncertainty that obliged all parties to engage in round after round of reactive struggle.

In this sense, contention—at least for a period of time—can often feed on itself. Along with the generalized sense of uncertainty, perceived threats and opportunities generally change the consciousness of field actors by exposing rules that had been taken for granted, calling into question the perceived bene-fits of those rules, and undermining the calculations on which field relations had been based (McAdam and Scott 2005: 18–19). As the commitment to the on-going structure of the strategic action field collapses, new actors can be expected to join the fray. In response to an emerging crisis, incumbents are apt—at least initially—to appeal to the status quo in an effort to try to stabilize the situation. For their part, challengers are likely to be the first to engage in innovative action, sensing an opportunity to advance their position in the field through novel means. Wholly new groups are also likely to emerge during the crisis.

One form of action that is ubiquitous during episodes of contention is framing (Benford and Snow 2000; Goffman 1974; Snow et al. 1986). All manner of combatants—sometimes including actors from outside the field—can be expected to propose and seek to mobilize consensus around a particular concep-tion of the field (Fligstein 1996; Snow and Benford 1988). Incumbents may well persist in trying to reconstitute the old order, often with the help of internal gov-ernance units and allies in proximate state fields. Indeed, the imposition of a *settlement* by state actors is a common, if not always stable, method for resolving an episode of contention. Very often the advantages—material, cultural, political—enjoyed by incumbents may be enough to overcome crisis and restore order. In rare instances, however, oppositional logics may carry the day as chal-lengers successfully sustain mobilization and slowly begin to institutionalize new practices and rules (DiMaggio 1991; McAdam, Tarrow, and Tilly 2001). Consistent with the distinctive "microfoundation" alluded to above, it is worth noting that the desire to resolve a field crisis often reflects "existential" motives as much as narrow instrumental ones. That is, all manner of field actors—even those who stand to benefit from severe and prolonged crisis—have a stake in restoring the shared sense of order and existential integrity on which social life ultimately rests. The important empirical implication here is that in researching an episode of contention and especially its resulting settlement, researchers should attend as closely to "existential" motives as narrow instrumental ones (e.g., to issues of meaning, identity, burnout, and general stress).

7. *Settlement*—Through either sustained oppositional mobilization or the reassertion of the status quo by incumbents and/or their state allies, the field begins to gravitate toward a new—or refurbished—*institutional settlement* regarding field rules and cultural norms. We can say that a field is no longer in crisis when a generalized sense of order and certainty returns and there is once

again consensus about the relative positions of incumbents and challengers (McAdam and Scott 2005: 18–19; Schneiberg and Soule 2005: 152–53).

We have already noted the role of state actors in restoring field order, but other external parties may be involved as well. In general, if proximate fields are the source of the destabilizing shocks that set contentious episodes in motion, they often provide the models for the settlements that bring these crises to a close. When field rules are uncertain, actors tend to be more receptive to new perspectives and to engage in search processes to identify alternatives. Proximate fields are a readily available and generally trusted source for new ideas and practices. So social movements experience "spillover" (Meyer and Whittier 1994) or "spin-off" movements (McAdam 1995); organizations appropriate the "legitimate" forms used in other fields (Clemens 1993, 1996; DiMaggio and Powell 1983: 151–52; Meyer and Rowan 1977); and judges justify new legal interpretations by analogy (Epstein 1987).

Other Perspectives

In developing the perspective on offer here we have borrowed elements from many existing theoretical points of view. We think it is useful to acknowledge our debts and common themes but also to highlight areas where we think we have added new insights or have some disagreements or critique. Our goal here is not to denigrate other perspectives but to suggest what we have to add to the rich thinking already out there. We do not view what we have done as just a synthesis of what already exists but instead a reconceptualization that draws on some elements extant in other theories but adds significantly to them as well. Our perspective solves a number of puzzles in the way that scholars have studied sociological forms of collective action, and it is that novelty that we wish to highlight. One way to do that is to distinguish our view from others by pointing out not only our debts to other perspectives but also where our concepts push forward the field theory project.

At several points we have alluded to what we see as significant differences between our theory and other alternative perspectives. But we have not done so in any detailed or systematic way. In this section we review some of the alternative perspectives that are most relevant to a field conception of social life, taking pains to acknowledge how closely some of our ideas align with those of other major theories/theorists. We then go on to suggest what may be missing from each of these perspectives and how our approach might redress those holes. In general, while all of the perspectives reviewed below imply elements of the field approach, none of them, in our view, constitute a general theory of social order that can account for such disparate phenomena as the alternative we propose here. We briefly consider the approaches proposed by Bourdieu, Giddens, institutional theory, network analysis, and social movement theory and suggest how our more general approach draws on each while extending them.

Bourdieu

Obviously, there is substantial affinity between Bourdieu's scheme and the one proposed here. Bourdieu is as responsible for the idea of situating action in fields as any scholar. His theoretical apparatus is one of the most developed (although it is not the only one[2]). We view our theorizing as developing both the theory of fields and the idea of action in order to explain more phenomena more explicitly. As such, we are not hypercritical of his approach but believe that he would take much of our argument as a useful way to expand the scope and power of field theory.

One of the places where our theory advances the theory of fields and action is our more systematic focus on collective actors. Bourdieu's three main concepts are habitus, capital, and fields. Almost all of Bourdieu's discussion of these phenomena is pitched at the level of individual actors who find themselves in fields (Bourdieu 1984; Bourdieu and Wacquant 1992). He has few accounts of how collective actors work or how cooperation and competition between collective actors actually structures fields (for an exception, see Bourdieu's *The Rules of Art* [1996]). In general, he has little to say about the architecture of fields beyond the general view that they contain positions that are structured by the relative power of actors. He also does not have much to say about the relationships between fields.

There are complex reasons this is so. In many ways, Bourdieu's theoretical starting points in classical social theory offered few clues about creating something like field theory, and this meant that he was breaking new and novel ground in the construction of his theory of capital, habitus, and field. He did so by creating a relatively simple but flexible set of ideas that offer a powerful organizing lens for research (see Sallaz and Zavisca 2007 for a review of how these ideas have been used in American sociology). His main theoretical contribution was proposing the concept of field and combining it with a theory of action. One of the problems he was trying to solve was a deep one for social theory and one that is close to the core of this project: the problem of agents and structures. His goal was to overcome the usual opposition between agents and structures and to demonstrate that both mattered if we are to understand what actors do. He was

---

[2] Martin (2009) examines the history of the idea of fields and argues that there are varieties of field theory in sociology that draw on different takes on the problem. Fligstein (2009) shows how much of new institutionalism in sociology, political science, and economics can be read as being about the problem of constructing mesolevel social orders, that is, fields.

not only one of the first to articulate these theoretical ideas but also among the first to deploy them in the empirical analysis of particular cases. Those cases, not surprisingly, were focused on how individuals acted in fields.

For us, the challenge is to extend these arguments and clarify the theoretical lenses we can use to analyze these sorts of phenomena in a deeper way. Our perspective widens the object of study and draws into it insights from other literatures. Bourdieu's focus on *individuals* acting in fields means that his theory is generally less about the problem of *collective* action (again there are some exceptions in his work, such as *The State Nobility* [1998]). Instead, his actors have a position in a field, they come to that field holding some form of capital, and they have their habitus, which gives them a cognitive framework with which to interpret the action of others in the field. This focus on individuals is very useful. But it does tend to obscure the all-important collective dynamics of fields. Our focus is on how people cooperate, how groups get things done, and how we are to understand the interaction that goes on between groups. This, needless to say, is our key point of departure.

Actors in Bourdieu's theory are generally only responsible to themselves and motivated by a desire to advance their interests within the constraints of the situations in which they find themselves. But fields also turn more centrally on coordinated action, which requires actors not to simply focus on their position in a field but to seek cooperation with others by taking the role of the other and framing lines of action that appeal to others in the field. We view these collective dynamics as complementary to the generally individual action that is Bourdieu's central concern.

One advantage of our approach is that it views both competition and cooperation as fundamental to field analysis. Thus, collective action, which depends on cooperation, will rely on actors being able to convince others that their view of the problems of the field and the identity they provide for others in solving those problems work for everyone. This kind of action is common in the social movements literature and the organizations literature because scholars in both of these fields are centrally concerned with the demands and dynamics of coordinated action. This is one of the main differences between the Bourdieusian perspective and the view of most scholars of fields in American sociology.

Another difference between Bourdieu's theory and the one developed here is our focus on the emergence or transformation of social spaces by collective actors. Most of Bourdieu's work was oriented toward establishing that fields exist, that they shaped the behavior of actors in profound ways, and that actors took what such systems gave. But his work was less concerned with the emergence of new fields and the transformation of existing ones (again with a few exceptions such as *The Rules of Art* [1996]). His one insight on the matter was that when the conventional wisdom (what he called "doxa") was called into

question, there emerged at least the possibility of field transformation or disso-
lution (Bourdieu 1977). But he had little or nothing to say about how this
happened and how collective actors produced new identities and frames to form
new fields or transform existing ones. We think that Bourdieu would broadly
agree with this aspect of our theory. Our approach, which explicitly relies on
social movement theory to understand the emergence of a field and its transformation, fills an important gap in field theory.

Finally, while Bourdieu was very aware of the fact that fields were connected
to one another, he rarely theorized the linkages between fields and the dynamics
that could result from the interactions between fields (although *The State Nobility*
[1998] certainly provides one of the few extant empirical cases of the interdependence of fields). For us, these linkages are fundamental to an understanding
of stability and change in existing fields. As such, these mechanisms need to be
explicitly explored and theorized. Indeed, this will be the sole focus of chapter 4
in this volume.

Giddens

Anthony Giddens's work shares many of the same assumptions about how
social life works as the perspective outlined here. Giddens's theory of structuration (1979, 1984) is very much concerned with the reflexivity of actors, even in
the most mundane reproduction of a system. Giddens also appreciates the role
that preexisting structures and systems of power play in the reproduction of
social life. For Giddens, social structures are rules and resources. Rules are
patterns people may follow in social life. Giddens defines two types of resources.
Authoritative resources control persons, whereas allocative resources control
material objects.

The theory employs a recursive notion of actions constrained and enabled
by structures that are produced and reproduced by those actions. Agents'
knowledge of their society informs their action, which reproduce social structures, which in turn enforce and maintain the dynamics of action. Giddens
defines "ontological security" as the trust people have in social structure; everyday actions have some degree of predictability, thus ensuring social stability.
Social change occurs when the trust that people have has broken down. The
agency of actors allows them to break away from normative actions, and
depending on the sum of social factors at work, they may instigate shifts in the
social structure. The dynamic between agency and structure makes such gener-
ative action possible. Thus, agency can lead to both the reproduction and the
transformation of society.

This phenomenological view of the duality of agency and structure shares
many common themes with Bourdieu's and the position we have elucidated.

Actors work to produce and reproduce their positions in social structures. They use rules (i.e., the rules of the field), resources (i.e., forms of capital), and their understanding of the field to make moves. Giddens also suggests that when structures appear to be broken down, actors can reimagine their worlds and bring about social change.

While we find this view to be attractive, we also think that it is a little vague. Giddens lacks several critical elements. First, he does not have a theory of collective action. Actors are instead located in nameless social structures where they are imposed upon to act. The motives of actors, their actual relationships to each other, and the desire to engage in collective action never appear in Giddens's view.

Second, Giddens lacks a conception of the arena of social action, that is, the concept of strategic action field. Instead, he has a much more general (and we would argue vaguer) idea about social structure. His use of rules and resources as structure makes it difficult to imagine how such structures are circumscribed. So, for example, in the theory of fields, there is always something at stake in the field. What distinguishes a particular field is that something is at stake and that the actors in the field are striving to control it. The theory of strategic action fields causes us to be able to ascertain who are members of a field, what their positions are, and what their moves might be. It also gives us insight into the fact that action is social and oriented toward others. Whether the goal of action is cooperation or competition, in a specific strategic action field, we can get closer to explaining the critical dynamics.

The lack of a theory of strategic action fields means that Giddens is also not good at understanding the common dynamics of individual and collective action that occur in fields. The theory of strategic action fields provides a way to understand if a mesolevel social structure is emerging, stable, or in the process of transformation. Without such a theory, it is hard to make sense of what actors are doing, as both individuals and collectivities. Our theory of strategic action fields specifies which state a field is in and therefore gives us leverage on the types of dynamics that are possible. In an emerging strategic action field, the problem of what the field is about, what exactly constitutes a resource, and the struggle over creating the rules all come front and center. The problem of gaining collective action, producing identities, and forging a field is what is up for grabs. Similarly, our perspective provides sources of social change in such fields. First, the connections between fields cause disruption in existing fields or new opportunities for field organization. Our view that reproduction in a field is not a rote process but instead the outcome of a round of interaction that does not necessarily only have to exactly reproduce a given order gives us a way to understand the piecemeal changes that can occur in particular fields. The theory of strategic action fields gives much more analytic leverage on how organized social life gets created and changes.

Institutional Theory

We owe a serious debt to institutional theorists in political science and especially sociology. Institutional theory in organizational studies (DiMaggio and Powell 1983; Meyer and Rowan 1977; Scott and Meyer 1983) is pitched at the same mesolevel as is our approach. Scott and Meyer (1983) use the term "sector" to describe fields as containing all of the organizations that one can imagine that might affect a particular organization. DiMaggio and Powell begin with the Meyer and Scott definition of a field containing all relevant actors. They identify three kinds of forces driving organizations in fields toward similar outcomes, what they call mimetic, coercive, and normative isomorphism. Their basic argument is that actors in organizations face uncertain worlds. In order to reduce this uncertainty, actors will be swayed by different kinds of forces. They may follow what they consider successful organizations. They may also follow the advice of professionals or experts on what they should do. Finally, they might be coerced by either other organizations or the government to conform to expectations. This has produced a powerful research agenda that has studied how new institutions spread in existing fields. We borrow much from this perspective: a concern with fields and the mutual constitution of fields by actors who come to take one another into account in their actions and who operate to give one another a sense of what to do and why to do it.

While acknowledging a serious debt to the institutional framework, we nonetheless see two problems with the perspective. First, institutional theory is really a theory of how conformity occurs in already existing fields. It lacks an underlying theory of how fields emerge or are transformed. The theory, by its very nature, is antithetical to the notion of agency. Actors follow rules, either consciously by imitation or coercion or unconsciously by tacit agreement (DiMaggio 1988; Jepperson 1991). DiMaggio's article (1988) is frequently cited as inspiration for the idea of institutional entrepreneurs. But its main argument is that institutional theory lacks a theory of agency, power, and conflict. The reason DiMaggio posits the idea of an institutional entrepreneur is that he is trying to make sense of what happens when a field comes into existence or is transformed. Here he suggests that this can only happen when someone comes along and figures out how to do something new and is able to convince others to go along with them. But even as useful as the concept of institutional entrepreneur is, it hardly constitutes a systematic theory of field stability and change. Without embedding strategic action fields in broader field environments, DiMaggio has no deeper structural account of the kinds of ruptures that typically catalyze entrepreneurial action. In the end we are left with a thinly veiled "great man" theory of agency. In short, for institutional theory in its Meyer–Rowan and DiMaggio–Powell variants to work it needs a theory of change like the one proposed here to complement its emphasis on stability and reproduction.

The leads to the second problem, which is that the institutionalist view greatly underestimates the role of power in the structuring of fields, even those that are stable. Indeed, in both the Meyer and Scott and DiMaggio and Powell versions of a field, actors do not have interests, resources, or positions that determine what they can get. They are not jockeying with one another in a game in which they are playing to maintain or improve their position but instead following scripts that tell them what to do. This problem means that not only does institutional theory lack a theory of emergence or transformation (that is consistent with its basic terms), but also it cannot even account for the piecemeal changes that we expect in the constant playing of the game as conditions change within a field or between fields.

Network Analysis

The idea of using network analysis as a way to model fields dates back to DiMaggio and Powell (1983). There has been a lot of interesting research into how networks function to shape the relations between, and fate of, the actors embedded in them. So, networks, we are told, can serve as a source of information (Davis, Diekmann, and Tinsley 1994), resource dependence (Burt 1980), trust (Uzzi 1996), or collusion (Baker and Faulkner 1993). In one of the most ambitious attempts to capture how networks and alliances help structure an entire field, Powell et al. (2005) argue that firms in the biotechnology industry appear to use networks to do all of the above.

For all of its virtues, however, network analysis is *not* a theory of fields. It is principally a methodological technique for modeling various aspects of the relationships between actors within a field. And while it can be a powerful tool to help map fields and especially to monitor changes in the composition of strategic action fields, it is mute on the dynamics that shape fields. There are, to be sure, network researchers who have sought to theorize the role that social ties, or other properties of networks, play in shaping social dynamics (Burt 1992; Gould 1993; Granovetter 1973), but no one, to our knowledge, has fashioned anything close to a network-based theory of fields.

So, for example, we remain very much in the same situation that social movement theorists find themselves in with respect to network analysis. While network analysis has been a staple of social movement scholarship, theory has not kept pace with empirical research. So while the field has amassed an impressive body of studies showing significant network effects, especially regarding movement recruitment, there is still no theoretical agreement on what it is about networks that explains the effect. Or as Passy put it succinctly a few years back, "We are now aware that social ties are important for collective action, but we still need to theorize. . . . the actual role of networks" (2003: 22).

Network analysis has the potential to be a powerful aid to the study of strategic action fields but only when informed by some broader theory of field dynamics. A structural mapping of field relations, however sophisticated, will never substitute for a deeper analysis into the shared (or contested) understandings that inform and necessarily shape strategic action within a strategic action field. In short, the analyst always has to provide the theoretical underpinning for what is important about the relationships (i.e., networks) being studied for any given outcome. If a field is really an arena in which individuals, groups, or organizations face off to capture some gain as our view suggests, then the underlying logic of fields is not encoded in the structure of the network but in the cultural conceptions of power, privilege, resources, rules, and so on that shape action within the strategic action field.

We close this section with a simple example designed to illustrate the difference between formal network analysis and the perspective on offer here. Network analysts have gotten extraordinarily good at empirically mapping overtime changes in network structure. The tendency is to interpret these changes in the relationships between actors in a network as substantively important changes in the field. If any set of relationships either disappears or emerges, then it is interpreted as a direct measure of an important change in the field. However, without understanding the ways in which these shifts are viewed by challengers and incumbents in the field, the analyst is powerless to tell us anything about their significance. So, for example, a shift in the relationship between actors might signify the improving fortunes of one actor in the field but nothing of significance concerning the field as a whole. Alternatively, the ascendance of a single actor might, under other circumstances, portend a dramatic restructuring of the entire strategic action field. The problem is that the technique of network analysis that only describes the change in that one actor's position cannot tell us which of these two outcomes is taking place. Only by wedding the structural sophistication of network analysis with attention to the meaning of the shifts for all relevant actors in the field can we tell if a change in the network structure has implications for the field as a whole.

Social Movement Theory

The final perspective we take up is social movement theory.[3] Looking at the key elements of the perspective sketched here, it should be clear that we have drawn heavily on social movement scholarship in fashioning our theory. A host of our

---

[3] In fact, a number of different theories of social movements have been proposed over the years (e.g., collective behavior theory, new social movement theory). Here the term "social movement theory" refers to the synthesis of *resource mobilization, political process,* and *framing theory* that has come to dominate the field over the past two decades.

key concepts—framing, political opportunity, rupture and settlement, episodes of contention, incumbents and challengers—have been borrowed directly from social movement theory. On the other hand, the framework proposed here is much broader in its application than social movement theory and different from the latter in a number of crucial respects. For starters, unlike the various organizational perspectives sketched above, social movement theory has never been oriented to the concept of "field." Second, as the name suggests, the study of social movements has become increasingly narrow and "movementcentric" in its focus (McAdam and Boudet 2012; Walder 2009b), while the theory proposed here emphasizes the critical interplay, not only of the actors within a field but also between the field and the broader field environment in which it is embedded. Finally, if institutionalists have been better at explaining stability and reproduction, social movement scholars have understandably sought to explain the dynamics of emergent conflict and change. Accordingly, social movement theory has very little to tell us about the processes that make for stability and order in strategic action fields. By contrast, the perspective sketched here aims to account for field emergence, stability, *and* transformation.

Each of the perspectives reviewed above captures an important aspect of the way in which strategic action fields work. The fact that scholars across these fields have found common grounds and borrowed from one another's theories implies that they resonate with other point of views. But all of these alternative perspectives fail to recognize their deeper theoretical affinity. The theory of strategic action fields is a far more general perspective that allows us to understand how new mesolevel social orders are produced, sustained, and come unraveled. Our brief consideration of these perspectives illustrates how, by ignoring this deeper level of convergence, each perspective offers an incomplete picture of how organized social life works.

Conclusion

A recurring theme in sociology is the existence of powerful social institutions or structures that are extremely resistant to change. "Greedy" institutions, class structures, states, corporations—all are viewed as enduring structures that defy change, even in the most turbulent situations. Capitalists always win, states always beat nonstates, and social movements are generally doomed to failure. Our view is that this perspective is at best partial, at worst, highly misleading. Strategic action fields represent recurring games. Even in stable fields, the game is being played continuously and the skill of challengers and/or destabilizing changes in proximate fields might render incumbents vulnerable and prevent reproduction of the field. At the very least, the rules, composition, and structure of the field will be in play constantly. Reproduction of the field may be the norm, but it is always accompanied by routine jockeying for position and incremental changes. As new actors appear and old ones disappear, rules get modified and incumbent/challenger relations are renegotiated. These kinds of piecemeal adjustments are the rule in virtually all fields, even the most stable.

This kind of incremental change is distinguished from those rarer, but still frequent, field foundings or transformations. Here, the order itself is altered. New fields suddenly emerge or old ones are transformed or perhaps even collapse and disappear entirely. These dynamics are different. Incumbents are struggling while challengers are emerging or rising up. It is at these moments that new identities and shared meanings define emergent interests to produce new and innovative social forms. But either way, collective strategic actors have to organize their groups, motivate their participants, and organize action vis-à-vis other groups. In settled times, the structural positions of actors may well determine their fate. If rules, resources, and political alliances favor incumbents, skilled strategic actors in challenging groups will do all they can to survive or improve their position. Backed by internal governance units and allies in proximate state fields, skilled strategic actors in incumbent groups will use the existing rules and resources to reproduce their advantage. But when resources or rules are up for grabs and when the existing order does not hold, skilled strategic actors fight hard to produce alternative orders.

The rest of our book lays out this theory in some detail. In chapter 2 we articulate the microfoundation for our theory—nothing less than a foundational perspective on how the nature and fundamental communicative/interactive capacities of modern humans inform our theory. In chapter 3 we move from the micro to the macro. As we noted above, all of the other approaches to the study of fields are, in our view, fieldcentric. That is, they attend exclusively to the internal dynamics of strategic action fields. We are concerned with this as well, but we are convinced that to truly understand a field and its dynamics, we must begin by systematically situating it in the complex network of "external" fields—state and nonstate—to which it is tied. Indeed, for us, the distinction between internal and external is largely illusory. Or more precisely, it is the complex interplay between the internal and the external that shapes the possibilities for field emergence, stability, and transformation. Then, in chapter 4 we link these macrodynamics to the prospects for change and stability in fields.

Chapter 5 applies the framework in two detailed case studies. Our goal is to use the framework to understand phenomena that at first glance seem to have little to do with each other. We illustrate many of our principles by reconceptualizing the twentieth-century civil rights revolution in the United States as a story of rupture in the national field of racial politics, triggered by destabilizing changes in three proximate fields. We contrast that case study with an account of the emergence of the market for mortgages in the United States since the 1960s and the eventual rise and fall of that market in the 1990s and 2000s. We hope the analytic utility of thinking of these cases in field terms will be clear from the extended narratives offered in chapter 5. In chapter 6, we address the methodological implications of our theory, offering something of a practical blueprint for anyone who would adopt the perspective as a basis for studying a given strategic action field. We bring the book to a close in chapter 7 by highlighting what we see as the central insights and implications of the theory on offer here.

2

Microfoundations

Rational choice theory has achieved widespread influence in a number of social science disciplines, most notably economics and political science. The perspective, however, has failed to gain much more than a toehold in sociology. Indeed, most sociologists are downright hostile to the theory. When pressed to explain why, those in the discipline are very likely to complain that the perspective is "asociological"—that the theory posits an atomized conception of the individual that does not accord with the "sociological perspective." But when it comes to the individual, what exactly *is* the "sociological perspective?" Beyond the rather facile assertion that humans are profoundly "social creatures," sociologists have done little to fashion a distinctive account of what that actually means. After all, lots of species are intensely social, perhaps none more so than ants (Gordon 1999). Surely we are not social in the same sense that ants are. Our closest evolutionary relatives—chimpanzees and gorillas—are also very social species, and social in many ways that mirror human sociability. But there are also myriad ways in which human social life is qualitatively different from that of even these closest evolutionary cousins. Bottom line: to dismiss rational choice theory for its failure to honor the extent to which we are "social creatures" is to evade the real question: what *is* the distinctive essence of *human* sociability?

We will not pretend to offer anything like a complete answer to that question here, but believing that any serious theory of human collective behavior must rest on a credible microfoundation, we use the first half of this chapter to sketch a bare-bones perspective on what we see as the distinctive essence of human sociability. We review the current literature on the emergence of modern humans to argue that language, culture, and the problem of meaning are at the center of what it means to be human. Then, we link this to sociological conceptions of sociability, making brief forays into the classical theories of Weber, Durkheim, and Mead. In the second half of the chapter, we explicate how what we term the "existential function of the social" enables the "social skills" that undergird the forms of strategic action that are central to the theory on offer here.

Meaning and Membership: On the Origin of the Existential Function of the Social

We begin by considering accepted knowledge about social organization and the evolution of primates. Modern humans belong to the general biological order of primates that may have emerged as long as 85 million years ago and includes a dizzying variety of extinct and contemporary species. This variety is nicely reflected in the smallest and largest of contemporary primates. The smallest is the Madame Berthe's mouse lemur, which weighs little more than an ounce; the largest the mountain gorilla, which can tip the scale at up to 450 pounds. So not discounting some common physical characteristics, it is clear that the order is not primarily defined by its shared anatomy. "Unspecified anatomically, primates are distinguished by *social organization* and evolutionary trends within the order tending toward increased dexterity and intelligence" (The Concise Columbia Encyclopedia 1983: 689; emphasis added).

Not surprisingly, hominids are the most social of all of the primate species. Split off from common primate ancestors about 15–20 million years ago, the hominid family is composed of four extant genera—chimpanzees, gorillas, orangutans, and humans. All of the species that today comprise these different groupings are highly social. Based on the archaeological record, however, it seems clear that for virtually the entirety of their presence on earth, the functions of hominid sociability were essentially materialist in nature. That is, hominids lived together for the material or survival advantages that group life conferred. This claim would seem to apply as much to our immediate human ancestors—the genus *Homo*, signaled by the appearance of *Homo habilis* roughly 2.4 million years ago—as to the other hominid genera. Indeed, and here is where it gets really interesting, for most of our own scant time on earth, the sociability of anatomically modern humans—that is *Homo sapiens*—appears to have been qualitatively materialist as well. That is, for roughly 150,000 years after the appearance of the species, *Homo sapiens* did not exhibit the capacity for collaborative, symbolic activity that we associate with modern humans. The emergence of culture in this more restrictive, existential sense only appears to have occurred somewhere around 45,000–50,000 years ago. It is to this puzzle that we now turn.

The consensus is that modern humans emerged in Africa around 200,000 years ago. These new arrivals would seem to be anatomically indistinct from us. Most important, their brain size was indistinguishable from ours. Yet, this clear anatomical break with the past does not appear to have been accompanied by a comparable change in behavior. In point of fact, we will need to fast forward roughly 150,000 years before we encounter clear evidence of the emergence of

modern human behavior. The evidence is overwhelming, appearing as a veritable explosion in the archaeological record of elaborate ritual burial and routine
production of art and ornamentation, among other indicators that we are clearly
in the presence of our existential, as opposed to materialist, kin.

What is the nature of this explosion and what are its implications for an understanding of the *social*? One common rendering of this evolutionary "moment" is
that it marks the emergence of "culture," in the human experience. But even if we
adopt a fairly narrow definition of culture, this account is demonstrably false. Tools
are typically regarded as a rudimentary element of culture and certainly all of the
prior species in the *Homo* line have been shown to produce and use tools. Indeed,
depending on how broadly one defines the term, there is evidence for tool usage
among our closest contemporary nonhuman relatives. For example, West African
chimpanzees have been shown to use stone hammers and anvils to crack nuts
(Boesch and Boesch 1993). Other species of chimpanzees have deployed other
tools—including termite fishing probes, pestles, and various levers—in foraging for
food (McGrew 1994). But even if we want to set the bar a bit higher in our
requirements for culture, it would be impossible to deny, say, Neanderthal that level
of evolutionary development. Beyond an effective and highly adaptable—if static—
tool assemblage, there are at least scattered claims made for rudimentary Neanderthal burial and perhaps even representational art. These include an incised piece of
bone from a 350,000-year-old site at Bilzingsleben in Germany and an alleged
outline of a female engraved on a pebble from the 230,000-year-old pre-Mousterian
site of Berekat Ram in Israel (Tattersall 1998).

If the "explosion" of 45,000–50,000 years ago does not represent the onset of
culture in the human—or even hominid—experience, how are we to understand
the breathtaking leap that seems to have taken place? While others have stressed the
emergence of symbolic thinking or high culture, we, as sociologists, are inclined to
underscore the *collective* aspect of the breakthrough. The sudden proliferation of art,
elaborate grave goods, and distinctive local tool assemblages speaks to an unprecedented capacity for *coordinated symbolic activity* and *collaborative meaning making*.
We refer to this in shorthand as the onset of the *existential function* of the social.
While hominids had heretofore banded together almost entirely for the survival
benefits afforded by group life, the collective now served another separable function:
the provision of group members with distinctive collective identities and shared understandings of the world.[1] This represents a qualitative break with the entire 15

---

[1] We need to make two clarifying points here. First, we are not suggesting that prior to the explosion of 45,000–50,000 years ago our human ancestors lacked any conception of group identify
or shared understandings of the world. They clearly did not. Groups that were fashioning tools and
hunting collaboratively clearly had to share both an inchoate sense of "groupness" and enough collective
knowledge—of tool making techniques, differentiated roles during a hunt, and so on—to survive

million–year sweep of the hominid experience on earth. We are finally in the presence of a form of sociability that we would recognize as broadly akin to our own.

We cannot overstress the significance of the *coordinated collaborative* and *intersubjective* nature of the activities reflected in the archaeological record from this period and beyond. A single example will suffice to make the point. It comes from an extraordinary burial at the 28,000-year-old site of Sungir in Russia. Ian Tattersall describes what the excavation of the site revealed:

> . . . two young individuals and a sixty-year-old male (no previous kind of human had ever survived to such an age) were interred with an astonishing material richness. Each of the deceased was dressed in clothing onto which more than three thousand ivory beads had been sewn; and experiments have shown that each bead had taken an hour to make. They also wore carved pendants, bracelets, and shell necklaces. The juveniles, buried head to head, were flanked by two mammoth tusks over two yards long. What's more, these tusks had been straightened, something that . . . could only have been achieved by boiling them. But how? The imagination boggles, for this was clearly not a matter of dropping hot stones into a small skin-lined pit. (1998: 10)

Tattersall goes on to intuit what the burial tells us about the people who carried it out, arguing for such things as a belief in an afterlife, the presence of material surplus, and the like. But, to us as sociologists, what the author does not mention is at least as significant as what he does. Above all else the site, to us, speaks of an extraordinary capacity for *coordinated, meaningful, symbolic, collaborative* activity. We use the term "meaningful" to underscore the fact that the ritual act encoded in the interment was clearly *full of shared meaning* for those involved. How many people did it take to boil and straighten the mammoth

---

in often harsh environments. It is just that all of these shared understandings seem to have derived from, and been overwhelmingly deployed in the service of, the material functions of the social. The capacity for meaning making as an end in itself appears to be only lightly developed prior to the explosion. Second, we are certainly aware that the greatly expanded capacity for collaboration and meaning making carried with it extraordinary evolutionary advantages that enhanced the survival chances of modern humans—at least in the short run. That said, it seems just as clear that many of the new ritual and artistic behaviors that followed in the wake of the explosion conferred no direct survival advantage on the group. Among the earliest known examples of jewelry is a collection of delicate beads made from ostrich eggs, taken from a Kenyan site—Enkapune Ya Muto—that dates to 40,000 years ago. "Their maker shaped the crude, circular pieces from fragments of ostrich eggshells, thinning each one and drilling a hole through the center. Many of them broke before they were finished. *An unknown Stone Age artisan spent hours crafting these decorations rather than searching for food, tending children, or making tools*" (Leslie 2002: 57; emphasis added).

tusks? Who contributed the 3,000 hours required to make and then sew the ivory beads on to the burial clothes? What did the various grave goods and the rituals involved in their production mean to the mourners? We will never know, but one can be assured that the members of the group shared an acute and elaborate sense of the event's significance. In sharp contrast to the earlier *Homo sapiens,* whose archaeological traces remain strangely mute, we are finally in the presence of voracious symbolists, people like us who possess both a clear capacity and an apparent *need* to fashion shared identities and meanings as a central component of social life.

Before we move on and discuss the implications—negative as well as positive—of the newfound existential function of the social, we cannot resist taking up the puzzling gap between the development of anatomically modern humans roughly 200,000 years ago and the onset of the social behavioral revolution of 45,000–50,000 years ago. How are we to account for this delay? We see three possible answers to the question. The first possibility is that the earliest "moderns" were, in fact, engaged in symbolic, collaborative activity, but we have not yet found the corroborating physical evidence to support the claim. Given the European bias in the record, this view is at least possible. We would do well to remember that modern humans only made it to Europe around 40,000 years ago. That means that the new species was confined to Africa and the Middle East for the first 125,000–150,000 or so years of its existence. Perhaps we simply have not searched long and hard enough in those locales to produce the requisite evidence of ritual burial and decorative art.

While possible, we think the first answer strains credulity. After all, while Europe has seen intensive archaeological investigation, so too has Africa and the Middle East. Indeed, Europe's fascination with Egypt and the Holy Lands made Northern Africa and the Middle East a central focus of archaeological activity from early on. Since Leakey's extraordinary finds in Kenya's Great Rift Valley in the early 1950s, East Africa has been the center of archaeological research regarding the origins of man. Given the research attention lavished on these areas, it seems highly unlikely that we have simply missed the evidence of the "explosion," especially given how extensive the evidence has been at the later sites. In short, we suspect that the paucity of evidence of symbolic, collaborative activity in these areas is real, reflecting its general absence in the lives of the earlier *Homo sapiens.*

How do we explain this? We see language, or the lack thereof, as the key to the gap. The second answer goes like this. While anatomically adapted to speech, perhaps early humans lacked the precise neural circuitry needed for fully elaborated language. So deprived, earlier *Homo sapiens* may still have possessed a marginally greater capacity for interspecies communication than Neanderthals, but nothing compared to what they would develop in time. While not identical, our view bears a strong family resemblance to the account of anthropologist Richard Klein (2002), who has long held that the symbolic revolution of 45,000 years ago must have been triggered by a random genetic mutation that improved the organization of the brain, affording humans the capacity for language and enhanced symbolic activity.

The third answer is really a variant of the second. While fully adapted to speech and language, it may be that the actual behavioral innovation lagged behind the anatomical emergence of *Homo sapiens*. This may not be quite as crazy as it sounds. Think of written language. Clearly humans had both the physiological and mental capacity for written language long before those capacities were translated into behavior. We do not think it is so farfetched to imagine that something similar could have happened with speech.

Whichever version of the latter two answers one favors, both accord well with the physical evidence and help explain some otherwise puzzling features of the archaeological record. The absence of significant ritual activity prior to 50,000 years ago becomes less puzzling if we assume that a fully realized capacity for human speech did not accompany the rise of *Homo sapiens* but only developed later. This might also explain a second intriguing anomaly in the archaeological record. While Neanderthals disappear from Western Europe barely 12,000 years after modern humans arrive on the scene, the two species appear to have coexisted in the Middle East for nearly 60,000 years, from 100,000 to 40,000 years ago. How can we account for these very different fates? Quite easily if we imagine that only the European *Homo sapiens* possessed a fully realized capacity for human speech and language. Without such a capacity, perhaps their Middle Eastern predecessors lacked the key evolutionary advantage needed to displace their Neanderthal rivals.

Whatever the case, the extraordinary evolutionary advantages conferred on modern humans by the acquisition of language and the related capacity for collaborative, symbolic activity are affirmed by the archaeological record before and after the creative explosion of 50,000 years ago. Consider the following stark contrast. Over roughly the first 150,000 years of the *Homo sapien* presence on this planet, the species was pretty much confined to Africa and the Middle East. The physical traces of their presence suggest an undifferentiated, fairly continuous way of life. Nor do their numbers appear to increase much during their long tenure in Africa. And as noted above, where they overlap with earlier human ancestors—for example, Neanderthal—they coexist with, rather than displace, them.

After the "great leap" of 50,000 years ago, the story could not be more different. Within at most 35,000 years—and possibly less—modern humans succeeded in peopling the globe. Within a scant 12,000 years of arriving in Europe, they—make that "we"—displaced the venerable Neanderthal who had lived

continuously in the region for at least 350,000 years. Our numbers expanded in
fits and starts before mushrooming explosively over the past three to four centuries. Finally, the "undifferentiated, fairly continuous" way of life of our earlier
Homo sapien ancestors quickly give way to the dizzying variety of cultures and
lifeworlds reflected in the archaeological record of the last fifty millennia. Over
this span, "humanity," to quote Klein, "was transformed from a relatively rare
and insignificant large mammal to something like a geologic force" (quoted in
Leslie 2002: 58). None of this is really all that surprising when you consider the
extraordinary evolutionary advantages conveyed by the acquisition of language
and the expanded capacity for communication and social coordination that followed from that endowment.

The Collective as Existential Refuge

One of the most interesting aspects of these discoveries is the way that they
dovetail with thinking in sociology, from Weber and Durkheim to Mead, Goffman, Berger and Luckmann, and Bourdieu. We note that no archaeologist or
anthropologist we are aware of directly views the sociological tradition as relevant to understanding the evolution of *Homo sapiens*. Yet their rich, speculative
accounts of those who carried out the burial at Sungir and those who executed
the extraordinary cave paintings at Lascaux and Chauvet are fully consistent
with collaborative meaning making as the defining quality assigned to modern
humans by a long line of sociologists.

Weber viewed humans as voracious meaning makers and collaborative symbolists. The ability of one person to understand another was the source of all of
social life for Weber (1978) and indeed provided the justification for the various
forms of organization that people fashioned. For Weber, meanings were of three
sorts: purposive/rational, traditional, and value oriented. The people who made
up a given society used these shared meanings to justify their actions in all social
circumstances. Durkheim (1995) noted that religion provided people with an
explanation of their place in the world and a set of understandings that helped
them cope with the uncertainties of life. In this sense, religion provided a sanctified affirmation and expression of the collective. Mead (1934), whose theory we
draw on substantively for our conception of social skill, saw language and socialization as the mechanisms that provided each of us with a sense of self and the
ability to take the role of the "other." He saw the essence of human sociability as
bound up with the capacity for empathy and the ability to use this capacity to get
others to cooperate on the basis of shared understandings. Later theorists, including such important figures for us as Berger and Luckmann (1967) and
Bourdieu (1977, 1984), have built on these insights and expanded their usage in

different contexts. It is useful for us to be explicit about the link we see between these foundational sociological ideas and our emerging understanding of the rise of truly modern humans. We pick up our evolutionary tale at the "moment" of language acquisition.

For all the obvious benefits that flowed from the language/consciousness "package," however, our evolutionary inheritance came with a cost. In liberating us from a primarily materialist existence, language/consciousness endowed humans with art, symbolic thought, and expanded reason but also new fears and threatening forms of awareness. These were two sides of the same coin. We regard existential fear and uncertainty as an unintended evolutionary by-product of whatever mix of genetic and/or anatomical changes triggered the cultural explosion of 50,000 years ago. What do we mean by "existential fear and uncertainty?" We refer to the proverbial "meaning of life" questions that only modern humans seem capable of asking. Only the most stubbornly nonreflective person can, from time to time, avoid the nagging, if generally inchoate, sense that his or her life is accidental, without inherent purpose, and destined to end in death. The philosopher Thomas Nagel (1986) terms these fears the "outer perspective," that state of detached reflection on what would appear at times to be the depressingly obvious "truths" about the human condition. According to Nagel, the capacity to stand outside and reflect on our situation is the basis for the "outer perspective" and the threatening mix of vertigo and fear that accompanies it.

Where exactly does this capacity come from? It is impossible to say for sure. Perhaps it is simply our greater capacity for abstract thought that allows us to formulate these questions. We are more inclined, however, to stress a strong link between language and these new fears. Language grants us the linguistic tools to make of ourselves an object. Instead of being the "I," the unconscious subject, the spontaneous actor, we can now step outside of ourselves and become "me," the object of our own reflection (Mead 1934). This is heady stuff and, if we can trust Mead and a host of others, the foundation for all role taking and thus the key to all those social skills that rest on our ability to "take the role of the other." We will have more to say about this later in the chapter. But this ability to stand outside of ourselves may well also be the source of our existential fears.

Our existential fears are thus rooted in the intimations of aloneness and meaninglessness made possible by our newfound capacity for expanded self-consciousness. It is perhaps not surprising, then, that our attempts to escape from these fears typically involve efforts to overcome or lose self-consciousness. Nietzsche (1988: 52–53), for instance, described the Christian desire for "redemption" as "the essence of all Christian needs . . . it is the most persuaded, most painful affirmation of it in sublime symbols and practices. The Christian wants to get rid of himself." Similarly, the timeless appeal of a love relationship would seem to rest on the desire to lose oneself in another. In general, the effectiveness of any collaborative existential project rests in its ability to inhibit self-consciousness by embedding the individual in a system of socially constructed meanings that substitutes the reassuring subjectivity of the "inner view" for the alienating effects of the "outer perspective." It is the meaningful worlds we fashion in concert with others that insulate us from the threat of the "outer perspective" and confirm our own significance.

This is what we mean by the "existential function" of the social. For most of us, most of the time, the latent threat of the outer perspective is held in check by the lived experience of the "inner perspective." Our daily lives are typically grounded in the unshakable conviction that no one's life is more important than our own and that the world is an inherently meaningful place. But one does not will this inner view into existence of his or her own accord. It is instead a collaborative product, born of the everyday reciprocal meaning making, identity conferring efforts we engage in with those around us. In this we function as existential "coconspirators," relentlessly—if generally unconsciously—exchanging affirmations that sustain our sense of our own significance and the world's inherent meaningfulness.

It would be hard not to see the elaborate burials that suddenly appear in the archaeological record at the time of the "explosion" as the quintessence of this kind of collective existential project. Consider again the interment at Sungir that we described above. Tattersall (1998: 11) describes sites like Sungir as "the most ancient incontrovertible evidence for the existence of religious experience." What are religions, at root, but elaborated worldviews and belief systems that offer reassuring answers to all those threatening questions. Are we alone? No, we are part of a special community of the faithful, a "chosen people," if you will. Is life meaningless? No, through our community we have privileged access to knowledge that renders the world a profoundly meaningful place. What of death? Do we cease to exist when we die? No, provided the community offers the appropriate ritual response, the deceased is assured of life after death. If death represents the most threatening embodiment of the "outer perspective," then a shared belief in an afterlife and collaborative practices designed to ensure its realization represent a powerful collective refutation of the threat. The elaborate and extraordinarily labor-intensive behaviors reflected in the Sungir interment speak eloquently to the emergence of the existential in the human experience. There is simply no narrow instrumental survival function served by such rituals. The thousands of hours devoted to straightening tusks and making and sewing beads could, after all, have gone into hunting, food preparation, shelter construction, or countless other activities directly linked to group survival. And why bury valuable goods and foodstuffs with the deceased when they could be used or consumed by the living? They did so because the binding, existential beliefs of the collective required it.

Let us be clear. We are not for a minute suggesting that all of the new behaviors that followed from the cultural explosion of 50,000 years ago speak to the existential motivations touched on here. Endowed with language and expanded consciousness, modern humans behaved the way they did primarily because they could not do otherwise. That is, they were now adapted to meaning making, communication, coordination, symbolic activity, and so on. This is simply what modern humans do. They also engaged in these new activities because they were instrumentally very effective. As noted above, there were great material advantages to be gained from their newfound capacity to communicate with each other and plan and carry out increasingly complex collaborative activities. Hunting or foraging expeditions could range over broader areas and involve more people. Productive roles within the group could (and, judging from the archaeological evidence, did) become more specialized, yielding survival gains for the collective. We could add other examples, but the point should be clear. Many of the new behaviors should be seen as trial and error efforts to devise more effective solutions to practical problems confronting the group. While Neanderthals survived by adapting the same general tool kit to a broad range of environments and climactic conditions, modern humans—by virtue of their new evolutionary endowments—became (and remain) relentless innovators.

In short, the materialist essence of human life was no less compelling after the cultural leap than it had been before. It is just that a second, quite different, social function/activity was now evident in the archaeological record. It would be a mistake, however, to see the material and existential functions of the social as separate from each other or to attribute preeminence to one or the other. Marx famously characterized religion "as the opiate of the masses," insisting that beliefs and ideologies (read: the existential aspects of the social) were dependent upon and indeed an expression of the underlying material logic of society. We disagree. In our view, the human capacity and need for meaning and identity is as much a structuring force in social life as the material demands on the collective. It is precisely because modern humans need and are relentless in their efforts to fashion shared meanings (like Christianity) and identities (like being a Christian) to restrain existential doubt that these constructions are available to those (like capitalists) who would appropriate and exploit them for their own purposes. In short, the material/instrumental and the existential are inextricably linked. Even as strategic actors are working to advance their interests, they are simultaneously exercising the distinctive human capacity for meaning making and the construction of collective identities. People do what they do both to achieve instrumental advantage and to fashion meaningful worlds for themselves and others. This, we will argue, is as true today as ever. Any adequate theory of human strategic action must take this mix of instrumental and existential motives into account.

There is, however, an interesting and important difference between instrumental and existential motives in our comparative awareness of the two. That is, in representing modern humans as "voracious meaning makers," as relentless existential actors, we are not claiming that we behave in this way with all that much conscious awareness of our "true" motives. How can we explain this general lack of awareness of our need and proclivity for existential projects? Indeed, there would almost seem to be a contradiction inherent in asserting that existential doubt/fear is a central motivating force in social life and yet produces little conscious awareness on the part of the individual actor. How can we be motivated to act on the basis of motives of which we are only dimly aware? One need not be a Freudian to believe such a thing possible. Two factors help resolve this apparent contradiction. The first is simply our typically inchoate experience of existential doubt. If the devout generally sense the divine via little more than "rumors of angels" (Berger 1990), then most of us only apprehend the threat of aloneness and meaninglessness in fleeting moments of dread and despair for which we have few words and fewer explanations. Lacking structure and coherence, these moments are not quite real and therefore generally elude full consciousness.

Just as important, the fears sensed in these moments are sufficiently threatening as to encourage their suppression. As Nyberg (1993: 83), writes, people seem to "know very well that we need hope to survive, that there are things we must strive not to know, even if that attitude looks to others like denial or self-deception." Since our basic existential fears threaten hope, most of us "strive not to know them." We do this, not only through individual denial, but by "investing" in collaborative existential projects that assert the orderly, purposive nature of the world. Indeed, the viability of these projects is directly related to our capacity for denial. Nothing poses a greater threat to our beliefs than a conscious awareness of the existential motives underlying them. How much more meaningful to marry for love than for existential assurance How much more satisfying to find religion through the redeeming grace of Christ than as a conscious hedge against the abyss. With all due respect to Pascal, it is not simply unseemly to profess a belief in God as a kind of existential side bet but patently ineffective as well. To do so is to acknowledge the self-interested, constructed nature of "faith," thereby leaving the issue of existential doubt unresolved and denying oneself the comfort that "true faith" affords. Faith as a cognitive and emotional commitment to the demands of any existential project would appear to rest on precisely this combination of self-interest and social construction, but to be effective these motivational and sociological dynamics must remain opaque. The effectiveness of any meaning project, then, rests on a kind of existential sleight of hand. Even as people are working purposefully to fashion and sustain meaningful social orders, they must simultaneously experience this as something other than their handiwork.

We close this section with an important aside. After rereading what we wrote, we were struck by the generally "upbeat" tone of this section. To be sure, we acknowledged that the language/consciousness "package" that serves as the physiological basis for the existential function of the social was a two-edged sword, conferring great evolutionary advantages while simultaneously burdening the species with new fears and threatening forms of awareness. But in emphasizing our voracious capacity for meaning making, we could be read as arguing that existential despair is really no match for the cultural creativity of the species, that our worst fears and doubts inevitably succumb to the collective understandings and identities that sustain us. In point of fact, the existential "under toad" is a formidable opponent, inflicting despair, loneliness, anomie on all of us at one time or another, sometimes with tragic consequences.

But this admission constitutes only one aspect of the "darker" side of the perspective on offer here. Indeed, there are several other sobering implications of the argument. We will confine ourselves to just one other. Even when the forces of collective meaning and identity triumph over existential doubt and despair, they often do so by investing deeply in conflict with other groups and their associated meaning projects. Beginning with Simmel (1955), sociologists have long recognized the "functions of social conflict" (Coser 1956). Mead (1934) was quite aware that the valorizing existential projects of groups could contain an element of "us" versus "them" where "they" were defined as "heathens," "savages," "infidels," or some other evil or dangerous collective requiring eradication.

Answers to the most basic existential questions often seem clearest during wartime or at other times of savage social conflict. Who am I? I am a holy warrior doing battle with an evil enemy. What does it all mean? It is a cosmic battle between good (us) and evil (them). However we might recoil in value terms from Nazism, it is critically important to our perspective that we recognize just how profoundly meaningful the movement was to its adherents. Hitler was nothing if not a supremely skilled social actor adept at fashioning unambiguous "truths" that valorized the lives of believers and sanctified their presence in the world. In doing so, his is only an extreme example of the opposition between the existential and material functions of the social that is unique to our species. That is, conflict is sufficiently attractive as a source of meaning and identity that we appear willing to destroy each other to achieve its existential benefits.

Social Skill

If the genetic and/or anatomical changes that occurred 45,000–50,000 years ago were responsible for burdening modern humans with new existential fears and challenges, they also afforded us the mental, linguistic, and social skills needed to respond to these threats. Central to our perspective is the concept of "social skill," that complex mix of cognitive, affective, and linguistic facilities that render individuals more or less effective as skilled strategic actors supremely well adapted to the demands of collective action. Drawing on the distinctive micro-foundations sketched above, we want to use the balance of the chapter to expli-cate the concept of social skill as a necessary prerequisite for what is to follow in later chapters.

Our goal is to provide a distinctly sociological understanding that uses the existential capacity and need for meaning and membership as the core for un-derstanding how people create and sustain mesolevel social worlds. We argue that the need for meaning is at the basis of people's efforts to get and sustain collective action. But in order to have meaning function in this way, it is necessary to have a model of what people do in their everyday interactions in strategic ac-tion fields to produce collective action and create such meaning. Such a model must posit a *Homo sociologicus*, who requires meaning as the ground of his or her being and achieves that meaning by engaging in collaborative action with others. At the risk of redundancy, we reiterate a crucially important point made above. In stressing the central importance of meaning making in group life, we are not for a minute suggesting that issues of power, interests, and status are somehow marginal to our perspective. They are anything but. But seeking out instrumental gain, social status, and power are inherently linked to the problem of meaning. We seek out these things because we want to prove to ourselves and others that we are worthy as people. In doing so, they provide us with meaning and the sense that our lives have purpose. By "winning," we confirm to ourselves and others that life is not meaningless (or at least we manage to keep that doubt at bay). Meaning making is inextricably bound up with the contests for power, status, and other interests.

In order to make sense of what people actually do to attain collective action, we introduce the notion of social skill. Social skill can be defined as the ability to induce cooperation by appealing to and helping to create shared meanings and collective identities. Skilled social actors empathetically relate to the situations of other people and, in doing so, are able to provide those people with reasons to cooperate (Goffman 1959, 1974; Mead 1934). Skilled social actors must under-stand how the sets of actors in their group view their multiple conceptions of interest and identity and how those in external groups do as well. They use these understandings to provide an interpretation of a given situation and to frame courses of action that appeal to existing interests and identities. Their appeals elicit cooperation from members of their group and produce generally negative accounts of the identity of those with whom the group is competing.

Part of what creates and sustains fields is the ongoing use of social skill by actors. All fields require the active participation of individuals and groups to continue to function. This raises the question of how groups are held together and how action in a strategic action field is structured. Everyone who is a member of a social group derives existential benefits from being in the group. It is on the basis, and very often in defense, of these benefits that group members collaborate with one another and compete with those with alternative views of the strategic action field.

People routinely deploy social skill as part of a meaning making project. They do so with a mix of motives. Of course, they might gain materially from their actions and this might be one of their core motives. But people engage in collective action for less clearly instrumental reasons as well. Creating or affirming shared meanings and identities through collaborative action is among the most satisfying and affirming of human activities. Being part of a group and reveling in the lived experience of "we-ness" is one of the most important ways that individuals come to have a positive view of themselves and hold their existential fears at bay. Having a successful marriage or relationship, raising children, cooperating with others at work, all provide us with the sense that life is meaningful and we play an important part in it. From this perspective, there is a false distinction between instrumental and altruistic action. Collaborative meaning making sounds very altruistic, but it is also the ground of all collective instrumental action.

The concept of social skill is rooted for us in symbolic interactionism (Goffman 1959, 1974; Joas 1996; Mead 1934). Actors' conceptions of themselves are powerfully shaped by their interactions with others. When interacting, actors try to create a positive sense of self by fashioning shared meanings and identities for themselves and others. Identities refer to sets of meanings that actors have that define who they are and what they want in a particular situation. Actors in dominant positions who are efficacious and successful may have high self-esteem. Actors in dominated positions may be stigmatized and forced to engage in coping strategies to contest their stigmatization (Goffman 1963).

Mead (1934) argues that some social actors are better than others at inducing cooperation. This is because they are able to create a positive sense of self that resonates with others. We say that these actors are more socially skilled. Skilled social actors produce meaning for others, because by doing so, they produce meaning for themselves. Their sense of efficacy comes, not from some narrow conception of self-interest (although skilled actors tend to benefit materially from their skill) but from the act of inducing cooperation and helping others attain ends. They will do whatever it takes to induce cooperation and if one path is closed off, they will explore others. This means that skilled social actors are neither narrowly self-interested nor motivated by fixed goals. They generally do not have individual fixed interests but instead focus on evolving collective ends. They keep their goals somewhat open-ended and are prepared to take what the system will give. This more open stance toward the world and their own aims means that skilled strategic actors often behave very differently than ideal type rational actors, who are narrowly pursuing their own fixed interests and goals in some contest with others.

As Giddens (1984) has pointed out, all human beings are capable of skilled social performances. They need to be somewhat socially skilled in order to survive. But we all know people who are more socially skilled than others, that is, have the ability to get others to cooperate. They appear in universities, politics, and the world of business. Sometimes they are leaders or managers in that they hold formal positions of power, but sometimes they do not. The assertion, here, is only that some people are more capable at taking the role of the other and using this intersubjective understanding of others to fashion shared meanings and identities to mobilize collective strategic action.

Skilled strategic actors mostly find themselves in fields that are already structured. As a result they often do not have much choice as to their position in the field, the resources available to them, or the opportunities they might have to either reproduce or change their situation. Still, even within these constraints, skilled actors have considerable latitude for action. If they are in incumbent groups, they will use their skill to maintain group solidarity, to sustain and affirm the shared identities and meanings that undergird the collective, and, in general, to maintain the status and material advantages enjoyed by group members. If they are in challenger groups, their social skills may be sorely tested but still potentially very consequential. In such situations skilled actors seek to maintain solidarity and a positive collective identity in the face of lots of challenges. From a more narrowly strategic perspective, they must continue to fashion lines of action that maintain what opportunities they have while searching to exploit any emerging vulnerabilities they discern in their opponents. Social skill may be a property of individuals, but the use of social skill is heavily constrained by the individual's position within the field in question. That is, successful deployment of social skill will depend on the actor recognizing her or his social position, being able to take the perspective of other actors (both those with whom they are trying to cooperate and those with whom they are competing), and finding a set of actions that "make sense" given their position. One way of thinking about this is that one needs to separate out the role a person occupies in a particular strategic action field from the ability of the person to enact that role and effect an outcome.

Much of sociology wants either to reduce people to positions in social structure (thereby denying them the ability to be self-aware actors) or alternatively to view them as highly agentic, at every moment creating and re-creating society whether they know it or not. The theory of social skill and its relationship to the theory of fields implies that both the individual skills actors have and the positions they occupy in social space affect their ability to engage in cooperation, competition, and collective action. Action depends on both the structural position and opportunities actors have and their ability to recognize how they can mobilize others in order to maximize their chances for both narrowly instrumental and broader existential gain. In any given situation, actors' ability to improve their group's situation may be highly or minimally constrained by their position in the structure. Either way, the challenge will be to use their social skill to exploit whatever opportunities may be available to them. They must also continue to motivate others and provide meaning and identity to sustain group solidarity and morale.

It is useful to elaborate more clearly how we deploy the idea of social skill in our argument and how it differs from more rationalist arguments. The concept of social skill helps solve three important problems in our theory of fields. First, it provides a microfoundation for the theory as a whole. For all our objections to rational choice theory, we have long admired the stark set of behavioral assumptions on which the perspective rests. The essence of human social life, according to proponents of the theory, is rational calculus and action in pursuit of narrowly instrumental ends.

In contrast, for us, the essence of human sociability is collaborative meaning making. This is not to deny the more narrowly instrumental/material ground of human existence. It's just that, for us, the material and the existential cannot be disentangled. For starters, material ends are always conceived by, and enacted through, groups. Without participating in groups, there would be no material rewards. The meaning projects of fields are what allow groups to function and pursue and distribute rewards. This is because the act of creating material objects requires collective action. And collective action requires identity and meaning in order to convince individuals that they are part of something real, important, and tied to their "interests." The existential projects of groups help explain a number of key features of social life that rational accounts take for granted. For all its heuristic appeal, individuals are rarely, if ever, calculating *outsiders*. Even the most selfish of "loners" is motivated by ends that are, at root, collective constructions. They seek out affirmation of their worth by striving to get what others have. They seek out the admiration of those whose respect they crave and seek to punish those who are their enemies. Further, these individuals are generally obliged to pursue these aims within collectives in consort with others.

This brings us to our second point. In rational actor models, individual participation in collective action can never be taken for granted. Indeed, the default option for rational actors is to refrain from collective action and resist collective commitments that might impede their ability to realize their ends. This tendency to "free ride" can only be overcome, we are told, when organizers provide selective incentives that make it rational for individuals to affiliate with the group or action in question. In short, collective entanglements only make sense if they aid the individual in realizing narrow instrumental aims. Our stress on the existential functions of the social leads us to embrace a starkly opposing view. For us, affiliation with groups and other collectives is a highly desired end in and of itself. Ultimately the central sources of meaning and identity in our lives can only be conferred by collectives. Accordingly much of our social skill is deployed in the service of fashioning and safeguarding these collective existential projects.

This leads us to our third and final point. By focusing on social skill, our theory shifts the emphasis from motives to action and the contributions that skilled actors make to the emergence, maintenance, and transformation of social orders. This runs counter to almost all social theorizing that begins with individuals reacting, in a self-interested way, to their positions in social structure. So, for example, in Bourdieu's theory of the habitus, the most sophisticated current theoretical view of the link between individuals and social structure, individuals' reaction to a particular situation depends upon their position in a particular field, the resources available to them, and their perception of strategic options based on socialization and lived experience.

In our theory, however, actors are never simply self-interested. Most of us, most of the time, are motivated to affirm our membership in this or that group— for example, family member, employee, congregant—by helping to reproduce the order in question. Admittedly sometimes we do so with an eye to preserving the narrow instrumental goods conferred by these collectives, but most of the time we are simply expressing our affiliation with the group, preserving and extending its identity, and generally honoring its existential hold on us.

Social Skill in Action

Having gone to pains to show how our foundational sense of human sociability informs our conception of social skill, we want to turn in this section to a much more focused discussion of some of the forms of socially skilled action that we see routinely deployed in fields. We see all of these forms of action as reflecting not only the deployment of social skill but also, at a deeper level, the motivating force of the existential function of the social.

The literature has identified a number of important tactics that socially skilled actors use to engage in cooperative and competitive behavior in groups (Bourdieu 1977; Coleman 1986; DiMaggio 1988; Fligstein 1996, 2001a; Goffman 1959, 1974; Leifer 1988; Nee and Ingram 1998; Padgett and Ansell 1993; White 1992). The basic problem for skilled social actors is to frame "stories" that help induce cooperation from people by appealing to their identity, belief, and interests, while at the same time using those same stories to frame actions against various opponents. This is the general problem of framing that Goffman (1974) identifies. These stories are sometimes about meaning and membership, that is, existential issues and questions of group identity, and sometimes about "what's in it for me."

One of the most important vehicles for framing is the direct authority to tell someone what to do. Long ago Weber (1978) noted that authority was the probability that a direct command was obeyed based on the position of legitimacy of the person giving the command. By holding a position in a particular social group, actors will find it easier to attain cooperation from others. But even if one has a formal position in a group, one must still induce cooperation in subordinates (Barnard 1938). This means there has to be a broader repertoire of other tactics that skilled actors use in order to structure interactions with those within and across groups.

Agenda setting is the ability to set the parameters of the discussion for others (Kingdon 1995; Lukes 1974). If a skilled actor can get others to accept what the terms of discussion are, much of the battle has been won. Agenda setting is usually attained by behind-the-scenes action to convince multiple actors and groups that a particular agenda is in their interests. When the groups meet, the agenda is set, the terms of discussion are set, and the identity and interests of actors are framed. This ensures that actors have to come to understand their interests within certain bounds, thus closing off many other courses of possible action.

Skilled actors understand the ambiguities and uncertainties of the field and work off of them. They have a sense of what is possible and impossible. If the situation provides opportunities that are unplanned but might result in some gain, skilled actors will grab them, even if they are not certain as to the usefulness or the gain. This is a pragmatic, open-ended approach to strategic action that is akin to what Lévi-Strauss calls "bricolage" (1966). It follows that skilled actors will take what the system will give at any moment, even if it is not exactly what they or others might ideally want.

Indeed, skilled social actors often end up convincing others that what they can get is what they want. In order to do this, skilled actors have to convince others who do not necessarily share interests that what will occur is consistent with their identity and interest. This can be done by selling groups on some overriding values that all accept or convincing them that what will happen will serve their narrow interest, at least to a degree. Since interests and preferences can be formed as fields form, it is necessary to link broader frames to groups' existing conceptions of interest.

The skilled social actor will engage in brokering more than blustering (Gould 1993). This works in two ways. First, strategic actors present themselves as neutral in a situation, acting as if they are simply trying to mediate the interests of others. Second, strategic actors present themselves as more active in selling the group collective identity and appealing to others to find a way to get people to go along. Their solution is sold either to help keep the peace or to ensure that the field does not collapse. To be a broker, skilled actors have to convince others that they are not motivated by narrow self-interest and will gain personally from finding a negotiated solution.

Since the goal of skilled action is to attain cooperation from others, socially skilled actors often appear hard to read and devoid of interests of their own (this is what Leifer 1988 and Padgett and Ansell 1993 have called "robust action"). Opposition can quickly mobilize against someone who appears to want something for narrow individual gain. On the other hand, if someone appears open to others' needs and not wedded to any particular course of action, others will very likely find the situation more conducive to negotiation or other forms of cooperative action.

One main problem for socially skilled actors is to find a way to link actors or groups with widely different preferences and help reorder those preferences. This aggregation process, once it gets going, can take on a life of its own. Once a number of actors come on board, others will likely follow. The trick is to bring enough on board to set in motion the proverbial bandwagon effect. This is most frequently done by fashioning a resonant collective identity (Ansell 2001). Such an identity allows groups to attach their divergent interests to a common project.

Skilled actors will be pursuing a number of lines of action going simultaneously. Many of these—perhaps most of them—will peter out or fail to materialize. But as long as these aborted lines of action are not viewed as serious failures, all one needs is a few successful lines of action, or victories, to convince others to come along. After the fact, other actors or groups will likely only remember the successes even if one had to try various lines of action to get a few to work. Part of this illusion of action is to try and convince others that their vision contains more reality than they might think. If you can convince others that they have more power or control to get others to go along, then once something gets set in motion, others will fall in line.

Another common ploy of strategic actors is getting others to believe that some line of action was actually their idea. If the ploy works, the payoff is tremendous commitment to the initiative by the nominal architect of the plan. A related tactic has the skilled actor setting up situations in which others are subtly encouraged to take the lead and buy into what they have come to believe was their idea. By getting actors who are relatively isolated to cooperate and convincing them that their cooperation was their idea, the strategic actor gets others to cooperate without appearing Machiavellian.

Padgett and Ansell (1993) have argued that a good way to secure cooperation with disparate groups is to make alliances with people with few other choices or isolate particularly difficult outliers. The preferable action is to include as many outliers as possible into the field and gain agreement on an overarching worldview and collective identity. One good way to do this is to be the node that connects these outliers to the network. Then, the skilled actor is the source of information and coalition building. Occasionally, certain actors or groups are so disruptive that the best tactic is to isolate them. Even if there are a number of upset but isolated actors, they generally remain disorganized. Since these types of actors are usually incapable of strategic action themselves, they remain isolates.

Conclusion

In this chapter, we have parsed the rich literature on human evolution to offer a highly speculative, sensitizing perspective on the origins of what we have termed the "existential function of the social"; that "moment" when collaborative symbolic activity assumed central importance in social life. The intent was to provide at least the bare bones of a microfoundation for the theory being developed here. We have linked this underlying microfoundation to strategic action in fields via the concept of social skill; that is, the ways in which skilled actors use empathy and the capacity to fashion and strategically deploy shared meanings and identities in the service of institutional projects within fields.

The theory of social skill and fields is applicable to a range of sociological phenomena that share common characteristics. The subfields in sociology that are best analyzed from this perspective are concerned with organized groups that have a reason to set up rules for a particular social space. The social phenomena in which self-conscious actors strive to organize groups toward collective ends include institutional politics, religion, social movements, the economy in which firms and governments create markets, and the nonprofit sector of capitalist economies. All of these arenas of action contain actors who seek to construct institutions to guide their interactions in order that they might forward their existential and material interests. They want to create new social spaces where their groups can dominate or prosper. In all of these empirical terrains, we observe formal organizational rules, laws, and informal practices being used to guide interaction. Now, of course, the goals of actors are very different across states, markets, religion, the nonprofit sector, and social movements. But in all of these arenas, we see actors striving to attain cooperation within their groups and to stabilize interactions across groups.

Our claim that the framework on offer here applies to most public arenas or institutional spheres in modern society is intended to be quite provocative. While some scholars have gestured toward a more general theory of institutional action, few have tried to broaden the scope of their own theorizing to accommodate phenomena as diverse as those touched on above (for an attempt, see Powell 1991). Our stress on the centrality of meaning making and its expression in the form of social skill implies that in both settled and unsettled fields, the competing meaning projects of groups will structure the interactions both within and across groups. Since even in settled strategic action fields there will be contestation, we expect that some group of individuals will always be trying to change the definition of the situation and the meanings that inform action in the field. This will result in ongoing change to the nature of group interaction, the meanings for actors, and the positions of groups and individuals. In less settled times, we expect that the possibilities for innovative action will increase. New identities, new political coalitions, and even new strategic action fields can emerge. Social skill in both cases is what bridges the gap between what individuals are doing and the structures and logics that result from their efforts.

With these foundational underpinnings in hand, we would like to close the chapter by offering some additional clarifying comments on the concept of social skill before briefly revisiting the metaperspective on human sociability with which we opened the chapter. We begin with a conundrum related to the distribution of social skill across social space.

Our perspective rests on the assumption that socially skilled actors exist in every field. They are equally likely to populate incumbent and challenger groups. If socially skilled actors exist both in incumbent and challenger groups, one could argue that whatever advantage skill might convey, it would be offset by the presence of equally skilled actors in the other group—leaving the incumbent in a dominant position. Indeed, this is frequently the case and we have no problem acknowledging that very often the social skill of challengers and incumbents is roughly equal, allowing the contest to be decided on the basis of the superior resources and/or political endowments of the latter. But even if the overall structure of the field remains largely unchanged, skill may still make a difference. Even in the most stable of fields, we can expect to see constant jockeying for advantage and efforts to marginally improve one's position in the strategic action field. Social skill will be important to these as well as to major convulsive moments in the life of a field.

Then again, there *are* those "convulsive moments." At such times, strategic action fields are unstable and present new opportunities for challengers to better their positions. It is at these moments that the ability of socially skilled actors to mobilize resources and to frame innovative lines of action to secure cooperation may prove decisive. Challengers who are more attuned to moments when their position might be significantly improved will work diligently to locate and exploit such opportunities. Quite simply, we expect the role of social skill to be more decisive in situations of greater field flux than in relatively stable times.

Still, the role of social skill and the ultimate outcome of field contention in such moments remain unpredictable and depend not just on the distribution of social skill across groups but also on resource endowments, political allies, and events in other proximate fields. We could imagine a situation in which similarly sized and resourced groups face off and the superior social skills of one of the combatants lead to the defeat of the other. But we can also imagine cases in which the resource endowments of the groups are really not so equal and the more advantaged group prevails independent of differences in social skill. Lots of other outcomes are possible as well, depending on the mix of factors noted above.

The problem of determining when social skill is decisive in the way that a field becomes organized or in the ability of challenger groups to improve their positions is mostly a question of empirical analysis. But what our perspective does say is that it is always important for actors to be mobilized, even strong incumbent actors. Thus, the problem of using social skill and using it effectively is always an issue in strategic action fields. The constant jockeying for position and the piecemeal changes in strategic action fields very much reflect skilled social actors looking for an edge, any edge, and occasionally changing the nature of their position in the fields.

Even small changes can sometimes be turned into larger changes if multiple groups align with an innovative new collective identity or collective action frame. Social skill depends on the ability of actors to transcend their narrow worldview, take the position of the "other," and figure out how either to get the "other" to cooperate or to effectively blunt or counter the "other's" advantages. This dynamic within strategic action fields is on ongoing part of the game. It only makes sense that most of the time in settled strategic action fields, incumbents can reproduce their advantage primarily through superior resources or the actions of internal governance units or other political allies. Even settled strategic action fields have moments of turbulence, however, presenting socially skilled actors with opportunities to successfully challenge even the most entrenched incumbents.

We would like to close the chapter where we began, by underscoring the distinctive microfoundation on which our general perspective rests. In truth, most sociologists have little or nothing to say about the fundamental behavioral assumptions that ground their work. Implicitly, however, we think we discern two very different metatheoretical perspectives lurking behind most sociological scholarship. In the distinct minority are rationalists who see calculus and individual/collective interests as the driving force in social life. Juxtaposed to the rationalists are most sociologists who embrace one or another version of what Dennis Wrong (1961) long ago termed the "oversocialized conception of man." The actual microfoundations of this view have never really been articulated, but that has not stopped the perspective from being broadly modal within the discipline. What do we mean by the "oversocialized conception of man?" We simply mean that most sociologists stress the critical importance of various forms of social influence—norms, socialization, collective identity, social scripts, "taken for granted" organizational routines—in shaping human social life.

As card-carrying sociologists, we would never deny the power of such influences in social life. But in asserting the distinctive microfoundations spelled out earlier, we part company from most of our disciplinary brethren in two significant ways. First, we seek not to simply assert the power of social influence but to account for it. We maintain that the tendency of humans to hew to social norms, to conform to group pressures, reflects nothing so much as the existential functions of the social. That is, our desire to belong and to believe that the world is an ordered, meaningful reality renders us susceptible to social influence. By conforming to group norms we affirm membership and meaning and, in turn, restrain existential doubt.

This latter account differs from most generic sociological perspectives in a second sense. By seeing humans as possessing both the capacity and the *need* to engage in collective meaning making, we are asserting a much more active, agentic view of social life than would appear common in sociology. The image implicit in most sociological work is that of unconscious conformity to norms or adherence to "taken for granted" routines. If humans are inclined to accommodate various forms of social influence—and we certainly think they are—we see them doing so much more thoughtfully and with conscious regard for the material and existential stakes involved in their actions. This more active, purposive view of the species is consistent with our stress on social skill and the active fashioning, stabilization, and transformation of strategic action fields.

From the micro we now turn to the other extreme. Having explicated a microfoundation to help account for the capacities and motivations that shape strategic action within fields, we now seek to place those fields in the broadest possible macrocontext. For if certain species capacities shape contention in strategic action fields, they do so in response to constraints and opportunities that arise outside of the field as much as dynamics internal to it.

3

Macroconsiderations

As we have noted, ours is hardly the only theory of fields to be found in contemporary social science. More and more scholars in a range of disciplines appear to be drawn to the concept and the idea that much of organized life is carried out in constructed social orders, which have come to be known as fields. Among the works we most admire in contemporary sociology are the various analyses of emergence, contention, and change in this or that field (Armstrong 2002; Duffy, Binder, and Skrentny 2010; Rao, Monin, and Durand 2003; Scott et al. 2000). But while our conception of strategic action fields draws on and shares much in common with these and a host of other works, ours is a much more ambitious theory-building effort than any previous work in this vein. The scope of this ambition can be seen most clearly in this and the previous chapter. In chapter 2 we sought to ground our perspective in a distinctive microfoundation. Believing that sociologists are too quick to insist that theirs is a distinctive disciplinary perspective on social life without systematically articulating such a perspective, we have tried to at least move in that direction in chapter 2. We have tried to suggest the ways in which the human species is both adapted to, and seemingly dependent upon, the kind of collaborative action and meaning making that is central to fields. What's more, we have sought to suggest the ways in which the social skill exhibited by field actors expresses these species capacities and needs, even as it powerfully shapes the emergence, reproduction, and transformation of strategic action fields. To our knowledge, no other field theorists have sought to embed their perspective in the kind of microfoundation we have sketched in chapter 2.

In this chapter, we move from the micro to the macro. In doing so we seek to put the single field that is almost always the focus of scholarly attention into a broader field systemic context. If anything, the macroperspective on offer in this chapter is even more central to our theory of fields than is the microfoundation sketched in the previous chapter. For in our view, the state of a field at any given moment is simultaneously shaped by dynamics "internal" to the field and by events in a host of "external" strategic action fields with which the field in question has very close and sometimes dependent ties. Indeed, we have put quotation marks around "internal" and "external" to indicate just how difficult it is to draw these boundaries and to argue that any analysis of a field that fails to take the issue of "external" relations seriously is bound to be badly truncated and incomplete. Yet, virtually all analyses of fields produced to date suffer to a greater or lesser extent from this "fieldcentric" bias. That is, they invest deeply in an internal analysis of field dynamics without fully understanding the extent to which these dynamics are inextricably linked to events elsewhere in the dense latticework or system of interdependent fields that comprise modern society. Our goal in this chapter is to begin to fashion a systematic macroperspective on the relationship between fields and this broader field environment that so powerfully affects the developmental history and trajectory of any given strategic action field.

Toward that end, the chapter is organized into five sections. We begin with a general discussion of the various ways that strategic action fields can be embedded in the broader system of fields and how these forms of embedding powerfully shape the prospects for stability and change in all fields. Here we distinguish between three different dimensions or patterns of embedding. The first pattern is one in which a number of fields are nested hierarchically in each other, in a system that resembles Russian dolls. Any large corporation will exhibit this pattern. The second distinction we introduce concerns the formal power relations that characterize the link between any two fields. Here we distinguish between dependent and interdependent fields. In the first case, one field exercises clear authority or power over the other, while, in the second, the two fields exert more or less equal influence on each other. There are, of course, lots of fields, indeed the great majority, that are not tied together at all. So, in fact, we can speak of "dependent," "interdependent," and "unconnected" fields. Finally, we emphasize the quantity of ties that characterize the embedding of any given field. Some fields are embedded in a dense latticework of other fields, while others are comparative "isolates," with ties to relatively few strategic action fields.

In the second section of the chapter, we offer a brief "excursus on formal organization" designed to render the concepts of formal organization and bureaucracy in terms of our perspective. Formal organizations are perhaps the most ubiquitous form of collective action in the modern world, and clarifying how they relate to the idea of strategic action fields is important theoretically. Section three is devoted to an extended discussion of the modern state—conceived here as a dense and interconnected set of fields—and its role in helping to found, stabilize/certify, reproduce, and undermine/transform the great majority of nonstate fields. We then take up the issue of "internal governance units" (IGUs). These are bodies internal to a field—often established at the time of the field's founding—that are designed to ensure its smooth functioning and reproduction.

They serve a variety of administrative and regulative functions that will be discussed in more detail in the section. The section follows the one on the state because, among their other functions, many of these governance units also serve as the field's liaison to and lobbying arm vis-à-vis various state actors and fields. Finally, we close the chapter by briefly discussing the proliferation of fields, the expansion of higher education, and the rise and spread of professions as three related and interdependent processes characteristic of modernity. As fields slowly emerged as the fundamental organizing technology of public life, the need for skilled social actors to "populate" them grew apace. Actually we see these processes—the proliferation of fields, the growth of higher education, and the development of professions—as mutually reinforcing historical processes.

The "Embeddedness" of Strategic Action Fields

Fields do not exist in a vacuum. They have relations with other strategic action fields and these relations powerfully shape the developmental history of the field. It is useful to consider how these relations affect the stability and instability of strategic action fields. One of the central insights of our theory is that the basic structure of any given strategic action field is the same as any other field regardless of whether or not the field is made up of individual people, groups, organizations, or nation-states. It also follows that the relationship between any two fields, even if they contain similar groups (say, two industries composed of firms), is to be understood in terms of the same relationships. The relations between strategic action fields are of three types: *unconnected*, hierarchical or *dependent*, and reciprocal or *interdependent*. The links between fields are shaped by a number of factors: resource dependence, mutual beneficial interactions, sharing of power, information flows, and legitimacy. Where no obvious links exist between fields along any of these dimensions, we can say that fields are unconnected. Hence, we could say that the commercial fishing industry in the United States in the 1950s and 1960s and the civil rights movement in the same period were unconnected fields.

It is useful to develop some analytic terms by which to distinguish the relationships between fields. Earlier, we argued that fields were composed of individuals, groups, divisions, organizations, industries, nation-states, and even international organizations. One of our important ideas is that there can be a form of embedding whereby actors that make up smaller collectivities are located within larger strategic action fields that contain larger collectivities. We described this as the "Russian doll" quality of strategic action fields. Higher level strategic action fields can be usefully decomposed into their units, which themselves would be strategic action fields. The relations between such groups can be cooperative or hierarchical. This means that higher order groups can sometimes command lower order groups. But it is possible for lower order groups to dominate these relationships as well. This can happen because sometimes the lower order strategic action fields are dependent on higher order strategic action fields, and at other times, the higher order strategic action fields can be dependent on lower order strategic action fields. There can also be cooperative relationships within groups of strategic action fields organized as Russian dolls.

It is useful to give some examples. Consider a firm. Firms are nested strategic action fields in which there are hierarchical dependent relationships between the component fields. Each plant and office is a strategic action field in its own right. Typically firms are organized into larger divisions in which management controls resource allocation and hiring. These divisions themselves report to a central office where they vie with other divisions for resources. But these relationships can be cooperative as well as hierarchical and competitive. One can imagine a situation in which divisions of the organization are roughly equal in size. This might motivate them to form a political coalition to lobby and co-opt top management.

There are also examples of nested fields in which lower level strategic action fields exert strong control over the higher order fields. Take, for example, professional sports leagues. Here, each team constitutes a field in its own right and in turn competes with all other teams for players, coaches, and victories in the broader league strategic action field. But often in sports leagues, the nominally higher order central administrative organization that is supposed to oversee the sport winds up being dominated by one or more of the most powerful, resource-rich teams in the league. In this case, lower order fields (e.g., dominant teams) can have power over the entire strategic action field. For example, Leifer (1995) argues that the New York Yankees dominated baseball in the United States and created a system that came to favor them over a period extending from roughly 1920 to 1970. Strategic action fields can be organized with groups made up of similar types of collective actors. These linkages can be hierarchical and dependent or more cooperative. Take, for example, the United Nations, a forum in which representatives of nation-states meet to discuss common problems. Theoretically, all of the states are equal by virtue of their being sovereign states. They cooperate on many common issues, issue resolutions, and jointly sponsor various aid and educational programs. But some states clearly have more power than others. The United Nations has a Security Council that clearly privileges the countries that have permanent membership. In the end, then, a relatively small number of incumbent nations exert inordinate influence over the operation of the broader organization.

Fields operating at the same level of group organization can also have a more cooperative or reciprocal structure. Pierre Bourdieu describes the interdependence of the elite university system and the large corporations in France in his book *The State Nobility* (1998). One can conceive of the collection of universities in a given country as a strategic action field. Here, universities will vie for position in a status hierarchy to form a field of incumbents and challengers. In France, the elite universities known as grandes écoles dominate the university system. A system of entrance exams guarantees that only highly vetted individuals end up in these universities. These students go on to supply the main officials for the government and large corporations. The world of large corporations in France has a hierarchical structure as well. The government has spent the past thirty years building up a set of partially state-owned large corporations. These firms are viewed as "national champions" because they are supposed to secure the markets of the country and be competitors in world markets as well. They form a set of incumbents that largely structure a host of specific strategic action fields populated by variable numbers of other firms.

The question that Bourdieu poses is what is the relationship between the incumbent units within these two realms? He argues that the grandes écoles need to be able to place their graduates in government and large corporations in order to maintain their position of prestige in the system. This makes them dependent on both corporations and the government for their legitimacy. This would make the grandes écoles appear to be overly dependent on their "customers" and possibly insecure in their positions. But Bourdieu suggests that both the firms and government need the grandes écoles as well. In order to justify their positions in the economy the firms need to appear to be hiring the best and the brightest students. This means that to maintain their legitimacy, both the state and large corporations rely on the grandes écoles to certify the best students in the country. This produces a symbiotic and cooperative relationship between fields organized by large, incumbent organizations.

Given the many possible relations between strategic action fields, it is important to know when two fields are related to each other and to be able to characterize the nature and closeness of that relationship. At this point in history, it is probably the case that all organized social space on this planet can be reached via connections through other social space. This was not always the case. Indeed, one definition of modernity is what Giddens has called the shift in time-space distanciation (1990). Our modern conceptions of time and space have been greatly altered by improvements in technology, communications, and transportation that have increased our ability to be aware of and even control distant events. A similar point can be made about social space. If we consider something like the spread of AIDS in the world, we can see the literal connections between social spaces of a particular sort. Yet it is clear that some social spaces are closer together than others and that some social spaces are farther apart. While in the past, this was very much limited by geography, it can clearly be seen that geography, from a theoretical point of view, is really a stand-in for propinquity in social space.

In the modern world, however, it is possible for fields that are not directly linked in geographic space to be socially connected. So, for instance, scholars in one academic department who are active in their disciplines are likely to have more information about what is occurring in other departments around the country in their disciplines than they do in departments one floor away. From our point of view, nearness in social space is, therefore, the crucial and hidden variable.

Two strategic action fields can be said to be directly related to one another if they share direct social relations. A direct relation is one in which actors in two strategic action fields sustain routine interaction that effectively links the fields. Indirect ties occur when actors in two fields are connected via ties to actors in a third strategic action field. When these indirect relations are hierarchical or dependent, the indirect ties can have strong effects even though no direct interaction occurs. When two groups have the same relation to a third group, their relations will be dependent upon the nature of the shared relation. Closeness can be defined in terms of the number of relations, both direct and indirect. The more relations that exist, the closer the strategic action fields are to one another.

It is worth considering for a moment the relationship between the number of ties that a field has to other strategic action fields and its vulnerability to change pressures emanating from the broader field environment. One can think of the number of such ties as constituting a continuum from no connections to a very large number of connections. At first blush it would seem logical to imagine that fields characterized by large numbers of ties to other fields would be more prone to instability, precisely because these ties could serve as conduits for destabilizing change pressures arising in nearby connected fields. But stability/instability depends upon much more than simply the number of ties that link a strategic action field to the broader field environment. What is critical is the degree to which particular resource dependencies can or cannot be managed within the constellation of fields. If tightly coupled fields offer actors in other fields lots of alternative partners and hence less resource dependence, the more connected the field, the more likely that it will have alternative means to weather a particular crisis. It will be able to expand those connections or perhaps search for links to new strategic action fields to stabilize itself. In looking at how connectedness to other fields is likely to affect stability, one needs to closely examine the nature of the links between strategic action fields. A densely connected strategic action field is more likely to be destabilized when its linkages place it in a more dependent position and it has fewer opportunities to forge stabilizing ties to other strategic action fields.

A similar argument can be made regarding a situation in which there are few linkages between strategic action fields. If a field is not closely tied to a large number of strategic action fields, then the chances that a crisis in a particular field will eventually spill over into many other (particularly distant) fields will be reduced. Because there is little or no dependency between strategic action fields, distal fields are somewhat insulated from such crises. An example of this is the savings and loan crisis in the United States during the 1980s. Within the space of about three years, the entire savings and loan industry collapsed in the United States. This destroyed an industry that had supplied capital for home ownership for almost 70 percent of mortgages in the country, and the loss for the whole industry was estimated at about $200 billion (Barth 1991). But the effects of the collapse of the industry were quite geographically local (mainly in the Southwest United States), and the larger economy was barely affected. Indeed, the economy continued to expand even while losses piled up in some parts of the real estate market. This suggests that the strategic action field of the savings and loan indus- try was not all that connected to many other fields. Of course, the crisis in the housing meltdown in 2007–2008 did spread across a wide variety of strategic action fields, not just in the United States but also around the world. The nature of these connections has yet to be fully explored in the scholarly literature. But it is clear that there was both tight coupling between a large number of banking fields and few alternatives for banks that were destabilized by the downturn in one of their markets. We will explore this case and the interconnections between fields in greater depth in chapter 5.

But not being connected very widely can also be a disadvantage for a partic- ular strategic action field. If a field is highly dependent on only a few other stra- tegic action fields and those fields experience crisis, there will be few alternatives for the target strategic action field. So, for example, when oil prices rose from 2004 to 2007, all industries that were dependent on the price of oil found them- selves in a difficult situation. The airline industry was totally dependent on jet fuel, and the price of oil figured heavily into its costs. As a result of their inability to pass the costs on to consumers or to reduce their dependence on oil, almost all airlines suffered large losses and many went bankrupt. Our argument suggests that both the number and nature of the links between fields condition the broader prospects for field stability and instability.

We do not want to overstate the degree to which social space is independent of geographic space. We simply want to argue that the key to understanding physical space is to appreciate how it comes to be occupied by complex and dense sets of social spaces. It is much easier to evolve a new social space if one is in direct physical contact with other people who have the knowhow and tools it takes to help found the new social space. The current view of urban agglomera- tion implies that the creation of new social space is likely to be concentrated where lots of firms, industries, educated people, and government are located (Arthur 1988; Krugman 1991). These actors learn from each other, compete with each other, and are able to produce new, nearby social spaces as they figure out how to take advantage of the opportunities to do so. Indeed, the growth of cities is one of the forces that clearly are involved in the proliferation of strategic action fields.

An Excursus on Formal Organization and Bureaucracy

Before we go any further, we would like to clarify the relationship between the concept of the "strategic action field" and that of "formal organization" or bureaucracy (we use the latter two terms interchangeably). The notion of a field is the more generic of the two concepts and is also a good deal more abstract. Formal organizations are "objective" entities in the world, with clear boundaries and legal designations. Fields are constructed social orders that define an arena within which a set of consensually defined and mutually attuned actors vie for advantage. These definitions highlight the differences in the two concepts, but there is a healthy overlap between the two as well. For starters, formal organizations are often the central players in strategic action fields. A good many of the quintessential examples of IGUs are also formally constituted organizations. But the most important point about fields and formal organizations for us is that the hierarchical nesting of formal organizations can constitute an interdependent system of strategic action fields.

At the same time, however, formal organizations are a very specific kind of field. This is because of their particularly rigid, formalized structures—structures that define the relationships between subunits within the field and the rules regulating field conduct more precisely and legalistically than is true for other kinds of fields. Formal organizations do this by deploying structures that define who has the authority to make decisions and prescribing consequences for those who do not abide by these decisions. These definitions are, of course, contested and often spark power struggles, but they also typically routinize the conflict and make these struggles more susceptible to rule-driven solutions. We want to say a bit more about how these two concepts intersect.

In *Economy and Society* (1978: 901–44), Max Weber outlines his theory of bureaucracy. He identifies a bureaucracy as a form of organization with a leader and a permanent staff who are all supported by salaries. They are recruited because they have the requisite skills and credentials to hold their jobs and they maintain those jobs because of their presumed competency. The activities and careers of people in bureaucracies are governed by rules that are supposed to be applied without regard to the person or group to which they are applied. Bureaucracies first emerged in governments as they worked to routinize the tasks of governance. Weber argues that bureaucracies have existed in other times and places besides modern society, including ancient Egypt and China. The prerequisite for organizing a bureaucracy is a material surplus sufficient to support the officials needed to staff the system. This means that producing bureaucracies was difficult throughout most of human history, as most populations lived very near subsistence. Indeed, bureaucracies were fragile because of their dependence on a large surplus. But Weber also notes that once in place, bureaucracies are difficult to destroy and dislodge because they are ruthlessly efficient at enforcing rules and reproducing themselves. Once such a surplus exists, bureaucracies work to enlarge, expand, and sustain themselves.

Each bureaucratic level within an organization can be conceptualized as a strategic action field. The role structure of each level of the bureaucracy is heavily prescribed. Indeed, the manager of an office, her or his principal assistants, and the people who work in the office are located in a hierarchical authority structure that heavily circumscribes their activities. The relations between levels of bureaucracies are also heavily rule governed and controlled by the authority relationships that knit the system together. In stressing the prescribed structures and formal rules of bureaucratic systems, however, we are in no way suggesting that large formal organizations exhibit a rigid, top-down conformity. Bureaucracies exhibit the characteristic political dynamism of all fields. Lower order participants can act both individually and collectively to impair the functioning of the unit and to challenge the nominal authority of higher-ups. They can also form coalitions to dictate how the work is organized and how relationships are structured vis-à-vis other units within the organization. Specific bureaucratic divisions or other subunits can also make claims that their contributions to the organization's central tasks are more important than others, thus justifying a larger share of bureaucratic resources and/or influence over organizational decision making.

Notwithstanding the possibilities for pushback and opposition by lower level units and given the authoritative control possible both within each level of the organization and across levels, formal organizations probably do exhibit a bit more stability than other kinds of strategic action fields. As long as higher level units retain control over resources and key political alliances both within and external to the organization, lower order units will remain functionally dependent on higher order ones. So while they might contest rules issued from above, actors in these lower order offices or divisions will understand the nature of the hierarchy and will tend to acquiesce. In terms of the formulation in the first section of this chapter, formal organizations are sets of hierarchically organized strategic action fields characterized by a high degree of resource dependence.

Bureaucracies are not just hierarchical but nested as well. Within a large formal, organization, there will be competition for resources between units of the bureaucracy. Units that are larger and have more constituents within or outside of the organization will generally be able to control more resources. In the case of a government bureaucracy, for example, a Department of Motor Vehicles, this stability does not depend on who is being served (i.e., citizens) but instead on the relationships to the higher levels of the organization and to all of the other state fields on which the department is dependent. All resources to the office flow through the higher levels of government. These higher levels determine wages, staffing, and facilities. If the higher level strategic action field in the bureaucracy decides to cut staff, the lower level field has little choice but to comply. Viewed as fields, bureaucracies tend to be very stable to the extent that higher level incumbent units retain control over the resources on which lower level units depend.

What happens, however, in state bureaucracies if those higher level units lack the resources to support the activities of lower level units? In some developing societies, the ties between the levels of government bureaucracy can be attenuated by the inability of the higher levels of the organization to secure sufficient resources to maintain the employment of the lower levels. One obvious response for people who work in the lower levels is to engage in forms of corruption, that is, bribery, payoffs, and other illegal acts. It is difficult for higher levels of the organization to stop this. Quite simply, they lack the resources to secure the loyalty of their own employees. Indeed, the higher-ups may themselves be dependent on forms of corruption to supply or supplement their incomes. There is evidence that such corrupt bureaucracies, once in place, not only are hard to dislodge but also affect the overall economic development of a society (Evans and Rauch 1999).

Large for-profit firms face a different kind of challenge in their efforts to maintain a stable top-down authority structure. Their challenge stems from the fact that at least some subunits are not simply embedded in the firm but in a competitive external market as well. Success in that external market is likely to embolden the division to make greater claims on the material, status, and political resources of the firm as a whole. And unlike a state bureaucracy for which profit is irrelevant, higher-ups in for-profit firms are clearly vulnerable to challenges by nominally lower level units that can legitimately claim to be significant profit centers for the larger organization. Since the survival of the organization depends, to a considerable extent, on the profitability of the firm, such challenges are likely to be at least partially successful, serving in the process to restructure incumbent–challenger relations within the overall firm strategic action field.

Even in the absence of the profit motive, government bureaucracies are vulnerable to a somewhat similar challenge from particular lower level state fields. If, in the final analysis, the survival of firms depends on their profitability, the bottom line for governments is their ability to retain control over the legitimate use of violence that represents their ultimate basis of power. This grants to the military (or other social control forces) potentially disproportionate or even decisive importance, especially under conditions of mass unrest or rival claims to sovereignty. Under these conditions, any effort by the military to secure more resources or formal authority for itself within the broader system of state fields is likely to be successful. Coup d'états are an extreme expression of this vulnerability, but even in the absence of a formal military takeover of state authority, we can identify lots of instances in which the military has improved its standing within a broaden system of state fields by demanding more re-sources or governmental authority during times of civil unrest. The growing authority of the military in the wake of Egyptian president Hosni Mubarak's ouster in the spring of 2011 is but the most recent notable example of this phenomenon.

The State as a System of Strategic Action Fields

Having sought, in the previous section, to render the concepts of formal organi-zation and bureaucracy in terms of our perspective, we seek to do the same in this section with the concept of the state. It is useful to be more explicit in our thinking about the state as a set of strategic action fields. Our basic theory and account of field dynamics apply as much to state fields as any other strategic ac-tion fields. But the state as a set of strategic action fields differs in one important respect from other fields. State actors have advanced the claim that they alone can define, or at least ratify, the rules for public strategic interaction in a given geographic territory and that these rules can be enforced by the use of physical violence. Of course, this claim is plastic as to exactly what it means and to what spheres of life it applies. Even if a given state claims sovereignty over an issue or territory, its ability to exercise that authority is always open to contestation. Like any complex collection of fields, the state, at any given moment, will typically have some strategic action fields in formation, others that are stable, and still others that are in crisis.

As previously noted, the state's unique claim to exercise sovereignty within a designated geographic territory means that state fields have tremendous poten-tial to shape the prospects for change and stability in virtually all nonstate strate-gic action fields within those geographic coordinates. The relationship between state and nonstate fields is not entirely one sided however. As we argue below, the stability of even the most powerful state depends at least in part on the sup-port it derives from incumbents that control certain key nonstate fields.

In this section we explore the processes by which state fields come into exis-tence, how they affect the prospects for change and stability in most nonstate fields, and how, in turn, the stability of state fields are affected by the support they receive, or challenges they confront, from especially important nonstate fields. We do this by means of the following three questions:

1. What is involved in the state's claim to define the rules for legitimate action in other strategic action fields? And how did this claim come about historically?
2. What role do states/state fields play in shaping the prospects for stability and change in nonstate strategic action fields?
3. How are states, in turn, supported—or, at times, undermined—by events within nonstate fields?

The Nature of State Fields and Their Claims to Sovereignty vis-à-vis Nonstate Strategic Action Fields

What is involved in the state's claim to define the rules for legitimate action in other strategic action fields? The modern state is not much more than 350 years old if we date its emergence from the Treaty of Westphalia in 1648 (Krasner 1988, 1995). From our perspective the modern state is a set of strategic action fields that claim to make and enforce authoritative rules over a specified geographic territory. It is itself a powerful form of collective action that has been invented to produce and control strategic action fields to create the structure of the state and society more generally. The "technologies" involved in the building and organizing of the modern state have evolved in a piecemeal fashion. Institutional entrepreneurs in specific state strategic action fields, particularly those involved in taxation and warfare (Gorski 2003; Rosenberg 1958), developed bureaucratic organizations as a way to exert control over the economy and society. But they did so by advancing a set of claims about the legitimacy of their right to make the rules for all of society. As people who worked for governments discovered how to organize and reproduce strategic action fields, the form has been borrowed and modified by skilled strategic actors to organize innovative, new forms of state governance. In earlier eras, the general functions and preeminent legitimacy that presently attach to the state were exercised by other strategic action fields including the Church, monarchy, nobility, and village or tribal elders. To the degree that they ran the state, it was run in their interest.

Today, the state's legitimacy is based on its providing public goods for its citizens, including protection from attack by foreign states, public order, the rule of law, and the arbitration of public controversies. The strategic action fields of the state are still organized, to a greater or lesser extent, to serve the interest of those groups or classes that dominate state structures. In the case of totalitarian states or dictatorships, for example, leaders, their family, and their cronies benefit from the state's dominance over the economy and society. But state strategic action fields are also organized to support the interests of those incumbents in nonstate fields who have had a hand in the structuring of state strategic action fields.

New state fields have frequently emerged in response to chaotic conditions in society. The expansion of policing and the creation of standing armies are two examples of this dynamic. A host of other state fields have emerged as an indirect by-product of the expansion of the rule of law to new arenas and new groups in society. The conferral of new rights or legal protections is inevitably accompanied by considerable conflict and contention *and* the creation of a host of new state fields to safeguard the gains achieved. This has resulted in something of a self-perpetuating cycle of legal expansion—the creation of new strategic action fields by groups intent on taking advantage of the new opportunities open to them, which forces states to fashion new regulatory and compliance fields to oversee the resulting nonstate fields.

This leads us to consider how the conception of the modern state as the final arbiter of the rules by which all of society would function came about. The central challenge in constructing a stable strategic action field has typically involved devising a set of enforceable rules that ensured the reproduction of those rules by the groups and interests at stake. The problem of defining the rules for other fields, or the general problem of constituting meaningful social action (e.g., what kinds of social space would it make sense to form for a given social group), was often also contained within the same strategic action field. In a mundane example, for most of this century, steel companies in the United States saw their primary business as steel production and did not consider invading nearby social space to produce copper, oil, or natural gas. The firms in the steel industry's strategic action field defined reasonable and unreasonable actions and what kind of social space should or could be organized. The problem of who got to define the rules by which strategic action fields would operate more generally is a historical question. In tribal societies, the reproduction of the tribal identity prevailed. The crucial difference between tribal societies and the steel industry was that tribal leaders controlled the definition of all social spaces (i.e., the potential for all strategic action fields) in the social territory of the tribe while the steel industry only controlled itself and the nearby social spaces and would never have tried to extend that control beyond those social spaces.

This suggests that the claims to define legitimate action in all strategic action fields were not originally associated with a formal state but instead the group or its religion. One could argue that any social institution that could make this claim and had a way to enforce it (whether it be through norms, effective political administration, or violence) acts as a state. More formally, a state is a set of strategic action fields in which actors engage in political strategic action oriented toward defining what will constitute the rules of interaction in all social space in a given territory. The view that the origins of the modern state were warrior bands is misleading (Tilly 1975). This view focuses on states exacting tributes, and from our perspective this is not the essence of state activity. These warrior groups operated as states only internal to their own society. They were frequently not oriented toward holding particular territory or enforcing rules in that territory. Instead, they were oriented toward plunder. Our conception of the state does not exclude totalitarian or authoritarian regimes. But it does imply that a claim of the leaders of the states is precisely to control the organization of strategic action fields in a given territory.

The modern state claims to produce rules of strategic interaction within a geographically delimited territory. Instead of controlling a tribe or a people who might be nomadic or spread across judicial locations, the modern state views its mission as the definition and defense of geographic borders. The claim of a modern state also involves exercising a monopoly over the means of violence within those same borders (Elias 1994; Weber 1978). There are procedures defined (i.e., laws) that govern action and make possible new forms of action. There is a bureaucratic apparatus to enforce and adjudicate claims. Also, there is an attempt to define separate spheres of action such that one can tell where the state begins and other strategic action fields end (even in socialist societies). Finally, there will often be a claim to represent the interests of the nation (however that is conceived, i.e., as an ethic group, a religion, language, common heritage, or some other form of identity), even in authoritarian regimes.

The modern state formalizes the problem of creating new social spaces in two ways: it provides for or enables expansion into known and unknown social spaces, and it limits that expansion by setting the rules by which that expansion can occur. It does so by creating procedures to create new social spaces and govern existing ones and by providing procedures to enforce both the claims of the state and the claims of actors in nonstate strategic action fields. The extension of these rules, procedures, and techniques of field creation happened over a relatively long historical period. The process turned on a series of changes that were the result of successfully deploying state and nonstate strategic action fields: the pacification of a territory, the growth of cities, and the creation of a market economy. All of these innovations relied on the creation of strategic action fields to control populations, to produce incumbents and challengers, and to work out the problem of internal governance within strategic action fields. The formalization of the rights of states, the extension and elaboration of the rule of law, the institutionalization of procedures for adjudicating conflicts within and across strategic action fields, and the growth of the private economy all reinforced one another and encouraged the rapid growth and institutionalization of more and more state and nonstate fields.

The Impact of State Fields on Nonstate
Strategic Action Fields

We turn now to the relationship between state and nonstate strategic action fields. It is our contention that it is almost impossible to talk about action in a strategic action field without reference to its relationship to one or, indeed often, multiple state fields. This is because the stability (and instability!) of any nonstate strategic action field depends to some degree either indirectly or directly on its linkages to the state. But this does not mean that all of these dependencies are achieved easily and without conflict. There is the potential for both conflict and symbiosis in the linkages between state and nonstate strategic action fields.

Let us start by considering why nonstate strategic action fields tend to flourish where there is already a certain amount of social stability produced by state fields. Generally, the existence of state fields means that government actors have effectively circumscribed and tamed a geographic area within which nonstate actors can operate. The presence of state fields creates the kind of predictability and security that allows nonstate actors to create new fields without fear of having themselves or their property threatened. They can rely on the state fields to provide security and reliability in the enforcement of law. This makes all kinds of action possible that were previously difficult to achieve. Social stability also means that making investments in formal organizations in nonstate fields makes sense because it is possible to make long-term commitments to paying a staff. Finally, in moments of crisis, actors in nonstate fields have recourse to appeal to state actors to help restore stability and order in their field. In times of crisis, incumbents in previously stable nonstate fields can typically call on their allies in state strategic action fields to help restore the status quo.

But the relationship between state and nonstate strategic action fields is also marked by a fair amount of mutual distrust and hostility. It is useful to consider some of the sources of this conflict. State and nonstate strategic action fields compete for resources all of the time. States want to use societal resources to continue to fund state strategic action fields. The outside constituencies of these state strategic action fields are fully supportive of this practice, because they want to continue to derive the benefits of the goods and/or services that the state is providing. On the other hand, those segments of the population who are being taxed to support state programs from which they do not derive benefits have reason to oppose the practice. In short, any given state strategic action field serves particular interests and yet taxes all social groups to support their activities. We will have much more to say about challenges to state by nonstate fields in the next section.

One of the most interesting features of modern states is their gradual expansion through the accretion of new strategic action fields designed to solve emergent political/administrative problems. It is worth expanding on this point a bit. If we begin with the idea that the state is a system of strategic action fields that claim to set the rules for those collectivities that define a spatially delimited population, then the ability to actually do this will depend on the capacities of state strategic action fields. The building of these capacities is an ongoing project, one that reflects the different kinds of crises that beset a particular society. One of the distinctive features of the modern state is the separation of political governance from the economic and social bases of society. In small-scale hunter–gatherer societies, these functions were fused. Feudalism, as well, gave political, economic, and social power to the local nobility. But as societies grew in size (and this was true in empires as well as modern societies), the differentiation of the state from the rest of society could be observed. So, for example, a private economy often emerged in empires to produce luxury goods and sell staples such as cloth and food. Within the state, the governing bodies were composed of "notables," but as empires required staffs to function, bureaucracies emerged to coordinate tax collection, the army, a legal system, and a system of surveillance over the hinterland. The great empires of antiquity, Egypt, Persia, China, and India all created elaborate bureaucratic structures to expand their control and separate local economies and social orders from the state.

Although they represented a dramatic shift away from the fragmented, multilevel system of authority characteristic of medieval Europe, the first truly modern states (e.g., England, France) now seem small and ineffectual compared to their modern counterparts. But once the fundamental principle of centralized governance had been accepted—however grudgingly—and the basic state structure was in place, the potential for state expansion soon became obvious. As all manner of groups and interests came to look to the state to solve problems and adjudicate claims, the creation of new state strategic action fields arose as pragmatic solutions to new political/administrative problems.

These problems could also be generated by conflicts between state strategic action fields over jurisdiction. Within the state, there is constant conflict over which bureaucracy controls which set of issues. As a result, modern governments are constantly shuffling and reshuffling their executive bureaucracies to better organize control over various arenas of social life. The structuring of the strategic action fields of the modern state also highlights the role of collective action by citizens outside of the state in the expansion, redefinition, or reorientation of state strategic action fields. As various groups pressed for privileges and rights, government strategic action fields were created to organize new features of social life. Governments began to provide for collective goods such as roads, schools, and police. The creation of these organizations generated employment opportunities and encouraged new groups to make demands on the state to regulate and expand the rights and roles of actors in other nonstate fields. This produced a historical layering of the state over time as regimes sought to create new forms of governance in response to particular crises.

The separation of the economic and social spheres of life from the political sphere is a product of modern times. We speculate that this separation was less the conscious decision of actors and more the result of a set of conflicting claims to sovereignty within a given territory. Again, the relative weakness of European states in the Middle Ages meant that there were competing claims as to who could control what features of life. So, in places where the Church reigned supreme, religious and political power might be fused. In places such as northern Italy and central Germany, where merchant states had emerged, states were not very strong and local notables, including merchant families, ruled. They frequently created a system of courts to solve economic disputes and bought the help of mercenaries to engage in armed struggle when necessary (Greif 2006; Spruyt 1996). Of course, kings and noble families continued to claim both economic and political privilege. The largest of these political units would go to war and attempt to take control over lucrative trade networks. This plurality of powerful strategic action fields meant that the separation of economic from political affairs was a result of the historical accident of the fragmentation of sovereignty across Western Europe. When kings finally sought to bring larger political units together, they required the cooperation of local authorities, who variously included merchants, the nobility, and the clergy. The states they built tended to bear the imprint of the coalition of groups that were party to the national project in that particular country.

In the modern era, one of the main catalysts for state expansion has been social movement activity. The definition of social movements as groups that practice noninstitutionalized politics (Tarrow 2011 perfectly captures our view of these processes. As states developed, relatively few groups were initially granted legal and political rights within the new polity. Those who were excluded had only one way to express their grievances: by practicing politics outside the confines of the state fields. Here, they could riot, protest, organize, and engage in various forms of insurgent action. The strategic action fields of most states have been continuously challenged in the modern era by more and more groups. If these groups are powerful enough, they could change the strategic action fields of the state or generate new fields oriented in part to their demands. This produces new forms of governance subject to the claims making of previously excluded groups.

This gradual accretion of state fields is sometimes hard to unpack. It is possible for older institutions of the state to remain in place for long periods of time. Laws governing family relations, property rights, and inheritance, for example, might show great continuity over long historical periods. Laws regarding social welfare programs and particular benefits change much more quickly. Strategic action fields organized to regulate various aspects of business exhibit both stability and change. Newly formed governments born of social movements or revolutions might act to radically shift a large number of the fields of the state. So, in the case of modern political revolutions, many of the layers of the state either disappear or are radically altered. Of course, new strategic action fields are formed as well. But even here, scholars have noted continuity in the way that so-called radical governments end up preserving state structures that carry the legacy of the old regime (Pierson 2000; Skocpol 1979). This is because the strategic action fields of the existing state have constituencies in and outside of the current government. The only way that strategic action fields get destroyed is if the constituencies they serve either disband or disappear.

The advantage of this view of the modern state is that it guards against the tendency to reify the state. The state is definitely *not* a unified actor. The myriad fields that comprise the state wax and wane as they compete for resources and support from other state and nonstate strategic action fields. In one historical moment, one could imagine a state where the military function predominated, in another, the religious, and in still another, the social welfare. The strategic action fields within the state are dependent on their links to strategic action fields outside of the state. But the strategic action fields outside of the state are also dependent on the state for legitimacy. These mutual processes of dependence mean that actors within the state will make claims to lead the state on the basis of the relative strength of these ties and the strength of the groups supporting the state.

The Dependence of States and State Fields on Nonstate Fields

To this point we have primarily stressed the crucial role that state actors/strategic action fields play in the emergence, stabilization, and, on occasion, transformation of nonstate fields. And indeed, no broad group of fields typically has more power to shape the prospects for stability and change in other strategic action fields than do state fields. But the relationship between state and nonstate fields is, by no means, one sided. If the stability and indeed survival of nonstate fields depends to a considerable degree on the certifying support of allies in state strategic action fields, the reverse is true as well. That is, all states (and state fields) depend for their existence on the support they derive from myriad ties between state and nonstate strategic action fields. Especially important, in this regard, are the ties that link the state to a host of key economic fields that exercise disproportionate influence over the nation's economy. Absent the tacit support—if not outright backing—of the incumbents in these crucial economic fields, most states would struggle to survive. Indeed, although we typically attribute the collapse of states to the withdrawal of popular support—to the exercise of "people power"—it is often the defection of these key economic incumbents and the fields they dominate that actually precipitates regime change. Consider the ouster of Ferdinand Marcos as the president of the Philippines in 1986 (McAdam, Tarrow, and Tilly 2001: chapter 4). The term "crony capitalism" was often used to describe the essence of Marcos's rule in the Philippines. While overly simplistic (and pejorative), the term nonetheless captures a stark truth about the regime. Through the provision of various subsidies, favorable tax policies, and out and out corruption, Marcos early on mobilized the support and loyalty of the dominant actors in the country's key economic fields. Coupled with the crucial backing of the United States, it was this support that kept Marcos in office for the better part of two otherwise tumultuous decades. And in the end, it was the defection of these elites that helped to precipitate the mass unrest that finally drove Marcos into exile in February of 1986 (Hedman 2006; McAdam, Tarrow, and Tilly 2001: chapter 4).

The 1979 overthrow of the Somoza regime in Nicaragua turned on a very similar process of elite defection as the one seen in the Philippines (Booth 1982; McAdam, Tarrow, and Tilly 2001: chapter 7; Selbin 1993; Wickham-Crowley 1989). Indeed, the withdrawal of support by key economic incumbents has not only been identified as critical in the Nicaraguan case "but in more general comparative analyses differentiating trajectories of successful from those of unsuccessful revolutions" as well (Dix 1984; Midlarsky and Roberts 1985; Wickham-Crowley 1989, 1992).

These examples conduce to a more general point. Modern nation-states rest on myriad ties between state and nonstate fields and, more precisely, on alliances forged between nonstate incumbents and their allies in state strategic action fields. But these alliances depend on the ability of the incumbents in both fields to honor the terms of exchange on which the relationship is based. Key state allies can be expected to support the status quo in a given nonstate strategic action field, but only up to a point. Should the field devolve into sustained conflict and incumbents lose the ability to facilitate routine field reproduction, their counterparts in proximate state fields can be expected to intervene to help restore stability through the certification of new incumbents and/or the imposition of a new settlement. But the reverse is true as well. If key state actors/ strategic action fields lose the ability to ensure the overall environmental stability that is essential to the smooth functioning of a given nonstate field, incumbents in the latter may well precipitate efforts to replace their state allies, restructure the malfunctioning state strategic action field, or, in the case of a broader breakdown in state order, join with others to bring about regime change.

It is important to distinguish between the exceedingly rare instances of the latter and the more routine forms of state/nonstate contestation that are ubiquitous in modern societies. If we are right, there are always multiple conflicts ongoing within nonstate economic and societal strategic action fields. These strategic action fields are always being created and destabilized. Routine influence by the already existing nonstate strategic action fields will pressure the political actors within the state to act to adjudicate disputes in the interests of existing organized powers that be in the strategic action fields. But if the challengers in a nonstate strategic action field get powerful enough, they may not accept the authority of the state strategic action field to adjudicate the issues. If enough challengers present demands to stop supporting incumbents so brazenly, they begin to challenge the legitimacy of state authority, resulting in a crisis of legitimacy for particular state strategic action fields. These kinds of crises are going on all of the time and they can cause real change in state strategic action fields.

We would expect the level of general contention in the strategic action fields in society and the level of contention in state fields to be highly correlated. The implication here is that if the crises in the economy and society get severe enough, they spread to the strategic action fields of the state. This creates the perception of a legitimation crisis, and this general perception can precipitate crises in other fields. What does it take to raise the level of contention in society more generally to create such a crisis? Clearly it takes events that affect large numbers of nonstate fields in such a way as to undermine the power of incumbents and grant leverage to challengers. Large-scale economic crisis can sometimes produce this effect. Countless economic fields can devolve into crisis, triggering responses by state actors in support of incumbents in those economic fields. In such a situation, some incumbents are likely to be displaced as challengers mobilize to demand that more be done to stabilize the system.

Another source of generalized societal crisis is foreign invasion. The literal disruption of daily life by war and civil unrest undermines the ability of state strategic action fields to continue to ensure the delivery of goods and services. When this happens, incumbents in nonstate fields are threatened as well. Indeed, war or civil unrest begins to undermine important economic and social strategic action fields, further weakening incumbent control over the regime.

These kinds of moments are not as rare as we tend to think. But even in more settled times, there are routine, low-level conflicts going on constantly in state and nonstate strategic action fields. Incumbents and challengers constantly face off in both state and nonstate fields. And strategic interaction linking state and nonstate actors is going on all the time as well. If things go badly for nonstate incumbents, they are very likely to appeal to their allies in proximate state fields for help. At any given moment, even in settled times, some number of state fields will be engaged in mediating crises in a host of related nonstate fields. It is these disputes and their resolutions that cause politics to be an ongoing process and that act to build the state in a piecemeal fashion over time.

Internal Governance Units

In the previous section, we sought, among other things, to underscore the decisive and varied ways that modern states—themselves complex collections of strategic action fields—affect the founding, stabilization, reproduction, and transformation of virtually all nonstate fields. From formulating laws that regulate the establishment of new fields, to "certifying" (McAdam, Tarrow, and Tilly 2001) the "winners" of struggles to control fields, to launching investigations that destabilize power relations within a strategic action field, states routinely shape the prospects for stability and change in all manner of nonstate fields. But to this point in our discussion of the relationship between states and fields, we are guilty of perpetuating something of a fiction. We have consistently referred to the relationship between this or that state actor and some nonstate field. In point of fact, fields as a whole typically do not interact directly with state actors. Particular members of the field—incumbents more so than challengers—may have cultivated relationships with specific state actors, but typically much of the interaction between the strategic action field and the various state fields germane to the field is carried out by what we have termed "internal governance units," or IGUs.

By IGUs we mean organizations or associations within the field whose sole job it is to ensure the routine stability and order of the strategic action field. It may seem odd to be discussing IGUs in a chapter devoted to the *external* environment in which strategic action fields are embedded. We do so, however, because quite often these units have one foot in the field and the other outside. For among the many functions exercised by IGUs, one of the most important is external field relations. Consider the following diverse set of examples: the commissioner's office of any major sport, a trade or industry association, the ethics committee of a state bar association, accrediting bodies in higher education. All of these are IGUs, but their personnel spend much of their time in routine interaction with counterparts in a host of external state and nonstate fields. So the commissioner of baseball routinely testifies before Congress on matters as diverse as the antitrust provisions accorded baseball and the league's drug policies. The heads of national trade associations typically spend far more time lobbying legislators on trade policy, talking to their counterparts in other countries, or crafting pieces of legislation than they do interacting with incumbents and challengers within the field. In short, at least some IGUs are more outwardly focused than attuned to events in the strategic action field. These units constitute the lobbying arm and public face of the field as well as its liaison to state and nonstate fields crucial to the long-term stability of the strategic action field. Their central mission is to cultivate favorable relations with important actors in these fields and to use these relationships in any way they can to advance the interest of the strategic action field.

These external functions do not, however, exhaust the missions of IGUs. Indeed, IGUs are probably oriented to as many internal as external field functions. Although our main focus here is on the latter, we want to briefly touch on these internal functions to give the reader a more holistic sense of the various ways that IGUs seek to promote the long-term stability and routine reproduction of the field. Besides their external liaison and lobbying functions, IGUs can serve any one of five major internal functions:

- Administration—some IGUs provide routine administrative services to members of the field
- Information—others serve as information clearinghouses for the members of the field and sometimes for external audiences as well
- Regulation—other IGUs seek to ensure conformity to the rules of the strategic action field by monitoring and regulating the behavior of members
- Enforcement—still others are charged with enforcing the rules by apprehending and sanctioning those who violate them
- Certification—finally, there are other units that monitor and control access to the field by accrediting or otherwise certifying field membership

In bringing this section to a close we reiterate an important point touched on in chapter 1. On occasion, IGUs are imposed on a strategic action field by state actors, typically to curb the power of one or more incumbents and to create a more level playing field for all members. In such instances, these units serve—at least initially—as neutral arbiters of field relations. More typically, however, IGUs are created, oftentimes during the founding of the field or at times of crisis, to institutionalize the worldview and advantages of incumbents. Accordingly, most IGUs function as conservative institutions, promoting the routine reproduction of the field and, by extension, the advancement of incumbent interests. The mere presence of these units, however, confers legitimacy on the field through the appearance of order, rationality, and equity.

Higher Education and the Professions

We wish to consider one final set of macroinstitutions that we see as power-fully implicated in the creation, maintenance, and transformation of strategic action fields. Among the main beneficiaries of the increasing complexity of modern society are the educational institutions that have arisen and the pro-fessions and new occupations that have emerged to manage that complexity. Universities, graduate programs, and professional schools have expanded their activities dramatically in the past 100 years. As late as the early part of the twentieth century less than 3 percent of the U.S. population had received any college education whatsoever. By the turn of the twenty-first century, a quarter of the adult population had earned a four-year degree and another quarter had attended at least some college. We see the relationship between this expansion of schooling and the proliferation of strategic action fields as reciprocal. On the one hand, the proliferation and increasing complexity of strategic action fields produces a demand for individuals who have high-level organizational skills. But these newly educated individuals also have the social and technical skills to fashion new strategic action fields and work to expand existing ones. As the overall structure of these strategic action fields expands, this, of course, creates more demand for the educated professionals to manage the system.

The exponential increase in schooling is related to the increasing com-plexity of modern work. But this complexity is made possible by the archi-tecture of strategic action fields, which allow more and more fields and more and more complex relationships between fields. We want to argue that the increasing growth of strategic action fields—especially in the economic sector and the state—have greatly increased the demand for people with not only particular technical skills and knowledge (e.g., in electrical engi-neering or material sciences) but also more general skills that allow them to analyze and solve problems pragmatically and then coordinate and manage people. Indeed, most of the enormous growth in managers and profes-sionals over the course of the twentieth century was less technically driven than it was a product of the need to manage the increasingly complex social dynamics within and between state and nonstate fields. Even in highly tech-nical firms, such as those in Silicon Valley, only a small percentage of the people who work there actually have technical jobs. Most manage produc-tion, sales, or relations to suppliers and customers. Indeed, between 1900 and 2000 the percentage of the American workforce employed as either managers or professionals increased nearly sevenfold from 5 to 33 percent (Gordon 1996).

The expansion in higher education is also related to the growing demand for social skill. As strategic action fields have grown in size and number, the need for skilled collective actors has increased dramatically. Generally speaking, it is the expanding class of educated professionals who have been called upon to satisfy this demand. Thus, they tend to be the entrepreneurs who key the development of new strategic action fields. Here, they create new forms of organizing and work to promote the coordination of activities within their organizations and between their organizations and their competitors and their suppliers, customers, and government. They are also trained to go to the state to legitimate and defend their actions. Even in more settled social space, they maintain the pecking order by analyzing the conditions in the strategic action field and working both to ensure the efficiency of their own group and to maintain relationships with their competitors and the state. This has created a kind of accelerating upward spiral that has been expanding on and off in the advanced industrial economies for the past 100 years.

People who are highly credentialed work for political parties, social movement organizations, government, firms, and nonprofits. Their role in these various spheres of social life is to facilitate and coordinate various forms of collective action. In essence, they are using social skill to sustain or transform existing fields and start new ones. Such actors not only work within a particular strategic action field to help innovate, produce, and reproduce their orders, but they also work at the borders of orders.

Conclusion

In this chapter, we have considered the broader macroenvironment within which strategic action fields are embedded. We began by theorizing the relationships between fields. We argued that fields are either disconnected or stand in a dependent or interdependent relationship to one another. This parallels our argument about the dynamics of a particular field by pointing out that the edges of fields are governed by similar principles. In addition, we noted that fields can be hierarchically embedded in one another. This embedding resembles a Russian doll. So, one can start with the field of international arms control; embed national governments in such a field; decompose those governments into a set of fields that comprise military establishments; go deeper into those establishments and find separate armies, naives, and air forces; and continue still further downward to the individuals who make up a platoon of soldiers. Like any given strategic action field, the *links* between all of those fields are governed by principles of hierarchy or cooperation and need to be managed by actors with social skill. Finally, we have considered how the density of connections between a given field and the broader network of strategic action fields affects its relative vulnerability to destabilizing exogenous shocks.

We then sought to clarify the relationship between the concepts of field and formal organization. We began by noting that formal organizations are not only the constituent elements in many strategic action fields but also a collection of nested fields in their own right. Formal organizations are a particular kind of field that operates within and across strategic action fields. They tend to be hierarchical and rule bound and to produce quite stable strategic action fields as a result. Formal organizations are in many ways the fundamental building block of the modern world and, of course, are constitutive of many strategic action fields. One place where formal organizations play an especially central role is in the strategic action fields of the state. We devoted a long section to a discussion of the critical importance of the nation-state to an understanding of field dynamics. Conceptualizing states as complex and hierarchically organized systems of fields in their own right, we went on to describe the decisive ways in which states can be implicated in the founding, stabilization, reproduction, and transformation of state and nonstate fields. The relationship between state strategic action fields and nonstate strategic action fields is not, however, entirely one sided. Just as state actions can sometimes destabilize relations and precipitate crises within nonstate fields, so too can particularly important strategic action fields—say major industries or emergent social movements—occasionally undermine state fields or even entire state systems. More routinely, strategic action fields create organizations or associations—termed "IGUs"—that seek, along with their internal functions, to stabilize and manage relations with important state actors and other external fields. We devoted a short section to a description of the routine liaison, lobbying, and public relation functions of these IGUs. Typically IGUs help maintain the internal order of an existing strategic action field while also lobbying and otherwise acting on its behalf vis-à-vis a number of proximate state fields.

Finally, we offered a brief account of the close temporal connection between the proliferation of fields in the modern period and two related social trends: the expansion of higher education and the rise of professions. The increasing production of educated people and the mobilization of various professional "projects" is both a cause of the expansion of strategic action fields and an effect of the demand for such people to create and sustain strategic action fields and the organizations that comprise them. Such actors have proliferated dramatically over time. They also play pivotal roles in linking actors across strategic action fields.

This overview of the relationship between strategic action fields and broader macrostructures and processes is an important part of our theory. It is what takes the stripped-down abstract idea of how people organize social space in the first place and produces an account of how all of this works at a much larger, more complex systematic level. The great proliferation of strategic action fields in modern society is the outcome of these processes. People have invented new things to do, new ways to consume and produce, and in doing so, have had to invent new ways to organize. These proliferate, are borrowed, and are disseminated, mostly through networks of professionals and managers. This ferment opens up new opportunities for action. As a result, social space is constantly being organized, reorganized, and transformed. In the next chapter we offer a more systematic framework for analyzing and understanding stability and change in strategic action fields.

4

Change and Stability in Strategic Action Fields

This collaboration was born of the common theoretical/empirical challenge we faced in making sense of change and stability in the cases we were studying. More than anything else, our shared desire to fashion a systematic theory of fields was motivated by a fundamental concern with order and change. So everything that has come before in this book is really a prelude to this chapter. In chapter 1 we sought to lay out the basic elements of our perspective. In chapter 2 we were concerned with providing a microfoundation that would help us understand the kind of skilled social action we see reflected in the creation, stabilization, and transformation of fields. Convinced that the prospects for field stability, conflict, and change are generally shaped as much by events outside the field as in, we devoted chapter 3 to a detailed examination of the broader macroenvironment in which fields are inevitably embedded. Having put these various pieces in place, we are finally ready to more systematically explore the topic of stability and change in strategic action fields.

Current Debates

One of the most important ongoing debates in social movement studies, organizational theory, and political sociology is the nature of social change in strategic action fields. One perspective emphasizes the continuity of actors in fields and posits piecemeal social change and continuous learning and change on the part of actors (Powell et al. 2005; Steinmo, Thelen, and Longstreth 1992; Thelen 2004). This perspective also takes the position that these ongoing changes are typically not caused by "exogenous shocks" that arise outside of the field of interest. Instead, the impetus to change is the ongoing interaction within the field, what might be called the "contest for positioning."

Proponents of this first perspective reject the idea of routine field stasis or equilibrium. Whatever stability is achieved in a given field is seen as a product of constant maneuvering by incumbents and challengers alike. If incumbents are able to retain control over the field for an extended period of time, it is because they have made skillful use of their material, existential, and political advantages to safeguard or reproduce their positions. This perspective rejects the idea that fields are so institutionalized that all change is unlikely and instead views the reproduction of the status quo as the outcome of actors using their position, the rules, and the resources they have to defend their positions. Implicit in the perspective is the idea that incumbents and challengers are engaged in an iterative strategic dance, continuously modifying their strategies and tactics in response to the earlier moves of other actors in the field.

The other perspective depicts field change as much more dramatic, much more decisive, and generally triggered from without. Proponents of this alternative perspective tend to view field processes as a form of punctuated equilibrium. Here, the only moments of real change occur when fields are either formed or transformed though crisis. These rare, but highly consequential, situations result in entirely new or radically transformed fields (Arthur 1988, 1989; Fligstein 1996; Hannan and Freeman 1977; McAdam 1999; White 1981). These moments, as noted above, are usually the product of destabilizing change processes that arise outside the field in question. These events are what create opportunities for the existence of a new social space or the destabilization of an existing order. At these moments, all aspects of the field are up for grabs, for example, its raison d'être, its composition, which forms of action are legitimate, and what kinds of shared understandings and identities are to structure the field. It is at these moments that "entrepreneurs"—skilled social actors who can forge new identities, coalitions, and hierarchies—wield maximum influence. However convulsive and transformative, change is expected to be short lived. Once a new settlement is in place, we are told, fields quickly coalesce and their rules and power hierarchies become institutionalized. This prevents radical change and promotes the routine reproduction of the status quo.

On the surface, these two conceptions of social change seem incompatible. But we argue that with a deeper understanding of field dynamics we can make sense of the conditions under which *both* can occur. Our central insight is that the emergence of a field is akin to a social movement moment in which entirely new things can occur. It is the fluid quality of such moments that make radically innovative new forms of action and organization, mobilized around appeals to new collective identities, possible. In this kind of situation, one may observe pivotal events that bring about a kind of punctuated equilibrium. In a short period of time, fields can coalesce into a congealed social, political order. Similarly, when fields are collapsing, the situation once again becomes fluid and many new things are possible. The rules that hold fields together and the resources that help groups maintain their positions are up for grabs, encouraging skilled social actors to engage once again in novel framing and innovative forms of action.

If one is observing an already existing field, the dynamics of interaction are likely to be quite different. Actors will engage in strategic action to make changes in response to what others are doing in the field. There is always a great deal of dynamism involved in holding an order together; but we expect change in stable fields to be more incremental, more imitative, and, generally, in reaction to the moves of others. Indeed, the well-established empirical fact that actors tend to imitate each other in stable fields can be interpreted as a process of both adapting and learning. Reacting to others' moves by either matching or complementing them is a way to preserve one's position in a field. We are not, however, suggesting that simple reproduction is the only thing that happens in established fields. On the contrary, while transformative change typically does await the destabilizing force of exogenous change pressures, lots of consequential jockeying for advantage and incremental shifts in position are the norm in even the most stable of strategic action fields.

The issue of the source of change is a bit more complicated. Part of the problem is defining what is internal and what is external to the field. It is certainly the case that incumbents and challengers can learn new strategies and tactics in their ongoing battle for position. They can invent new identities for themselves and others and move the field in novel directions. But the usual impetus to do so stems less from the competition within the field and more from how the terms of that competition are altered by events or actors outside the strategic action field.

Proximate strategic action fields—both state and nonstate—are ordinarily the source of both stability and change in a given field. Under normal conditions, the formidable resource advantages—material, existential/symbolic, and political— enjoyed by incumbents are simply hard to overcome on the basis of internal dynamics alone. New inputs from outside the field are thus normally required to change the balance of power within the field. These inputs can include dramatic events or other exogenous shocks that suddenly and decisively alter relations within the field, or infusions of new resources and/or ideas from external sources that greatly improve the strategic position of challenging groups. One other very specific, but fairly common, external event that can alter power relations within politically sensitive fields is a significant transfer of formal political authority from one party—or other governing authority—to another. So, for example, in the United States when control of the White House shifts from one party to another, the incumbent–challenger structure of a host of state fields—and not a few politically sensitive nonstate strategic action fields—can be expected to shift as well. All of these examples highlight the critically important role of external actors, fields, and events in the generation of potentially significant change pressures in the life of fields.

It is even hard to separate the more incremental shifts and positioning contests that we have described as "internal" to the field from what is going on outside.

Consider the example of the incumbent who is able, through skillful management and use of superior material resources, to safeguard the dominant position
within the field over a long period of time. It is tempting to chalk this success up
to internal dynamics alone, but what if it turns out that the majority of the incumbent's material resources come from stable ties to allies in proximate state and
nonstate fields? We are not suggesting that internal dynamics are irrelevant or
that the internal/external distinction has no meaning. The distinction remains
useful, and internal dynamics *always* matter. We have deployed the example simply to render the issue of internal/external more complicated and to underscore,
once more, the critical importance of external relationships in shaping the prospects for change and stability in any given field.

We will have much more to say about the sources of destabilizing change in
strategic action fields in the balance of the chapter. For now, however, we want to
return to the two stylized perspectives on field-level change with which we
opened the chapter and elaborate on our distinctive take on the matter. Quite
simply our theory incorporates elements of both perspectives. Which model of
change applies depends on the underlying conditions of the field and the degree
to which a stable order is in effect. It is this kind of deeper understanding of the
logic of strategic action fields that is at the core of our perspective. To make all of
this clearer, it is useful to explicate the general principles of field emergence,
stabilization/reproduction, and transformation. In the first three chapters, we
sketched the basics of a theory of strategic action and a broader view of social life
as organized around a complex and nested set of strategic action fields. But we
have yet to set this perspective in motion. In this chapter, we take up the following
logical sequence of questions:

- How do strategic action fields first emerge?
- How are these fragile, emergent strategic action fields stabilized?
- By what means are stable *settlements* effected and sustained in strategic action
  fields?
- What are the sources of *rupture* in such settlements?
- How is order typically restored in strategic action fields?
- Finally, what forms of skilled social action can we expect to see under each of
  these three field conditions (i.e., emergence, stability, and rupture/crisis)?

The Emergence of Strategic Action Fields

An emerging field is a socially constructed arena occupied by two or more
groups whose actions are oriented to each other but who have yet to develop a
stable order that effectively routinizes field relations. One can conceive of

emerging fields as social space where rules do not yet exist but where actors, by virtue of emerging, dependent interests and worldviews, are being forced increasingly to take one another into account in their actions. Concrete examples of such emerging fields would include the U.S. auto industry from 1890 to 1920 and medicine in the United States from 1910 to 1925 (Starr 1982).

Where does the impetus for new strategic action fields come from? There is no simple answer to this question. We begin by placing the matter in historical—indeed, prehistorical—context. As we argued in chapter 2, the possibilities for creating strategic action fields expanded exponentially with the advent of language and the rise of truly modern *Homo sapiens*. The capacity for organizing social space has been a consistent feature of the modern human experience. We believe, however, that the pace of field emergence is far greater today than at any prior time in human history. This is true for at least three reasons. First, much of human history involved relatively low population density, which meant that small human groups could live in relative isolation from one another, therefore obviating the need for the kind of strategic interactions that define multiple interdependent fields. Second, certain technological advances over the past three centuries have dramatically expanded the capacity for coordinated human action, making it possible to organize social space faster and with much great territorial reach than ever before. Indeed, throughout history, technological improvements in transportation and communication have been both a cause and an effect of field emergence.

Finally, to the extent that strategic action fields emerge in the interstices of existing fields, the third great spur to the establishment of fields is the existence of "proximate" fields. So, for example, "new" product markets are often founded near "old" product markets as part and parcel of the search to achieve stability for the firm (Fligstein 2001b). Or to take a concrete historical example, Spain's colonization of the Americas in the fifteenth and sixteenth centuries set in motion a period of competitive colonization involving all of Spain's European rivals, a process that was to be repeated during the second great colonial expansion of the nineteenth century. In short, the organization of fields inevitably stimulates the emergence of other fields. So to the extent that the world is far more organized now than, say, 500 years ago, the pace of field emergence—and the conflict it inevitably produces—is that much greater as well.

These three factors—population expansion, technological advance, and the pace and extent of social organization—have, we believe, been the general motors of field emergence throughout human history. In the modern period, one other process bears mention as well. The rise of modern nation-states—themselves strategic action fields but with special authority to determine the legitimacy of, and set the rules for, most other public arenas—has created another central vehicle for field emergence. As we argued in chapter 3, the state creates new strategic action fields and provides opportunities for actors in the economy and society to create new social space. Indeed, as we explained, this is a reciprocal process, with the organization of new nonstate fields often creating the need for new state strategic action fields to provide oversight and regulation of the new nonstate fields. So often the passage of a new law, or the issuance of a major judicial ruling, creates new opportunities for strategic action by established or emergent collective actors. Similarly, organized groups can take their grievances to state actors and lobby to produce rules to promote their interests in existing fields or to establish new fields on terms favorable to them.

In the modern period, then, state action constitutes a fourth major catalyst of field emergence. These four factors often work in concert. For example, one common dynamic has been for technological change—much of it state sponsored—to set in motion state-directed efforts to take strategic advantage of the new possibilities for field establishment created by the advance. Globalization and European integration conform, in part, to this dynamic. To the degree that states interact with other states and large-scale organizations in the economy and nonprofit sectors come to operate across national borders, the possibility for the emergence of international fields increases. For instance, ongoing economic and political integration in the European Union has created countless new strategic action fields in the economy and the social and political life of European citizens (Fligstein 2008). European integration has spawned any number of new multinational policy fields made up initially of existing national organizations but soon supplemented by emerging multinational public interest groups, which constitute new fields as well (Fligstein and Stone Sweet 2002; Marks and McAdam 1996, 1999).

We now consider the internal processes by which strategic action fields get established. For a new field to emerge, the actors involved in the negotiation of the initial *settlement* must achieve a degree of consensus on four issues. First, they must arrive at a general, shared understanding of what is going on in the field, that is, what is at stake (Bourdieu and Wacquant 1992). Here, we would expect that actors in a settled strategic action field would share a consensus as to what is going on. Such a consensus does not imply that the division of spoils in the field is viewed as legitimate, only that the overall account of the terrain of the field is shared by most field actors. Second, there is a set of relatively fixed actors in the field whose roles and comparative status/power are consensually defined by others in the strategic action field. Third, there is a set of shared understandings about the nature of the "rules" that will govern interaction in the field. By this we mean that actors understand what tactics are possible, legitimate, and interpretable for each of the roles in the field. This is different from knowing what is generally at stake. This is the cultural understanding of what forms of action and organization are viewed as legitimate and meaningful within the context of the field. Finally, there is the broad interpretive frame that individual and collective strategic actors bring to make sense of what others within the strategic action field are doing.

Here, rather than positing a consensual frame that holds for all actors, we expect to see different interpretative frames reflecting the relative positions of actors within the strategic action field. We expect that actors will tend to see the moves of others from their own perspective in the field. In most fields, for example, we expect that dominant or incumbent actors will embrace a frame of reference that encapsulates their self-serving view of the field, while dominated or challenging actors will adopt/fashion an "oppositional" perspective. The reactions of more and less powerful actors to the actions of others thus reflect their social position in the field, and their interpretation will reflect how someone in their position who perceives the actions of others as directed at "people like them" will react. Their reactions to those actions will be drawn from the repertoire of behaviors that are legitimate under the rules in reaction to others given their position in the field.

For a field to emerge, these social understandings have to be created. An emerging field is an arena occupied by two or more groups whose actions are oriented to each other but who have yet to develop the four features of a stable field. Such arenas might be quite conflictual. The identities of groups may change substantially over time as groups are formed, enter or exit the embryonic field, or die. There may be no agreement on what the shared social space is about. There is no a priori reason that any social space has to become organized. Lots of potential fields fail to coalesce at this stage. If groups cannot find common ground (i.e., build coalitions) or one group cannot figure out a way to dominate the strategic action field, the field can drift for a long period of time in an unorganized state. We suspect that a great many "field projects" never materialize or only develop after several abortive attempts. And even when a field does coalesce, it may take years or even decades to do so. Indeed, the two examples of emergent fields touched on above—the U.S. auto industry and organized medicine in the United States—took something like thirty and fifteen years, respectively, to develop.

One of the thorniest problems involved in theorizing about fields is conceptualizing the field settlement. Some theorists posit that a field settlement is achieved when broad agreement on a set of rules and "institutional logics" comes to be shared by most actors in the strategic action field (Scott 2001). This view would seem to suggest that fields are far more cooperative than competitive and more about consensus than conflict. Scholars working in the "new institutionalism" in organizational theory tend to emphasize these elements. On the other side, there is the view that fields are really about interests, conflict, and power. This perspective implies that all fields are characterized by a fairly stark hierarchy or power structure that is dominated by one or a small number of actors who set the rules and agenda for all other groups. This position has been most forcefully argued by Pierre Bourdieu (Bourdieu and Wacquant 1992).

Our solution to this problem is to argue that cooperation and hierarchy are both present in the organization of fields. We view fields as a continuum with those exhibiting high levels of consensus, coalition, and cooperation at one end and those based on stark hierarchy and stark differences in power at the other. A cooperative field of nonprofit organizations that exist to help the victims of natural disasters might operate at the cooperative end of the continuum, and a state headed by an all-powerful autocrat (think Muammar Gaddafi or Kim Jong-Il) would define the more hierarchical, coercive end. One common source of conflict in any field—regardless of where it lies along the continuum—concerns the relative acceptance of the terms of the field settlement. We can expect some players to want to change the terms of this by making the field more cooperative and others to aspire to more hierarchy, typically with their group at the top of the pyramid! Obviously most fields are not located at the ends of the continuum, but in fact contain elements of both coalition and hierarchy. Even in the most hierarchical fields, those who have the most social power often rely on at least tacit cooperation from those they dominate.

While affirming that strategic action fields typically exhibit a mix of coalition and hierarchy, it is nonetheless quite typical for a given field to emphasize one or the other of these organizational principles. It is useful to consider more systematically how skilled social actors, through strategic action and the deployment of resources, produce either hierarchically organized strategic action fields or cooperative strategic action fields. One of the main factors shaping the eventual structure of a strategic action field is the initial distribution of resources in the field. Where resources are highly unequally distributed across groups, one would expect that one group or a set of dominant groups would be able to impose their will on the field. The resulting strategic action field is likely to have a hierarchical structure. So, for example, in a new market, the largest entrants often have an advantage in surviving and ultimately taking over the market. This is because they have more developed products and deeper pockets to survive longer (Hannan and Freeman 1984). When groups have roughly equal resource endowments at the beginning of the field, this will result in conflict. Such conflict will be harder to resolve without the building of some kind of political coalition that will create a stable field. Such coalitions will require strategic actors to fashion a shared identity to bring disparate groups together in a novel fashion.

Here we offer a hypothetical example to illustrate what we mean. Imagine a city where there is a set of nonprofit organizations dedicated to feeding poor people. Depending on the evolution of the strategic action field, such a group of organizations could end up with a hierarchical competitive structure or a more dispersed cooperative structure. How could this happen? If at the emergence of the strategic action field, a single organization claimed to be the main group to feed the poor, they would do so by capturing big donors and getting city and county government to support their efforts. They would disperse their activities throughout the area and claim to be the only group that can really serve the community's needs. Smaller challenger organizations would find it hard to find donors, and if they located their food banks in areas where the larger group already provided service, they might find themselves with few clients and little political constituency. Alternatively, if at emergence there was no one dominant group, but a host of smaller groups who were dispersed both geographically but also in terms of their donors, they might find it makes more sense to divide the city. They could form a governance council that would formalize their territories and competencies. Instead of competing or producing a hierarchy they would form a political coalition to cooperate by dividing the city. We would expect the same strategic action field in two different places to have a radically different underlying structure depending on the initial resource endowments of the participants.

We emphasize four dynamics that typically shape the process of field formation.

1. Emergent Mobilization—Central to field formation—and indeed field dynamics more generally—is the process of *emergent mobilization*. So central is this concept to our theory that it makes sense to spend a bit of time describing the process and its significance for the creation of strategic action fields. Emergent mobilization refers to the process by which collective actors fashion new lines of interaction with other actors based on altered understandings of the opportunities or threats to group interests they perceive. Typically the process is set in motion by some exogenous change that is perceived by at least two actors as posing a significant new threat to, or opportunity for, the realization of group interests. The creation or *appropriation of organizational vehicles* sufficient to launch and sustain *innovative collective action* must follow if the process of field formation is to occur. Field formation takes place when this dynamic sequence results in sustained interaction between two or more actors intent on occupying previously unorganized social space.

This process is but a more general gloss on a model of "mobilization" familiar to social movement scholars (see McAdam 1999: xv–xxx; McAdam, Tarrow, and Tilly 2001: chapter 1). For what, after all, are social movements but emergent fields of a particular kind? More to the point, what social theorists need to recognize is that mobilization is not peculiar to social movements but a more general process evident in all strategic action fields at their initial formation and in times of crisis. That is, movement-like mobilization is the motor of field formation and the structuring dynamic during periods of field contention. We will have more to say about the latter phenomenon later in the chapter. For now we simply want to underscore a central image. Routine social life involves the reproduction of social relations through routinized patterns of collective action. Field formation and change necessarily involve emergent lines of collective action that result in new social relations, new identities, new normative understandings, and the like.

2. *Social Skill and the Fashioning of a Settlement*—For all our talk of change, emergent mobilization, etc., field formation turns substantially on the ability of skilled social actors to bring some kind of routinized order out of the initial chaos that typically characterizes incipient strategic action fields. In some cases this order may be imposed through some combination of superior resource allocations, state sponsorship, and the imposition of raw power. In most instances, however, fields are born of the concerted efforts of collective actors to fashion a stable consensus regarding rules of conduct and membership criteria that routinize interaction in pursuit of common aims. We term this set of understandings a "settlement." We can say that a stable strategic action field has emerged when the actors who comprise the field share an understanding of this settlement and act routinely to reproduce it. In such instances, social power and shared meanings have been mobilized to create a robust social order. In such strategic action fields, means and ends are widely shared and action is oriented toward preserving the set of stable understandings and collective identity that structure the everyday life chances of the affected groups.

Forging a settlement is quite an achievement, but even in the most stable of fields, a settlement must always be regarded as a work in progress. We should never forget that the political/cultural order of any field remains an ongoing social accomplishment, dependent on the *social skill* of the actors—especially the most powerful incumbents—who comprise the field. We will devote much more attention to the role played by social skill in the various field states (i.e., emergent, stable, and in crisis) in the final section of the chapter. For now, we mean only to flag the issue and note its importance to an understanding of field formation and strategic action field dynamics more generally.

We bring this section to a close with an important aside. This seems like the right moment to explicitly acknowledge the crucial importance of the "existential" dimension to the settlement process. Even with the microfoundation sketched in chapter 2, it is hard—even for us—to not lapse into the language of power interests in discussing field dynamics. But for us, the creation of a settlement ordinarily turns more on the cultural creativity of the meaning project that grounds the field than on the presumed instrumental logic of the initiative. Indeed, the latter—the "objective interests" served by the effort—are one of the crucial elements constructed as part of the meaning project. As much as anything, field settlements embody the seemingly unique human capacity for collaborative symbolic activity and *need* for meaning and membership.

A rather trivial example will help to make the point. We first met as assistant professors in the sociology department at the University of Arizona. Although we came to the university in different years, our memories of our first departmental meeting were identical, and a touch surreal. Both of us recall longtime department members invoking the spirit and letter of the "constitution" at various points in the meeting. At first we thought they must be talking about the U.S. Constitution, but it soon became clear that the department, at a particularly contentious moment in its history, had drafted an elaborate constitution of its own to restrain the authority of an autocratic department head. It turned out that the constitution had absolutely no legal standing at the university and that, in the university's eyes, the head retained full control of the department. The document's lack of legal standing, however, in no way undermined its instrumental *and* broader existential force within the departmental community.

How would we interpret this example in light of the perspective sketched here? During an episode of contention earlier in its history, a coalition of department members—who had not been previously allied—came together to challenge the authority of the head, who they viewed as overly autocratic. Together they drafted a constitution and used it in negotiations with the offending head to forge a new settlement whose terms were spelled out in the document. At first blush, this sounds like a simple instrumental struggle between the head and his allies in the department and an emergent coalition of challengers whose interests in exercising more voice in the department were in conflict with the head's desire to retain sole authority. And from a narrow instrumental perspective, this "reading" of the episode is certainly not wrong. But the "lived experience" of the constitution (and the conflict that produced it) by department members was much broader and far more existential than instrumental. The conflict and resulting constitution were the centerpiece of an elaborate founding (or more accurately, "refounding") narrative that bound department members together and was routinely invoked at nearly all department functions. This narrative served to valorize the collective and was definitely linked to ongoing status rewards within the department. Those who had actually participated in the drafting of the constitution enjoyed a unique kind of standing in the department, while the deposed head occupied a distinctly marginal position in the collective.

And the constitution remained very much a living document. A copy of it was brought to every faculty meeting and the adjudication of contentious issues often turned on constitutional readings of the opposing positions. Indeed, it was common for department members to frame new initiatives as efforts to more fully realize the broad aims of the document. Invariably each year a special constitutional committee was appointed to amend or otherwise update the document in light of recent departmental actions. Among the most honored formal positions within the department was that of "parliamentarian," whose job it was to offer readings of the document during especially contentious moments in department meetings. To new faculty members these institutional rituals seemed odd at best, cult-like at worst. Over time, however, we too were socialized into these routines and came to embrace the broader set of valorizing understandings and shared identity that knit the departmental community together. Indeed, both of us remember not only our sense of dislocation on first encountering these routines but also, years later, our irritation at new members who failed to properly "honor" the constitution and understand its significance in the life of the collective.

We have gone on this long, and in this detail, to make a single critically important point. At the heart of virtually every settlement (or resettlement) there is a meaning project of the sort featured in our example. It is the existential "ballast" (e.g., shared meanings and collective identity) supplied by the project that propels the broader effort forward and at least in part accounts for whatever success the group is able to achieve. Invariably, in our "objective" scholarly accounts of any field, this existential dimension is normally lost as we privilege the more narrowly instrumental elements of the story. We are convinced, however, that this submerged dimension was not only present at the founding (or refounding of the field) but also crucial to a full understanding of the structure of the field in routine operation.

3. *State Facilitation*—Field settlements can be effected through internal mechanisms alone. But in the modern period, especially in high capacity states, *state facilitation* of field formation is almost certainly the norm. State facilitation can range from aggressive sponsorship of field formation through the active backing of particular groups to passive certification of settlements effected primarily by nonstate actors. The anti–drunk driving movement affords an example of the former process, with officials in the Reagan administration essentially leveraging the field into existence through active sponsorship of Mothers against Drunk Driving (Edwards and McCarthy 2004). In the latter category we might include the far more reactive state licensing of doctors and other medical personnel following the resolution of the internal power struggle among groups with very different conceptions of how to organize the emerging field of medicine (Starr 1982).

4. *Internal Governance Units*—Except in the most informal of fields, most settlements involve the creation of *internal governance units* within a strategic action field. In strategic action fields, the power of incumbents is sometimes enough to maintain order. This is particularly true in bureaucracies and formal organizations in which those in authority can pretty much dictate what subordinates do. But even the most powerful bureaucracies almost always spawn internal

governance units such as human resource departments, ombudsmen, and branches of the organization that make sure that rules are followed (disciplinary committees, internal affairs departments). These internal governance units function to help maintain order in strategic action fields in many ways.

Very often the initial function of an internal governance unit is to stabilize the original field settlement. To facilitate and stabilize a settlement, field actors frequently put into place internal governance units. Both challenger and incumbent groups might find it useful to help create and participate in such units, particularly in response to crises. Indeed, internal governance mechanisms frequently emerge in crises in which certain members of a particular field are threatened. As a response, they bond together to produce some form of governance to solve that crisis and produce stability.

Besides the initial stabilization of the field, internal governance units serve many other specific purposes. To better understand their myriad purposes, it may be useful to discuss specific types of internal governance units. Internal governance units may be set up to generate and disseminate information about the field to both field members and various outside audiences. They can also act as the field's liaison or lobbying presence within select state fields. Trade associations and professional organizations are examples of these kinds of groups. Internal governance units may be set up to certify the activities of members. So, for example, bond rating agencies help bond sellers create an "objective" evaluation of a product. Certification boards control who can claim to be a member of a group. Here, groups such as professionals work to make sure that people without "proper" credentials cannot claim the status and rewards of field members. Internal governance units can operate as mediation services or private courts that adjudicate between member grievances. They can be set up to enforce rules and standards, and members accused of violating those standards may face fines and penalties.

Typically the establishment of internal governance units is justified by reference to the interests of the field as a whole. Very often, however, the units bear a strong imprint of incumbent interests and even personnel. So, for example, many international organizations, such as the World Bank and the International Monetary Fund, appear to have the interests of all of the world's citizens. They are there to help developing countries secure loans for valued projects and to help countries in financial duress find solutions to their problems. But such organizations are clearly more under the control of the most developed countries, particularly the United States. They frequently operate to protect private lenders and the financial system, and they act to lower the standard of living of people in poorer countries in the name of attaining financial stabilization. There is an informal norm that the head of the World Bank be an American and the head of the International Monetary Fund, a European. In short, to the extent that

incumbents substantially control the workings of one or more internal governance units, they strengthen their position within the field and enhance their
ability to fend off challenges from within and without. Not surprisingly, then,
battles for control over a field's internal governance units are almost always a
feature of major episodes of contention within a strategic action field.

In sum, field formation typically depends on the complex sequence of events
discussed above. Two or more groups intent on organizing previously unorganized social space begin to interact in an ongoing way. Whether some stable
settlement eventuates from this interaction depends on at least four factors:
(1) the resource (or other power) disparity between the parties (which
conditions the likelihood that a settlement will be imposed on the field); (2) the
social skill of the actors involved (which conditions the likelihood that a settlement will be reached through negotiation and consensus); (3) the extent
to which state actors intervene to help effect or impede a settlement; and
(4) the creation of internal governance units to help routinize and implement
the terms of the settlement.

Sustaining a Settlement: The Reproduction of Fields

If the initial settlement that defines the field proves effective in creating an arena
advantageous to those who fashioned it, then it is likely to prove highly resistant
to challenge. This is because *incumbents* (e.g., field actors who are favored by the
settlement) will be disinclined to mount a challenge to the status quo. Just as
important, incumbents are products as well as architects of the worldview and
set of understandings they have helped create. They are now dependent upon
this worldview, and this dependency restricts their ability to conceive of alternative worlds or courses of action. In the absence of a severe exogenous shock, it
would be very difficult for culturally "embedded" actors to shift worldviews dramatically, especially when their interests appear to be well served by the prevailing settlement. Even potential *challengers* (e.g., field actors who are disadvantaged
relative to incumbents) can be expected to help reproduce the strategic action
field on a daily basis, unless they see a real opportunity to advance their interests
by violating field rules and acting in transgressive ways. In essence, we see reproduction as the "default option" normally preferred by all field actors, challengers
no less than incumbents. In the absence of recognizable exogenous shocks and/
or strategic incompetence by incumbents, we expect the great majority of the
members of the strategic action field to conform to the prevailing settlement and
to act in ways prescribed by it, reproducing the field in the process.

The stability of a field, however, does not simply rest on the internalized
worldview of field members or the characteristic caution of challengers in the

face of the power and resources of incumbents. We would do well to remember that the founding and initial stabilization of a strategic action field is almost always accompanied by the creation of the kind of internal governance units just discussed, as well as the establishment of strong ties to allies in a number of key state and nonstate fields on which the new strategic action field is especially dependent. Even as the interests of incumbents are being encoded in field rules and procedures, an institutionalized support structure is being simultaneously erected to further insulate the field from change pressures. Internal governance units serve to monitor and enforce the rules enacted as part of the initial field "settlement." They also engage in various "external" activities—lobbying, education—designed to stabilize and promote the field and the interests of its most powerful members. To the extent that these external activities are successful, the field will also be able to count for support on powerful state and nonstate allies. The presence of these "internal" units and "external" ties can be expected to further stabilize the field. In the end, the presence of these structural supports will not be enough to forestall serious change pressures, but they certainly promote stability and reproduction in the short or even medium term.

In advancing this view, however, we do not mean to suggest that strategic action fields are inherently static worlds where conflict and change only occur on those very rare occasions when the field is destabilized by exogenous shocks. The reality is much more complicated and interesting. Instead ours is an inherently conflictual world where change is ubiquitous, incumbents worry daily about how to maintain their advantage, and challengers search for and seek to exploit any "cracks" they discern in the system. Constant adjustments are being made, and the field is always in some form of flux or negotiations. Incumbents and challengers are constantly accommodating changing conditions both in and outside of the field. Normally these adjustments have the effect of preserving the power and privilege of incumbents. But this process has limits and when these limits are reached, and the shared consensus on which strategic action fields depend breaks down, all bets are off. At these moments there is the possibility for significant change. If the challengers engage in successful strategic action, a new social order can be created. If the incumbents find a way to restabilize the field (including through the use of repression), a new settlement and the changes it encodes, may be necessary. In short, while perhaps only rarely destabilized by true exogenous shocks, some level of change and contestation is always occurring in fields. This, in turn, means that skilled social actors are always in a position to shape field dynamics. Let us start with field incumbents.

Skilled strategic actors in incumbent groups have an impressive array of tools to maintain their position. They have more resources and better social connections to actors in other strategic action fields, including the state. Their dominant position means that their role in producing the rewards in the strategic action field allows them to continue to benefit from the existing organization of the field. While such actors must be vigilant about what both other incumbents and challengers are doing, they will be in a good position to respond. Indeed, one reason that reproduction is possible even in situations of dynamic competition is that skilled actors in incumbent organizations can use their resource and cultural advantages to co-opt challengers and respond strategically to other incumbents.

One could argue that the social skill of actors matters a great deal less for incumbents in highly institutionalized strategic action fields. After all, if dominant groups are not threatened by either challengers or external threats, then their ability to reproduce their power is increased. The greater the power imbalance and the less frequent the external shocks or crises in the field, the less difficult it is for incumbent groups to reproduce themselves.

A case of this might have been the savings and loan industry in the United States from 1945 until the mid-1970s. During the banking crisis of the Depression, the government separated the mortgage business from the other forms of banking. The mortgage business became highly regulated in a number of ways. Most prominent was a restriction on how much interest banks could pay for deposits. This regulation was called "Regulation Q." The savings and loan banks took in deposits at a fixed interest rate and lent them out to potential homebuyers, also at a fixed interest rate. Their profit was therefore guaranteed as long as the rate at which they paid for money was lower than the rate at which they would lend money. As long as this was the case, the need for strategic actors to work very hard to maintain the advantages of incumbent savings and loans banks was minimal.

Strategic actors in stable fields who belong to challenger groups confront a much more difficult situation. Here, their survival is more fragile and the possibility of being taken over or disbanded is very real. Skilled challengers will do whatever they can to continue to exist in a field where they have few resources and few powerful linkages. One tactic they will very likely deploy is forming alliances with more powerful groups. If they can ally themselves with incumbent groups, they might be able to secure enough resources to survive. They can also seek out alliances with groups in other strategic action fields. This might prove to be a promising tactic to improve their position within the field. Powell et al. (2005) show how challenger biotechnology companies engage in exactly these forms of strategic action over time. Small firms often enter into alliances and joint ventures with large firms in order to promote their stability in the field. They also form alliances across strategic action fields to increase their stability.

A second tactic is to try and find a niche in the strategic action field where incumbents will not go because it is not worth their while. This allows challengers to not directly confront incumbents but instead work toward complementarities.

Carroll and Swaminathan (2000) describe the rise of the microbrewery industry in exactly these terms. In the second half of the twentieth century, the largest beer producers in the United States came to control a larger and larger part of the market. During this period, smaller, regional breweries either went out of business or were bought by the larger producers. But beginning in the early 1990s, the so-called microbreweries began to appear. These brewers frequently made and sold beer on the same premises. The success of the early microbreweries led to the proliferation of a large number of small producers working in the shadows of the large producers. Since their volumes were small and their marketing was based on their uniqueness, the larger companies more or less ignored them.

Settlements and Ruptures: Stability and Crisis in Strategic Action Fields

It is our contention that strategic action fields are normally destabilized, not by internal processes but by exogenous "shocks" to the field. There are exceptions to this rule—circumstances when internal processes alone account for the onset of instability and crisis. We will discuss these internal sources of change later in the chapter. But we begin with what we see as the modal source of destabilizing shocks to strategic action fields: external events or change processes.

We see three principal external sources of field destabilization: (1) invasion by outside groups, (2) changes in fields upon which the strategic action field in question is dependent, and (3) those rare macroevents (e.g., war, depression) that serve to destabilize the broader social/political context in which the field is embedded. We take up each of these sources of external change in turn.

1. Invasion by Outside Groups—Stable strategic action fields are subject to "invasion" at any time. Most such invasions pose no fundamental challenge to the prevailing settlement and set of field relations. We refer here to the routine entrance of new members into the field. Most of these new entrants are relatively resource-poor groups that hope simply to embed themselves in the field and to gradually improve their circumstances and standing over time. Examples of this type of routine entrance are common: the founding of new firms in established industries, the creation of new political parties in multiparty systems, etc.

Far rarer, but with much greater implications for field stability, are cases in which powerful outside actors seek to invade an established strategic action field with the goal of altering the settlement as a means of advancing their own interests. By "outsiders," we mean groups that have previously not been active players in the field. Outside challengers often make the most effective adversaries because they are not bound by the conventions of the strategic action field and instead are free to bring new definitions of the situation and new forms of action to the field.

Their ability to be successful in this effort will depend on a number of factors: the strength of field incumbents, the defection of challengers to the side of the invader, and, in the modern period, the attitude of relevant state actors toward the invading group. If the state refuses to protect the extant settlement and a number of challengers defect, the possibility for significant field transformation is high.

Examples of transformation through invasion are fairly common. So-called hostile takeovers are a form of invasion. So too is the entrance of a major foreign investor into a previously national industry. But it is not only economic fields that are subject to invasion. In the early to mid-1970s, the efforts of the Teamsters to unionize seasonal agricultural workers upset the relative stability that Cesar Chavez had been able to achieve within the farmworkers movement (Ganz 2000).

2. *Changes in Related Fields*—As we argued in chapter 3, all strategic action fields are embedded in a dense latticework of other fields, including fields governed by state actors. These relationships create dependencies between fields that normally serve to stabilize all affected strategic action fields. But these same dependencies are also a common—in our view, the most common—source of crisis in fields. Such crises arise when significant changes in *related fields*—that is, fields on which another strategic action field is dependent—disrupt the routine operation of the field in question. If sufficiently severe, these perturbations in the broader system of field relations have the potential to set in motion the same process of emergent mobilization discussed in connection with field formation. That is, if events in a proximate field are (1) interpreted by actors in a specific strategic action field as posing a significant *threat* to or *opportunity* for the realization of group interests and (2) that actor is able, through the *appropriation* or creation of an organizational vehicle, (3) to undertake *innovative action,* the result is likely to be a *rupture* in the existing *settlement* and the onset of a generalized crisis, or *episode of contention,* in the field.

Crisis in nearby strategic action fields is the most frequent cause of significant episodes of contention within fields. This is most often the case where there exist resource dependencies. If one strategic action field is dependent on another for either the production of inputs or the consumption of output, then crisis in the proximate field will produce crisis in the field in question. This creates a kind of vertical ripple effect across strategic action fields. Strategic action fields that do not have lots of linkages to other strategic action fields in order to control their resource dependencies are more likely to experience severe crises. The ability of strategic action fields to draw on different resources tends to insulate them from these kind of shocks. Conversely, strategic action fields that are highly dependent on one other strategic action field are more likely to endure bigger crises and be at risk for reorganization.

So, for example, at the end of the Cold War, the defense department in the United States underwent a certain amount of retrenchment. This was caused by a sharp drop in the resources being dedicated to defense. These cutbacks had the biggest effects on the strategic action fields that were totally dependent on the defense department. Military contractors were heavily affected as weapons programs were wound down or cut off. The Pentagon actually pushed the largest defense contractors into mergers in order to maintain capabilities to produce weapon systems. The contractors themselves had little ability to resist the pressure of their largest customer. They complied and the industry devolved into three large aerospace defense contractors.

The basic imagery, then, is of a society consisting of millions of strategic action fields linked by various types of relations. Given the large number of strategic action fields in society, it follows that even in the best of times there will always be a certain percentage of fields in crisis, subjecting some number of other related fields to destabilizing change pressures of their own. We see this kind of "rolling turbulence" as endemic to modern society. In short, a large number of strategic action fields in modern societies will always be in some form of crisis, and this will in turn place other strategic action fields at risk.

3. Macroevents—The final way in which fields can be destabilized from without is via large-scale *macroevents* that have the effect of creating a sense of generalized crisis, at the very least within a single society but oftentimes across many societies. The state is one of the central forces for change in strategic action fields because of its connection to many of the important strategic action fields in society. General political crises such as war, invasion, serious regime change, economic collapse, and the collapse of government have profound effects on the structuring of strategic action fields across society. This is because these crises undermine all kinds of linkages in society and make it difficult for groups to reproduce their power. In such instances, all manner of fields within the affected societies are expected to be destabilized by the generalized sense of crisis permeating the affected society or societies.

Though clearly unique in the number of strategic action fields affected, field crises generated by macroevents turn on the same mediating dynamics as the two forms discussed previously. So, once again we see attributions of threat/opportunity leading to the appropriation or creation of organizational vehicles for the purpose of engaging in innovative, contentious interaction with other field actors. In these rare instances, however, the perceived threat or opportunity that motivates action often has less to do with events in the field than with those in the broader society. In addition, the restabilization of relations within the strategic action field typically depends on the resolution of the broader underlying conflict and not simply skilled strategic action within the field.

The Chinese Cultural Revolution affords a perfect, if harrowing, example of this kind of generalized field crisis. The now extensive literature on the topic makes it clear just how far-reaching the effects of the crisis were on Chinese society (Walder 2009a). The conflict destabilized existing settlements in count-less work places, villages, cooperative farms, universities, and government agencies. Mao's support for generalized struggle against counterrevolutionary elements from parts of the population posed a stark threat to those in positions of power, while affording discontented groups a real opportunity to advance their interests by waging "class war" against their enemies. Both sides did so through the appropriation of existing structures and/or the creation of new ones.

Later in the chapter we take up the important topic of the restabilization of a strategic action field following a crisis. Not surprisingly, much of what we say there echoes our earlier description of initial field formation. So the social skill of field actors in fashioning a viable consensus among some subset of incum-bents and challengers is typically a key part of the story. So, too, is the role of state actors in helping to broker and/or certify a new order in the field to reduce the shared sense of uncertainty that fuels contention and begin to once again structure field relations. But all of this is made much more difficult in the case of generalized societal crises. It matters little if field-based actors have superb social skills when the broader political environment is as chaotic and unsettled as is typically the case in times of war or extreme economic stress.

Similarly, if the generalized crisis severely weakens the existing regime or devolves into a revolutionary situation with two or more contenders claiming sovereign authority, then the ability of state actors to help broker or certify a new settlement will be seriously compromised. Indeed, in such instances, the actions of "state" actors are more apt to promote ongoing instability than order. Here again, the analogy of the Russian dolls is helpful. Rather than serving as a stable container of all other fields, the largest doll (read: the state) is itself in crisis, subverting the efforts of actors in specific strategic action fields to put their houses in order. This was certainly the case in the Cultural Revolution in China, in which the ongoing struggle between different state/party factions ensured continuing instability in all strategic action fields linked to the state (Walder 2009a). In China this effectively meant *all* other fields. The point is fields desta-bilized through generalized societal crisis are likely to remain in flux until the broader crisis is resolved. More to the point, the resettlement of these fields is very likely to be temporally linked to, and bear a significant imprint of, the resolution of any attendant regime crisis.

We need to make it clear that not all ruptures in strategic action fields are the product of external shocks. Indeed, some field crises would seem to be owing primarily to internal dynamics. And while we think these *endogenous crises* are nowhere near as common as the *exogenous* variety, a full understanding of field dynamics requires that we have command of both. Our provisional hunch is that these "internal" ruptures typically reflect threshold or tipping point dynamics that grow out of entirely normal field dynamics. So unlike the sudden "shocks" that tend to catalyze exogenous ruptures, these endogenous crises tend to germinate slowly through the kinds of routine jockeying for advantage and incremental shifts in strategy and relations that are part and parcel of routine field dynamics.

To say that a strategic action field is stable and routinely reproducing the terms of an existing settlement should not be read to mean that change is not occurring in the field. On the contrary, as we have argued throughout, incremental change is the rule in even the most stable of fields. The absence of discernible threats to, or opportunities for, the advancement of group interests is expected to preclude the possibilities for successful emergent mobilization. But as James Scott (1985, 1990) argues, between open rebellion and slavish conformity, there lies a zone of strategic action that is rarely acknowledged by scholars, let alone theorized. So even while accepting the existing settlement, we should expect field actors to routinely engage in behaviors that are designed to improve their position in the field while guarding against any significant loss of strategic advantage. But even the most risk-averse actors can be expected on occasion to shift strategies, forge new alliances, or otherwise alter their patterns of interaction with key actors inside and outside the strategic action field.

All well and good; but what does this quotidian view of field dynamics have to do with the far more dramatic business of field rupture, contention, and change? The connection is straightforward. When aggregated over time, even incremental changes of the sort envisioned here have the potential to gradually undermine the relations and/or understandings on which a strategic action field rests. The individual changes are themselves so modest as to be virtually invisible. But the cumulative, threshold effects may be anything but, suddenly motivating the by now familiar pattern of emergent mobilization and contentious interaction discussed above.

Eric Leifer's *Making the Majors* (1995) provides a field analysis of the emergence of professional sports in America. So, for example, the formation of the first modern professional sports league, baseball, was a process of incremental change whereby the problems of the sport were resolved endogenously over a relatively long historical period. After the Civil War, baseball was an amateur sport played by almost 400 teams across the country. The competition between teams drove different cities and towns to seek out players who would make their teams better. This began a process of professionalization in which players would sell their services to the highest bidder. The problem of who the best players would play for and how they would be paid was the core issue that drove the dynamics of baseball until 1922. It was this problem that provoked a set of solutions that evolved over time. Once some people decided to field professional teams, the issue of who such teams would play and who would own the teams came to the fore. It is useful to tell a stylized version of the story.

In 1869, the Cincinnati Red Stockings decided to become a fully professional team. Brothers Harry and George Wright recruited the best players from around the country and beat all comers. The Cincinnati team won sixty-five games and lost none. The idea of paid players quickly caught on. Some wanted baseball to remain an amateur endeavor, but there was no way they could compete with the professional teams. The amateur teams began to fade away as the best players became professionals. In 1871, the National Association of Base Ball Players became the first professional baseball league. One of the most interesting features of the National Association was that the players owned the teams.

The National Association was short lived. It was undermined by a set of gambling scandals that drove customers away. Following the 1875 season, the National Association was replaced with the National League of Professional Baseball Clubs. The National League introduced one other important innovation. It was run by businessmen who established standards and policies for ticket prices, schedules, and player contracts. This proved to be a successful strategy that brought the fans back out to the games. In 1882, a rival professional league run by businessmen emerged, the American Association. In a few years, the two leagues decided to join forces rather than fight and agreed to honor each other's contracts with players. This created a series of fights between the players and the owners in which the players formed their own league. This failed. By 1903, the two leagues solidified their hold over the game by providing a common structure for the game, ownership by businessmen, and player contracts that would be honored by all teams.

The modern structure of baseball was cemented by a Supreme Court decision that allowed the two leagues to collude to control player movements and regulate the game. This solution also illustrates one of the principles of our theory: stable field solutions tend to get ratified by state actors. In 1914, the Federal League of Base Ball Clubs formed. It sued the now merged American and National Leagues for being a monopoly in 1915. The Supreme Court ultimately decided in 1922 that baseball was exempt from the antitrust laws because its business did not fall under the purview of the Sherman Antitrust Act. This decision solidified the power of the incumbents and ensured that the American and National Leagues—now known as Major League Baseball—could control the sport. This structure held until the free agent revolution of the 1970s.

Reestablishing Field Stability

As noted previously, all actors—even the most disadvantaged challengers— have a serious stake in social order. This stake would appear to owe as much to our physiology and psychology as anything else. This is not to say that we will avoid conflict and change at all costs. On the contrary, once set in motion, the genie of contention is not easy to put back in the bottle. Still, the myriad functions of social order are compelling, and strategic actors can generally be expected—even while still invested in conflict—to look for ways to restore it, preferably on terms favorable to them. How are fields restabilized after a period of conflict? By what means are new settlements effected?

Not surprisingly, our answers to these questions draw substantially on the central points made in the earlier section on field formation. After all, field formation no less than the resolution of a field crisis involves creating a stable order out of a previously chaotic action arena. Given this essential similarity, we can expect the *social skill* of incumbents and challengers and the stabilizing hand of *state actors* to be important in both sets of circumstances.

There is, however, a significant difference between the initial formation of a strategic action field and its restabilization following a crisis. The difference involves the presence in the latter situation of well-defined *incumbents* and *challengers*, whose relatively advantaged and disadvantaged positions within the field are expected to yield fairly predictable responses to any crisis. Generally speaking, incumbents can be expected to respond to any perceived *threat* conservatively, fighting tenaciously to preserve the settlement that is the political and cultural source of their advantage. They are likely to do so even when it is apparent to most observers that the system is doomed. This is partly because they have so internalized the self-serving account of their own advantage that they are blind to other perspectives. But it is also because their power and material advantage is fully dependent on the existing settlement, thus motivating them to fight to the bitter end to preserve their privileged position within the strategic action field.

Besides fighting tenaciously on their own, when confronted with a crisis, incumbents can be expected to enlist their allies in the internal governance units and in various key state and nonstate fields in an effort to restore the ruptured settlement or to help forge a new one that preserves as much of the incumbents' advantage as possible. This suggests another significant difference between crises in an established strategic action field and the chaos attendant on field formation. State actors (or those in related fields) may be called upon to ratify or perhaps even to help broker the initial settlement in an emerging field, but, in general, they are not likely to be deeply invested in the state of the strategic action field or strongly allied with particular groups within the field. However, as fields—especially large powerful fields—develop, we can expect the ties between the state and the strategic action field, and between the new and related fields, to grow more numerous and salient for all parties.

This is so for two reasons. Consider only state/field relations here. First, the stability of the state depends, at a very general level, on its ability to help maintain stability across a very broad range of fields. If too many strategic action fields are in crisis, general social/political stability will be threatened, with potentially fatal consequences for the regime in power. So, in general, states are invested in field stability. But they are also likely to resist change in specific strategic action fields because of particular ties to leading incumbents. As fields develop, savvy incumbents seek to ally themselves with leading state actors and vice versa; for their part, leading state actors—or those who aspire to such a role—see powerful incumbents in key strategic action fields as attractive allies. Although we have focused on state/field relations here, the same applies in the case of related fields. That is, the stability of any given field is partially a function of the stability of all strategic action fields with which it has established significant dependent relations. Under normal circumstances, this will motivate field incumbents to intervene in related fields to help forestall or resolve crises. The fact that these incumbents are already likely to have strong ties to counterparts in these related fields only reinforces the tendency toward defense of the status quo.

The point is field development does not simply involve the maturation of internal relations. Over time, fields also become more embedded in the broader institutional fabric of society through the self-interested ties that develop between key incumbents and leading actors in state or other related fields. The practical implication of this is that when the stability of a given strategic action field is threatened, its incumbents are likely to be able to activate key external allies—especially state actors—to help defend the status quo. This does not mean that they will inevitably be able to blunt the challenge and restore the original field settlement. Even if incumbents are able to mobilize powerful external allies, the challenge to the field may be too strong for the powers that be to overcome. Or it may be that external allies, sensing the inevitable collapse of the settlement, shift their allegiance to other parties to the conflict. Finally, it may be that challengers within the field have successfully allied themselves to other external actors whose intervention helps precipitate the crisis and foreshadow a new settlement in the strategic action field.

In summary, incumbents can be expected to resist significant change in the field and to bring their own considerable resources—existential as well as political and material—to bear on the outcome of any struggle for control over a given strategic action field. Given these great advantages, it is hardly surprising that one very common—perhaps modal—outcome of contention within a field is simply the reestablishment of the prior order. That brings us to the challengers. In the face of the obvious advantages enjoyed by incumbents, how should we expect challengers to act when afforded an opportunity to do so? The first point worth making is that we should expect many "objective" opportunities for successful challenge of a strategic action field to go unheeded. That is why we have placed the processes of collective attribution, social construction, and appropriation at the center of our model of emergent mobilization. There are two important implications here. First, challengers may perceive and construct opportunities for contentious action where none objectively exist. Our point is that such anomalous readings of "objective" environmental conditions are bound to be rare, as such interpretations are unlikely to find many adherents and/or sufficient environmental receptivity to survive the predictable response of incumbents and their allies.

Similarly, we fully expect the opposite to happen as well, that is, circumstances rife with "objective" opportunity that fail to produce so much as a ripple of emergent contention by challengers. Indeed, such cases may even be modal. So daunting are the multiple barriers—psychological, cultural, organizational, and political—to mobilization that we are convinced that many "opportunities" for successful challenge die before they produce change. But should challengers overcome these barriers and engage in emergent mobilization, what steps will they need to take to achieve a new, more advantageous, settlement and restore overall field stability? While admitting a broad range of possible outcomes, we nonetheless see two stark challenges confronting any who would challenge the cultural logic and legal/organizational structure of an existing strategic action field. The stark internal challenge is to fashion an alternative order attractive to a good many groups in the field. The eventual external challenge is to secure allied backing for the proposed new settlement. We briefly take up each of these challenges.

1. *Forging a Winning Coalition*—Several times we have mentioned the fact that all actors have a certain stake in social order. Without evoking the more determinant conceptions of "false consciousness," the fact remains that existing settlements represent an often imposing cognitive barrier to contentious action. After all, such settlements define stable, predictable worlds and sources of meaning and identity for all participants in the strategic action field. To overcome this barrier, challengers must fashion alternative conceptions of control that simultaneously undermine the existing settlement, while providing a new animating vision for the field. In their discussion of the construction and promulgation of "collective action frames," social movement theorists have long recognized the critical importance of this process (Benford and Snow 2000; McAdam 1999; Snow and Benford 1988; Snow et al. 1986).

2. *Seeking State Allies and the Ratification of Change*—Prior to the rise of centralized national states, framing, coalition building, and other internal mobilization processes might have been sufficient to impose a new settlement on an existing strategic action field. Even today, under circumstances of limited state capacity, these same internal processes may be sufficient to bring about the transformation and resettlement of a particular field. But under conditions of moderate to high state capacity, the resolution of most episodes of field contention will necessarily involve both successful internal mobilization and

the eventual imposition and ratification of the new settlement by relevant state (or other external) actors.

But how can we reconcile the view of state actors as characteristically conservative and allied with strategic action field incumbents with their critically important role in ratifying change within fields? The question is not as puzzling as it might, at first glance, appear. Here we simply restate two points made in our earlier discussion of state/strategic action field relations. First, the ultimate stability and legitimacy of states depend critically on their ability to minimize instability across the myriad fields they oversee. This means that they are likely to *initially* help resist destabilizing change in any major strategic action field. That said, this same aversion to instability gives state actors a powerful motive to intervene to effect a new settlement if and when they perceive the old system as no longer viable. Under these conditions, they will be motivated to aggressively enter the fray to quickly restore order on terms favorable to themselves, regardless of the consequences to previous allies. This brings us to the second point made earlier.

We should not assume that state actors will remain loyal to the same set of strategic action field actors over time. So even a generalized preference for stability will not prevent state actors from switching allegiances, even if it contributes to change in existing strategic action fields. Finally, states are themselves composed of fields subject to the same dynamics discussed here. And when challengers successfully depose incumbents in an important state strategic action field, we can count on the newly installed authorities to aid their allies in other fields. So, for example, it is common practice for the two major parties in the United States to "clean house" in various state agencies when they reclaim the White House or state house from the other. Even in select nonstate fields, the reclamation of the White House by the "other side" will often lead to realignments and modifications of the existing order. Under various circumstances, then, state actors can be expected to aid change projects in strategic action fields.

The Relationship between Social Skill and the State of the Strategic Action Field

To this point in the chapter we have described the basic dynamics of field emergence, stability, and change. More specifically we have sought to explain the conditions under which fields emerge, sustain themselves, and are transformed through episodes of contention. Here we seek to link these three states to the social skills associated with each. Social skill functions as a microtheory for understanding what actors are doing in fields. It is the blend of preexisting rules, resources, and the social skills of actors that combine to produce fields in the first place, make them stable on a period to period basis, and produce transformation. Skilled social actors tailor their actions to the current state of the field (i.e., emergent, stable, crisis), their place in that field, and the current moves by skilled actors in other groups in the field. Social process matters, because even in stable fields, skilled social actors need to manipulate rules and resources in order to aid the reproduction of local orders. In the remainder of the chapter, we describe what we would expect skilled social actors to be doing under different field states and different locations in the pecking order of the strategic action field.

Social Skill and the Emergence of Fields

The emergence of new fields occurs when at least two groups seek to occupy previously unorganized social space. The absence of shared rules and understandings makes this an inherently unstable situation. Under these circumstances, skilled social actors will generally work to stabilize their group internally while also interacting with other would-be field members. Depending on their resource endowments, they may seek to impose an order on these other actors or, alternatively, to arrive at a more collaborative arrangement with these other groups. It is important to note, however, that in these situations, skilled social actors may very well fail to effect a settlement. Skilled actors may be unable to build political coalitions or be strong enough to enforce a local social order. All of the social skill in the world may fail to produce order where no one has enough claim on resources or where there is simply no way to forge the kind of shared understandings that stable fields require.

Order can be produced in two ways. First, the largest and most powerful groups can impose an order on the field. In this situation, preexisting rules and resources brought to the emerging field by groups may suffice to impose an order on the new field. This requires skilled strategic actors to use existing resources and rules, often based on power from other fields, to fashion a new order. It is possible for a single group to do this if it is strong enough. But quite often, no one group is dominant enough to be able to impose a settlement on all other contenders. In this situation, the contenders—or at least the strongest of the contenders—must find a way to cooperate in the imposition of an order. Skilled strategic actors can negotiate or signal to their principal competitors their intentions and help find a way to collectively impose order on the field. In this situation, the superior resources of a small number of groups will likely carry the day. This situation requires skilled social action, however, to convince nominal competitors that no order is worse than one in which they are somewhat disadvantaged.

The second way of producing order involves inspired skilled actors, who DiMaggio (1988) calls "institutional entrepreneurs" and who invent new cultural conceptions to help establish entirely "new" institutions. The trick is to fashion a political coalition under a new banner that unites disparate groups. The new cultural conceptions build on materials available to strategic actors that provide identities for collective actors that resonate with their prior conceptions of themselves. These new cultural conceptions can reorganize actors' identities and interests. By deciding who and how to be, groups accept a position in the order that may redefine who they are and what they want.

This makes it possible for new, unimaginable coalitions to emerge under new cultural frames and collective identities (see Ansell 2001 for an example). This process often occurs in instances of emergent collective action as new issues, collective action frames, and identities come together and coalesce to produce self-conscious social movements that command not only the narrow instrumental loyalties but also the primary existential commitments of their followers. That is, for many of the pioneering activists in any new movement, the movement community comes to serve as the central source of meaning and identity in their lives. But this is true not only of social movements narrowly defined but to a lesser extent also of all collective action projects that birth fields. Every field is born not so much of shared interests as of a creative cultural process that binds field members together through a constructed narrative account of the new collective identity that unites them and the shared mission that is at the heart of the field. It is in these moments that the close connection between the existential and the instrumental is clearest. Invariably, skilled social actors—institutional entrepreneurs, if you like—are to be found center stage during this process.

Social Skill and the Reproduction of the Field

Our perspective on social skill provides useful insight into the problem of social reproduction. Skilled social actors in stable fields are trying either to reproduce their dominance or to find openings to contest that dominance. In dominant groups, skilled social actors must ensure cooperation with their members inside their groups and across dominant groups. As long as they continue to deliver valued rewards for group members, skilled social actors are likely to maintain their power. Existing fields give incumbent actors a better chance of reproducing their advantage precisely because they imply an unequal distribution of rules and resources. In incumbent groups, skilled strategic actors orient their moves vis-à-vis others to the end of enhancing or maintaining their group's advantaged position in the field.

The relations between dominant groups are complex. Over time, one can expect that the skilled actors who exercise authority within dominant groups will try to better their positions vis-à-vis their principal challengers. This will also sit well with members of the group who will see that their leaders are trying to get an edge over their opponents. Thus, skilled actors in dominant groups will constantly be pushing the limits of current rules that produce order. At the same time skilled strategic actors have to be careful not to undermine the existing order by too direct a confrontation with the other principal dominant groups. This interaction can create a permanent tension within a field and the sense that the field is always on the verge of crisis.

Skilled strategic actors in dominated groups face difficult problems in stable times. They are likely to be the groups most disadvantaged by the skilled strategic actors within incumbent groups. After all, their position is weakest, and if dominant groups want to gain some advantage, they may choose not to confront other dominant groups but take on the dominated instead. Still, skilled challengers are not without options. They must find an identity for their group that will keep people committed to the group. Often, this is an identity rooted in opposition and control over "their" niche. Skilled strategic actors in dominated groups tend to take what the system gives.

It is possible in stable fields that the social skill of actors may not matter as much for the reproduction of the field. After all, dominating groups typically have resources, rules, and allies on their side relative to challengers. This is particularly true where there are few dominant groups, there are slack resources in the field, or success and failure are difficult to evaluate (e.g., schools and police departments). Here, the legitimacy of organizations in the sense of their right to exist may rarely be challenged (Meyer, Scott, and Deal 1981), and even when there is crisis, the organizations do not go out of business. It is also the case that for both incumbents and challengers these kinds of fields tend to attain a "taken for granted" status that further discourages innovative strategic action within the strategic action field.

Social Skill and the Transformation of Fields

As we have seen, existing fields tend to go into crisis as a result of changes that occur outside of fields, particularly in fields on which the field in question is dependent. Thus, a downturn in a field's major market or supplier, or in the case of governments, war or economic crisis, will have consequences for a particular local order. Crises are frequently caused by the intentional or unintentional actions of governments or the invasion of a field by outsiders. One can identify a real crisis in an existing field as a situation in which the major groups are having difficulty reproducing their privilege, as the rules that have governed interaction are no longer working.

Skilled strategic actors in dominant groups will typically respond to the onset of a crisis by hewing to the status quo rather than engaging in innovative forms of action. This happens for two reasons. First, at the outset it is difficult to tell a crisis that threatens the legitimacy of the whole field from routine contentious interaction. In such a situation, the first instinct of skilled incumbents will be to respond to the actions of others in the field, either challengers or incumbents, by engaging in actions that have always worked to their advantage. Second, since these actions have always reinforced the position of the dominant groups, skilled actors will continue to use them. Therefore, skilled actors will manipulate the same symbols, identities, and tactics that have always proved successful in the past.

If these fail over time and dominant groups struggle to reproduce themselves, the possibilities for new forms of strategic action open up. Challengers may find an opening (what social movement theorists call a "political opportunity") to force changes on the existing order. They may ally themselves with other dominant groups, invaders from other fields, or state actors to help reconstitute a given field. Occasionally, incumbents might defect to the side of challengers and help produce a fundamental structural change in the field. The social fluidity of this situation suggests that new bargains are possible. This makes the situation akin to what occurs in the moment of field emergence. It means that the largest groups might still be able to impose an order, albeit one that is based on different principles. But new visions for the field and new lines of innovative action are most likely to be undertaken by challenger or invader groups because they are the ones who are least committed to the old order. Those defending the status quo can accept a new order and adopt some new position in that order. But this will require their leaders to change their identity and interests in order to justify their new position. Following McAdam, Tarrow, and Tilly (2001), we term a sustained period of field uncertainty and conflict an "episode of contention." In the next chapter we offer extended examples of two very consequential episodes of contention in U.S. history.

Conclusion

The political–cultural approach to the construction of strategic action fields has many advantages. It gives us a generic social theory that can make sense of a large number of situations in the social world. The imagery we have provided views society as a vast multitude of strategic action fields that are connected in myriad ways. It also implies that much of the dynamism of modern society comes from the opportunities and crises that are constantly being presented to individuals, groups, and organizations and that enable them to occupy, create, and transform their local situations. This dynamism not only is internal to the logic of strategic action fields but also works at their edges. The dependence of strategic action fields on other strategic action fields and the overall dependence of modern society on an elaborate system of state fields provide a key source for both stability and change. We see five advantages to our perspective: (1) it offers a theory of social change that accounts for both routine piecemeal change and the much less common transformation of fields, (2) it provides a way to understand the role of political coalitions or hierarchy as the basis of social order for fields, (3) it suggests what actors can be expected to do under different field conditions, (4) it links the prospects for field stability and change primarily to the relationships that exist between the field and the set of external fields on which the field is most dependent, and (5) it highlights the especially decisive role of the state in promoting both field crisis and stability.

By viewing the formation of strategic action fields and their potential transformation as the outcome of a disorganized social space, we make sense of how sometimes very new things can happen when what constitutes groups, identities, and even resources is up for grabs. We have analyzed such moments as movement-like mobilization processes. New groups appear and they create new understandings about the nature of the field and unique coalitions and hierarchies to produce new mesolevel social order. Indeed, one of the most interesting aspects of such situations is the role of skilled strategic actors in being able to set up either a hierarchy or political coalition to govern a strategic action field. These processes occur in politics, society, and the economy.

But our theory also provides for constant, albeit piecemeal, change in stable fields. Here, the actors in strategic action fields are constantly jockeying for position. Challengers and incumbents are undertaking strategic actions to sustain and slightly improve their current position in the strategic action field, finding new accommodations with other groups, and working to reduce their resource dependencies on both groups within the field and outside of the field.

We equate the role of "entrepreneur" with skilled strategic action. As wielded by these entrepreneurs, social skill is expected to be consequential under all field conditions (i.e., emergence, stable, crisis). In "normal" times, strategic actors will use the tools available to them to maintain their position in the strategic action field. Incumbent actors will use their existing advantages to weather storms and crises in the field. Challengers will try different tactics to increase their odds of survival, including reducing their resource dependence on the powerful and alternatively allying with the more powerful actors.

The relationship between fields is, in our view, the central source of change in stable fields. If we grant that there are always new strategic action fields being created and old strategic action fields being destroyed, it implies that modern societies will feature a great deal of dynamism. It is this possibility of change that brings groups and actors together to try entirely new things. Finally, we view the state as a central actor simultaneously precipitating crises in some fields, defending/stabilizing the status quo in others, and helping to create new social orders in still other fledgling strategic action fields.

5

Illustrating the Perspective

*Contention over Race in the United States, 1932–1980 and the Rise
and Fall of the Mortgage Securitization Industry, 1969–2011*

In the first chapter we claimed that a unified conceptual framework would help account for empirical phenomena of interest to political sociologists and political scientists, economic sociologists, social movement scholars, and organizational sociologists. The framework we have proposed in the first four chapters is in many ways quite abstract. Readers might be excused for thinking that it is unclear how one could go about using the framework we have developed to analyze political and economic phenomena that appear at their root to be very different things. In this chapter, we use two detailed examples from political sociology/social movements and economic sociology to illustrate the usefulness of our thinking. The examples we choose are political contention over race in the United States from 1932 to 1980 and the rise and fall of the mortgage securitization industry from 1969 to 2011. The former is an iconic case familiar to students of American politics, social movement scholarship, and American history. The latter story concerns the industry that was at the core of the financial meltdown in the United States in 2007–2009. The purpose of this comparison is not a theory testing exercise but instead a lesson in how the theoretical concepts of the strategic action field approach can inform large and important changes in the major fields of society that at first glance seem to have little to do with each other.

We begin by considering how the ideas we have proposed can be applied to these two situations. In both of these arenas, there existed a stable strategic action field. Our effort here tries to characterize what the stable field was, who the players were in that strategic action field, what the "settlement" in place was, and how this set of understandings was maintained over time. Then, we consider how both of these strategic action fields were destabilized by exogenous shocks. We argue that these shocks came to destabilize the existing strategic action field, eroding the material and ideational advantages of the incumbents and creating new opportunities for all manner of combatants to contest the restructuring of the field. We then describe the two crises that resulted from the collapse of the previous agreement, paying special attention to the major parties to the conflicts and the roles they played in shaping the eventual settlement that brought the episode to a close. We describe the settlement for each case, identifying the new incumbents and challengers and the set of general understandings around which the settlement was forged. Finally, we show how these new settlements affected other strategic action fields. The successful reorganization of the field of racial politics in the United States and the reorganization of the U.S. mortgage market had profound effects on a host of proximate and more distant fields.

The Civil Rights Struggle, 1932–1980

The conventional account of the civil rights revolution is generally told as a social movement story. It revolves around the courage and agency of grassroots civil rights activists in the South. It is a powerful, inspiring story that almost always begins in Montgomery, Alabama with Rosa Parks's refusal to surrender her seat on the bus on that December day in 1955. The end of the story is less consensually fixed but tends to center on Martin Luther King's assassination in April of 1968, the meteoric rise and subsequent fall of the Black Panthers, the sad denouement of the 1968 Poor People's Campaign, or some other process or event that is thought to mark the "death" of the movement. In bookending the story in this way, however, the literature conveys the impression that contention over race in this period is synonymous with the mass movement that flourished from 1955 to 1970.

It should be clear by now that we favor a much broader view of social change and conflict, one that grants considerable, if not always equal, time to a much larger cast of characters and centers on the complex interplay of a good many state and nonstate strategic action fields. In an effort to render our perspective less abstract, we revisit the familiar civil rights story. Using the central conceptual elements of our theory, however, we recast the story in very different terms. Specifically, we structure our "revisionist" account of the civil rights struggle around the following five key concepts:

- strategic action field: before
- exogenous shocks
- crisis and contention
- settlement and the new strategic action field
- effects on other strategic action fields

We begin, however, by setting the case in the broader history of racial contention in the United States.

Setting the Stage: Contention over Race in the United States, 1781–1877

Notwithstanding the high-minded rhetoric of the founding fathers, African Americans did not share in the fruits of liberty that attended the birth of the nation. None of our celebrated founding documents granted blacks legal standing or assigned them new freedoms. Their subordinate status was perhaps best reflected in the process that was to be used in assigning the number of representatives each state would have in the lower house of Congress. For the purpose of enumerating the population, blacks who were slaves were to be counted as but three-fifths of a white person. This initial "settlement" of the "Negro question" was to hold—albeit with increasing tension—for the better part of the republic's first seventy-five years. "Rupture" finally came in the 1850s, as the vaunted Compromise of 1850 failed to achieve any kind of lasting consensus on the issue. Instead the decade was witness to a bloody guerrilla war between pro- and antislavery forces in Kansas, the Supreme Court's controversial 1857 decision in *Dred Scott v. Sanford*, John Brown's raid on Harper's Ferry, and the near fatal beating of antislavery senator Charles Sumner by proslavery representative Preston Brooks on the floor of the Senate following a strong abolitionist speech by Sumner. The chronologically last of these events—John Brown's raid—destabilized the field of presidential politics on the eve of the 1860 election, helping the long-shot candidate, Abraham Lincoln, secure the nomination of the abolitionist Republican Party.

What followed was a string of events that is familiar to generations of American schoolchildren—Lincoln's election, secession by the Southern states, the onset of the Civil War, Gettysburg, the Emancipation Proclamation, Lee and Grant at Appomattox, and Lincoln's assassination. Less well known are the eleven years of Reconstruction (1865–1876) imposed by the North on the South and the substantial, if troubled, racial equality that was achieved in the states of the former Confederacy during those years. Even *less* well known are the events surrounding the end of Reconstruction. The stage for those events was set when the 1876 presidential race between Rutherford B. Hayes and Samuel Tilden ended with no clear winner. In a successful effort to resolve the deadlocked election, Northern Republicans agreed to relax federal Reconstruction efforts in the South in exchange for Southern support for their candidate, Rutherford B. Hayes. The practical effect of the compromise was, once again, to render the "Negro question" a matter of regional rather than federal purview.

In Dahl's phrase, the compromise of 1876 was an important step in the process by which "the issue of the freed Negro was denationalized" (1956: 182). Schattschneider's famous statement is worth repeating here: "All forms of political organization have a bias in favor of the exploitation of some kinds of conflict and the suppression of others because organization is the mobilization of bias. Some issues are organized into politics while others are organized out" (1960: 71). In this sense, the compromise serves as a convenient historical referent marking the point in time at which the question of the sociopolitical status of black Americans was consciously "organized out" of national politics (McAdam 1999).

The Field of Racial Politics, 1877–1932

One of the trickiest challenges for anyone interested in studying a specific field is defining with some degree of conceptual and empirical precision what the contours of that strategic action field are. In some cases, it is easy. We have said that all formal organizations can be simultaneously analyzed as fields. There the boundaries of the field are perfectly clear. It is also reasonably easy to characterize and develop a viable operational definition of a mature industry, conceived as a strategic action field. Many other fields, however, resist easy characterization. Instead, analysts must carefully fashion a conception of the field based on deep knowledge of the case in question. Field research depends critically on this initial conceptualization of the field. Accordingly, we begin with the straightforward, but maddeningly complicated question: What do we mean by the "field of racial politics, 1877–1932?" We start by eliminating two unwieldy definitions of the field.

1. *White Supremacy*—While it is well accepted that white supremacy has been an important component of the American experience almost from the founding of the North American colonies, a case could be made that never was that belief more systematically encoded in all aspects of American life than during the period 1877–1932. For all its centrality to the history of the country, however, white supremacy cannot be conceptualized as a field. It is much more useful to think of it as a core belief, or central organizing principle, that was implicit or explicit in the settlements of countless thousands of strategic action fields during the period in question. It reflected white America's deep existential investment in the superiority of the white race during the era; the great majority of these fields were not narrowly material (e.g., political or economic) in nature. So threatened by the specter of the dominant black boxer Jack Johnson was the field of professional boxing that it conspired to bar African Americans from the field for some thirty years. Virtually all cultural fields followed suit. We could spend pages detailing the imprint of this belief on countless U.S. fields during this period, but

our punch line should already be clear. White supremacy was a component of myriad fields in the United States in this era but not a field unto itself.

2. *Jim Crow*—At first blush, Jim Crow might seem a more likely candidate to serve as the general definition of "the field of racial politics" in this period. But again, the designation is simply way too broad and amorphous to serve as an analytically useful conception of the field. Instead Jim Crow was an integrated *system of fields* designed to create a formal system of caste restrictions that regulated all aspects of Southern racial life, social and cultural no less than political and economic. The Southern state legislatures—each of them a field in its own right—served as the formal policy making engine of the system, enacting Jim Crow through thousands of discrete pieces of legislation over the life of the system. But the system was supported by all manner of economic, social, and cultural fields as well. Taken together, this dense latticework of fields was, in the absence of federal challenge, self-reinforcing and generally stable from 1877 until the early to mid-1960s.

Over time these various fields also spawned scores of "internal governance units" (IGUs), which strengthened Jim Crow all the more. In the period immediately following the end of Reconstruction, the legislatures of most Southern states created special committees to draft a flood of new segregation laws. These initial legislative efforts would, in time, grow into the highly elaborated "black codes" that embodied the Jim Crow system. Southern registrars served as another crucially important IGU during the Jim Crow era, ensuring the status quo of electoral fields in the region. They became expert at using all means at their disposal to ensure that the terms of the Thirteenth Amendment—granting blacks full citizenship rights, including the franchise—would not be honored within their jurisdictions. All manner of enforcement "units" grew up around various caste restrictions as well. These ranged from perfectly legal auxiliary police units—such as the labor detectives whose job it was to arrest black agricultural workers as they tried to board trains headed north—to "extralegal" vigilante groups such as the Ku Klux Klan. As the system came under increasing threat during the 1950s and 1960s, still additional IGUs—such as the White Citizens' Councils and the Mississippi Sovereignty Commission—were thrown into the breach to counter the mushrooming civil rights movement.

For all its importance, however, the distinctly *Southern* system of fields that came to be known as Jim Crow is also not what we have in mind when we refer to "the field of racial politics" characteristic of this period. Sitting in a sense "on top" of the Jim Crow system was a distinctly *national* racial policy field. It is this field that enabled the development of Jim Crow and that is the focus of our attention. Given the centrality of race in the American experience, this particular field has been a more or less continuous feature of the national political scene since the nation's founding. It is a field composed primarily of elected federal officials—including members of Congress, especially those from Confederate states—federal jurists, leaders of the two major parties, and, at times, *national* civil rights and segregationist groups, supplemented at especially contentious moments by other significant *national* interest groups (e.g., religious organizations, labor unions).

There have only been two periods in U.S. history during which a pro–civil rights coalition has dominated the national field of racial politics. One of course was during the legislative heyday of the civil rights struggle in the 1960s. The other was Reconstruction. If, however, abolitionist Republicans dominated the national field during the Reconstruction era, reducing the Southern political and economic elite to the status of disgruntled challengers, the Compromise of 1877 turned the field on its head. While the fully elaborated Jim Crow system would take ten to fifteen years to materialize, the impact of the settlement of 1877 was immediate. Ignoring howls of protest from the abolitionist wing of his party, the new Republican president Rutherford B. Hayes honored the bargain he had struck with the Southern members of the House and not only withdrew federal troops but also abandoned any pretense to a civil rights agenda during his one-term administration. Nor did his immediate Republican successors, John Garfield and Chester Arthur, do anything to reverse Hayes's policies. Republicans continued to dominate presidential politics in this period, but with the "party of Lincoln" increasingly aligned with "nativists" and conservative business interests, its abolitionist wing quickly atrophied, eliminating the only real threat to the growing power of the segregationist coalition. The crucial linchpin of the post-Reconstruction settlement was now firmly in place. There was now a shared, if tacit, understanding within the field that control over racial matters had once again devolved to the states. For seventy years no president dared to violate the unspoken terms of this unwritten "hands-off" policy.

If the field of racial politics was dominated by the white Southern political and economic elite after 1877, a host of other overlapping strategic action fields served to buttress the system as well. Conceived as fields, the two major political parties "enabled" Jim Crow. The Democratic Party was a strategic action field based on a strange coalition that included Southern whites, farmers from the Midwest, some fractions of the emerging merchant class, and members of the new urban working class, who were disproportionately newly arrived immigrants. Because of the pivotal role of Southern whites—they came to be called "Dixiecrats"—within the party, the issue of civil rights for African Americans was effectively tabled from the 1870s until the middle of the twentieth century. The Dixiecrats dominated the party because of the deep and abiding hatred felt by Southern whites toward the Republican Party (aka the party of Lincoln). This effectively eliminated party competition within the region, turning the South into the exclusive electoral preserve of the Dixiecrats. This granted the Southern wing of the party virtual veto power in the selection of presidential candidates.

Without the support of Southern Democrats, no president could be elected from the party. In our terms, this made the Dixiecrats the largest and most stable core incumbent within the Democratic Party strategic action field.

The Republican Party started as the party arguing for the abolition of slavery. After the Civil War, the party increasingly became the party of big business in America. The party favored minimal government, the gold standard, and generally anything that would allow private business to expand. Nominally, the party's alliance with African Americans continued in muted form after Reconstruction and throughout the period in question. But with Southern blacks denied the franchise and roughly 90 percent of blacks confined to the region as late as 1910, there was simply no electoral percentage in challenging Jim Crow. This left African Americans—and their few white allies within the party—as a marginalized challenger to the more important organized interests of various business groups and nativists increasingly concerned about the immigrant and "papist" hordes pouring into the country in the late nineteenth and early twentieth centuries.

The Southern cotton economy was another important strategic action field that buttressed the national field of racial politics. After the Civil War, the price of cotton was quite high. This created a huge incentive to reemploy the newly freed slave population in that economy. There was an impulse to redistribute land across the South to African Americans, but that program never gained leverage. Instead, in the late 1860s, a new system of farming emerged. The system was based on giving land to individual African Americans to cultivate in exchange for rent or a share of the crop at the end of the growing season. These new arrangements swept across the South (Fligstein 1981).

The return to cotton farming across the South had several long-term negative effects on the power of African Americans. First, blacks tended to be concentrated in the lowest ranks of the system as either sharecroppers or farm laborers. This put them at the mercy of plantation owners who controlled the conditions of lending and the settlement of debts at the end of the year. Local white economic elites worked hand in hand with local political elites to ensure that African Americans stayed on the land and remained in a marginal economic situation. Intent on retaining control over its agricultural labor force, countless Southern state and local governments passed laws barring Northern labor recruiters from the region and other statutes that made it illegal for "indebted" tenant farmers or field hands to leave the region. This led to a second long-term negative consequence. Confined to the South and denied the franchise within the region, African Americans were effectively barred from any meaningful role in electoral politics within the country. Finally, the South remained a monoculture economy dependent on the price of cotton. As that price rose and fell, the fortunes of both blacks and whites rose and fell as well. Since African Americans were most vulnerable, the down parts of the cotton cycle meant that they suffered most from disease and deprivation.

But so far we have not said much about the internal workings of the field of racial politics itself. If a long line of presidents colluded in the dictates of the field, they were not, in our view, the key incumbents. That honor goes to the Southern members of Congress. The one-party system in the South did more than simply reinforce the dominant position of the Dixiecrats within the Democratic Party strategic action field. The lack of electoral competition within the region also granted Southern members of Congress inordinate influence within the institution and, by extension, the broader national field of racial politics. The reason should be obvious. Facing little or no electoral competition, Southern senators and representatives were typically the most senior members of both houses. With committee chairs allocated on the basis of seniority, Southern segregationists were largely in charge of the country's legislative machinery. In a very real sense, these committee chairs served as the most effective IGU imaginable. Together they served as an "early warning" system alerting field incumbents to any ill-conceived legislative initiative proposed by the institution's beleaguered civil rights challengers. This gave them enormous power to subvert any legislation that they deemed threatening to "the Southern way of life," which, in turn, reinforced the reluctance of even progressive presidents to propose civil rights legislation in violation of the federal/Southern "understanding" on race. In short, throughout this period, Southern members of Congress were the key incumbents within the field relegating would-be civil rights advocates to the margins of the strategic action field.

In all, the post-Reconstruction settlement held for at least seventy years. If the withdrawal of federal troops in 1877 marks the clear onset of the new "understanding," the subsequent "rupture" is a bit harder to pinpoint. The decisive *public* break with the federal/Southern "understanding" on race came with Truman's embrace of civil rights reform in 1946. But this key event was preceded by a decade and a half of destabilizing change processes that powerfully impacted a number of proximate fields and, in time, through pressure from these strategic action fields, undermined the dominant position of the Southern political elite within the field of racial politics. It is to those changes that we now turn.

Destabilizing Changes: The Depression and the Cold War

The key external change processes that over time decisively undermined the field of American racial politics were the Great Depression and later the onset of the Cold War. We take up both destabilizing "shocks" in turn.

1. The Great Depression—The stock market crash of 1929 and the subsequent Depression weakened the racial status quo in a number of ways. To simplify, however, we can distinguish between the more immediate political and longer term economic/demographic effects of the downturn. All of the political effects follow from the stunning reversal of the fortunes of the two major parties in the wake of the crash. Just as the subprime mortgage crisis helped undermine Republican chances in 2008, so did the exogenous shock of the Great Depression destabilize the field of presidential politics in advance of the 1932 election. The resulting crisis effectively broke the stranglehold the Republicans had had on the White House since the turn of the century. Herbert Hoover, widely blamed for the Depression, was soundly beaten in 1932 by the Democratic challenger, Franklin Delano Roosevelt. The election, it should be made clear, had little or nothing to do with race and everything to do with the economy. That said, Roosevelt's ascension to the White House, the policies he pursued, and the symbolism that attached to his administration were to have tremendous implications for the nascent civil rights struggle and the politics of race more generally. The consequential political changes that followed from FDR's election include the following:

- The onset of a period of Democratic dominance in presidential politics that would not only reshape federal social policy but also encourage and empower progressive movements into the 1960s and beyond. The Democratic ascendance relegated the Republican Party to the role of challenger in the field of presidential politics for the better part of the next thirty-six years.
- The internal transformation of the Democratic Party strategic action field. By embracing pro-labor policies and granting labor leaders considerable voice in party as well as policy circles, FDR made incumbents of the party's Northern, liberal labor wing, undercutting the power of the Dixiecrats in the process. In effect, the modern Democratic Party dates to this period.
- The shift of black voters from the Republican to the Democratic Party. We now think of African American voters as the most loyal of Democrats. But the "black vote" was once the most reliable component of the Republican electoral coalition. The reason: loyalty to the party of Lincoln and opposition to a Southern-dominated Democratic Party. Even as the rest of the country abandoned the Republican Party in 1932, blacks favored Hoover over Roosevelt by a sizeable margin. FDR's New Deal policies and general support for progressives changed all of that, with black voters turning overwhelmingly to Roosevelt in 1936. The addition of blacks to the New Deal coalition further strengthened the incumbent Northern, liberal labor wing of the party and further undermined the power of the Dixiecrats.

- The realignment of the Supreme Court and the subsequent revolution in constitutional law. Reflecting thirty-plus years of Republican control of the White House, the Supreme Court that Roosevelt inherited was dominated by conservative jurists, who on several occasions ruled his New Deal programs unconstitutional. Frustrated, FDR spent much of his first term and part of his second battling the court and seeking to undermine its influence. In the end, however, he simply outlasted the aging conservatives, ultimately transforming the court and the broader field of constitutional law by posting liberal justices to the Supreme Court. Recognizing the opportunity this transformation presented, the National Association for the Advancement of Colored People (NAACP) fashioned and began to implement its long-term legal campaign to overturn "separate but equal." As a result, the pace of pro–civil rights decisions returned by the court increased from just eight between 1926 and 1935 to twenty-five over the next ten years (McAdam 1999: 85). *Brown v. Board* was still years away, but the key shift in the field of constitutional law had taken place. With it, the legal foundation on which the broader field of racial politics was structured was also decisively undermined.

It may be, however, that in shaping the civil rights revolution, the long-term economic and demographic fallout from the Depression was even more significant than its immediate political effects. By dramatically reducing worldwide demand for cotton, the Depression undermined the material logic and economic incentives so central to Jim Crow and the national field of racial politics. The importance of King Cotton to the national economy—at least prior to the Depression—was among the main reasons federal officials adhered to the racial "hands-off" policy in the first place. The Depression reduced the demand for cotton, which in turn greatly reduced the need for agricultural labor to work the system. This, in turn, helped to catalyze the Great Migration, which, between 1930 and 1960, saw nearly four million blacks move from the South to the North (Fligstein 1981; Lemann 1991). Like all migrations, however, this one was hardly random in its redistributive effect. Nearly nine out of every ten black migrants settled in one of seven politically key industrial states in the North and West (i.e., New York, New Jersey, Pennsylvania, California, Michigan, Illinois, and Ohio). By moving overwhelmingly to these states, blacks greatly enhanced their electoral and political importance. Taken together, then, the nominal *demographic* and *economic* consequences of the Depression had the effect of reinforcing all of the *political* trends described above. The decline of King Cotton and the Great Migration strengthened the hand of liberal Democrats and civil rights forces nationally and within the Democratic Party, while undermining the influence of the Dixiecrats.

2. The Cold War and the Renationalization of Race—For all the significance of Roosevelt's years in office, it is important to note that he himself remained fundamentally silent on racial matters throughout his four-term presidency, refusing even to endorse antilynching legislation on the many occasions such bills were brought before Congress. In sharp contrast, almost immediately upon taking office, FDR's successor, Harry Truman, became the first president since Reconstruction to publicly embrace the need for civil rights reform. He did so first in 1946 when he created a national Committee on Civil Rights and charged it with investigating the state of civil rights in the country and recommending "remedies for deficiencies uncovered." Two years later Truman issued two landmark executive orders, the first establishing a fair employment board within the Civil Service Commission, and the second calling for gradual desegregation of the armed forces (Leuchtenburg 2005; Sitkoff 1978).

What prompted Truman to act when Roosevelt had not? Comparing the field of U.S. party politics in which the two were operating only deepens the puzzle. While Roosevelt's electoral margins left him politically secure, Truman's status as a nonincumbent—remember he only took office when FDR died in 1945—made him uniquely vulnerable to challenge as he headed into the 1948 election. Moreover, with black voters now returning solid Democratic majorities, Truman seemingly had little to gain and everything to lose by alienating his party's strange, but critically important New Deal bedfellow: the Southern Dixiecrat. That, of course, is precisely what his advocacy of civil rights did. Angered by Truman's proactive support for civil rights, the Dixiecrats roiled the Democratic Party strategic action field by running their own third party candidate, Strom Thurmond, for president in 1948. The electoral votes of the once "solid South" were now in jeopardy of being lost. Considering that Truman himself had grown up as a white Southerner (McCullough 1992) and the "chilling effect" the Cold War had on the American left, one could hardly imagine a less propitious time to be advocating politically and socially progressive causes.

The key to the Roosevelt/Truman mystery lies not in America's domestic context but rather in the new pressures and considerations thrust upon the United States, and the executive branch in particular, in the postwar period. It is worth quoting Gunnar Myrdal's prescient 1944 remarks on the subject. As he imagined what the postwar world would look like, Myrdal argued that "the Negro Problem has also acquired tremendous international implications, and this is another and decisive reason why the white North is prevented from compromising with the White South regarding the Negro. . . . Statesmen will have to take cognizance of the changed geopolitical situation of the nation and carry out important adaptations of the American way of life to new necessities. A main adaptation is bound to be the redefinition of the Negro's status in America" (1970: 35).

The onset of the Cold War only made Myrdal's view that much more salient. Locked into an intense political/ideological struggle with the Soviet Union for influence around the globe, U.S. foreign policy makers quickly realized what a significant liability Jim Crow was to its critical foreign policy aims. This prompted calls—first from the diplomatic corps and State Department—for civil rights reforms to counter Soviet efforts to exploit American racism for its obvious propaganda value (Layton 2000).

Truman's civil rights initiatives were one response to these pleas. Another was the series of briefs filed by the U.S. Attorney General in connection with a string of civil rights cases heard before the Supreme Court beginning in 1948. The most important of these briefs was one filed in December 1952 in connection with a public school desegregation case—*Brown v. Topeka Board of Education*—then before the court. The brief makes clear the link between the Cold War and the postwar change in federal civil rights policy. In part the brief reads, "It is in the context of the present world struggle between freedom and tyranny that the problem of racial discrimination must be viewed. Racial discrimination furnishes grist for the Communist propaganda mills, and it raises doubt even among friendly nations as to the intensity of our devotion to the democratic faith" (quoted in McAdam 1999: 83).

If the Depression weakened the Dixiecrats' dominance within the field of racial politics, the Cold War marked the decisive rupture with the settlement that had held within the strategic action field for seventy years. Significant policy change would not come for many years, but the battle had been joined. If the end of Reconstruction had organized race out of national politics, it was the onset of the Cold War that effectively "renationalized" the issue and marked the beginning of the "episode of contention" over race that would extend through the 1960s. Drawing on the language of our perspective, we close this section with a brief summary of this crucial chapter in the unfolding civil rights struggle.

The chapter was set in motion by a fundamental restructuring of a particularly important field: the international system of nation-states. The restructuring was a direct outgrowth of World War II. Weakened dramatically by the war, neither Great Britain nor France was in a position to effectively influence the shape of the postwar world. Supplanting these perennial Western powers as the undisputed "incumbents" of the postwar world were the United States and the Soviet Union. The USSR attained this position by virtue of its decisive contribution to the allied victory and its effective occupation of Eastern Europe at the close of the war. U.S. dominance owed as much to its unchallenged economic position and military might—including the "bomb"—as its significant combat role during the war.

We care less about the causes of the restructuring of the international system, however, than its impact on a host of fields within the United States. The exogenous shock of the Cold War destabilized a number of key policy fields within the

United States. The two we have emphasized here are the U.S. foreign policy establishment and the executive branch of the federal government. Even before the end
of the war, a serious debate was under way within the State Department and the
U.S. foreign policy field in general over the shape of the postwar world and its implications for the formulation and execution of U.S. policy, domestic as well as
foreign. Those emphasizing the salience of the Soviet threat ultimately prevailed in
this debate. The stark nature of the threat prompted calls for a host of policy innovations, including impassioned pleas from the diplomatic corps—especially those
with postings in the Third World—for civil rights reforms to counter Soviet efforts to exploit American racism for its obvious propaganda value (Layton 2000).

Described above, Truman's embrace of various civil rights initiatives and the aggressive advocacy of civil rights reform through judicial means represented the
two principal domestic policy responses to the perceived Soviet threat. In turn, Truman's dramatic reversal of the prior "hands-off" policy with respect to race precipi-
tated a consequential episode of contention within the Democratic Party strategic
action field as Dixiecrats mobilized to counter the threat to "the Southern way of
life" posed by Truman's actions. In the end, the Dixiecrat revolt came to naught, but
not before threatening the stability of the party in a very serious way. The federal
embrace of civil rights reform also triggered increased mobilization by another
component of the Democratic coalition—civil rights forces—putting them on a
collision course with segregationists, the Democratic Party, and the American state.[1]

---

[1] Despite Eisenhower's Republican breakthrough in 1952, the basic dynamics we see operating
during Truman's presidency continued during Eisenhower's two terms in office. Given the loyalty
that black voters had displayed to Roosevelt and Truman, Eisenhower might have been expected to
evidence little enthusiasm for the issue of civil rights. But while he was famously quoted as saying
that no amount of civil rights legislation could change "the hearts and minds" of the public—im-
plying a preference for limited government involvement with the issue—the pace of federal civil
rights efforts actually accelerated under Eisenhower. There was, of course, the high drama of the 1954
Brown v. Board decision and the court's implementation decree of the following year. For his part,
Eisenhower continued the trend established by Truman, of using executive orders to accelerate the
desegregation of the armed forces and to press for the integration of public facilities in the District
of Columbia. He also ordered federal troops to Little Rock, Arkansas in 1957 when white mobs
threatened the integration of Little Rock High School. In helping to orchestrate the rising volume of
federal civil rights activity, Eisenhower's actions are not as surprising as they might seem. For starters,
the Cold War imperative that had motivated Truman was alive and well throughout Eisenhower's
term in office. But there were electoral motives at work here, too. Moderate Republicans—including
Eisenhower—sought to reclaim Lincoln's legacy within the party and to successfully compete for
the increasingly important "black vote." When Eisenhower captured nearly 40 percent of that vote in
1956, these dreams seemed entirely realistic (Lomax 1962: 228). The practical effect of this increasingly competitive situation was to render the black vote a more unpredictable and valuable electoral
resource, prompting both parties to intensify their efforts to appeal to African American voters. The
heightened party competition, in turn, granted all the more leverage to civil rights forces, encouraging increased activism as well.

The Episode of Contention and the Rise of the Civil Rights Movement

The fact that it has taken us this long in our account to take up the story of the mass civil rights movement only serves to underscore the need for the broader theory on offer here. The implication is clear: while the onset of the movement in Montgomery in 1955–1956 represents a crucial escalation of the ongoing episode of contention in the national field of racial politics, it is hardly its point of origin. Indeed, rather than Montgomery catalyzing the episode, the reverse is closer to the truth. It was the rupture of the federal/Southern "understanding" on race, occasioned by the Cold War and Truman's policies, that both encouraged and granted the *local* struggle in Montgomery so much significance. Without its embedding in the national conflict, it is not at all clear that Montgomery would have had the kind of impact it did. In short, it was the *nationalization* of the local conflict that shaped events in Montgomery and accounts for its singular importance in the history of the struggle.

If Montgomery did not actually trigger the broader episode of contention, it nonetheless represented a dramatic escalation and a significant new and qualitatively different phase of the struggle. Moreover, once the movement emerged, it became the dominant actor shaping the unfolding conflict. For that reason the mass movement and the evolving interactive dynamics of the civil rights struggle will be central to our analysis in this section. But episodes of contention are rarely the product of a skilled and unified challenger alone. Absent some level of ongoing uncertainty and lack of consensus within the strategic action field, even a skilled challenger will struggle to sustain the conflict. More accurately, it is the challenger's ability to reinforce the sense of uncertainty and prevent the reassertion, by incumbents, of the old consensus that is key to prolonging the episode. This, however, almost always depends on at least some level of ongoing environmental vulnerability. And so it was in the case of the civil rights struggle.

The key to the post-Reconstruction settlement had been the longstanding, tacit federal/Southern "understanding" that granted control over racial matters to the Southern states. The agreement came apart in the postwar period when certain federal actors "violated" the "understanding" by advocating the need for civil rights reform. They did so for two reasons. First, the Cold War transformed American race relations from a merely domestic matter to an issue of international geopolitical significance. Second, the increasing dominance of the party's liberal/labor wing, reinforced by the growing importance attributed to the "black vote," made the Democrats receptive to the civil rights issue. As long as these two environmental factors remained salient, the prospects for sustained contention remained strong, *provided the movement could devise ways to exploit them.* This brings us to the strategic genius and social skill exhibited by movement actors during the early 1960s zenith of the civil rights struggle.

The main parties to the conflict in the field during this period were civil rights forces, the white Southern segregationist countermovement, Southern elected officials, certain federal officials (especially in the White House, the Justice and State Departments, and the Supreme Court), the national and international media, and substantial "bystander publics" at home and abroad, whose attention and reactions to the struggle powerfully shaped the course of its development. The genius of movement leaders lay in their ability to, over time, devise and refine an interactive strategy that exploited the salient environmental factors touched on above, thereby sustaining the uncertainty and sense of crisis that are the hallmark of episodes of contention. This central interactive dynamic can be described fairly easily. Lacking sufficient power to defeat the segregationists in a local confrontation, insurgents sought to broaden the conflict by inducing their opponents to disrupt public order to the point that supportive federal intervention was required. As a by-product of the drama associated with these flagrant displays of public violence, the movement was able to attract favorable media coverage, generate broad public sympathy, and mobilize financial support from external groups.

The connection between this interactive dynamic and the two environmental factors described above should be clear. The salience of the "Soviet threat" was key to the success of this dynamic. In a very real sense the movement, during this period, was playing as much to the international as the U.S. media. Every time Southern segregationists attacked nonviolent demonstrations, the resulting images appeared on front pages around the world, fueling Soviet propaganda efforts to exploit the doubts about American democracy raised by the pictures. When this happened, federal officials were obliged to intervene to restore order, reduce the violence, and, most important, stem the flow of damaging information that played into the hands of Soviet propagandists. When, on the other hand, segregationists failed to take the bait—as they did in Albany, Georgia in 1962—the interactive dynamic was short-circuited. The result was this: no front-page images, no international outrage, no pressure on the federal government to intervene, local stalemate. In contrast, it is not a coincidence that the major victories achieved by the movement—for example, Birmingham and Selma—followed close on the heels of highly publicized supremacist attacks on nonviolent demonstrators.

Without discounting the critical importance of the Cold War context, however, the presence of liberal Democrats in the White House also has to be counted as key to the interactive dynamic sketched above. Both ideological receptivity and naked political calculus were at work here. With the Democratic Party strategic action field dominated by its liberal/labor wing during this period, there was a certain ideological consistency between the aims of the movement and the policy preferences of the Democratic administrations in office during the movement's heyday. Add to that the growing importance attributed to a rapidly expanding and increasingly loyal Democratic "black vote," and you add electoral calculus to the motivations for supportive federal intervention during the episode.

These environmental factors would have meant little, however, had the structure of the movement strategic action field not granted insurgents the ability to successfully exploit the environmental vulnerabilities described above. At the height of the struggle, the movement was dominated by the so-called big five civil rights organizations: the NAACP, the Congress of Racial Equality, the Urban League, the Southern Christian Leadership Conference, and the Student Nonviolent Coordinating Committee. These groups functioned simultaneously as the incumbent core of the movement strategic action field and the key challenger within the larger field of U.S. racial politics. Up until roughly 1965, these organizations operated as a political coalition within the movement strategic action field, and despite tensions and disagreements, shared a broad consensus regarding the means and ends that were to orient the movement. For them, the struggle was over the basic political and legal rights of African Americans. The goal was to secure these rights and to achieve the full integration of blacks into all aspects of American life. The main means to this end were to be nonviolent direct action, legal challenges, and interracial coalition. As long as this consensus and the strategic coalition it defined held within the movement strategic action field, civil rights forces were able to sustain the episode of contention and achieve a remarkable litany of legal and legislative victories.

A New Settlement

So why did the episode come to an end? Having generated so much momentum and achieved so much, why did the movement begin to decline right at the apparent peak of its power? From the high-water mark of Selma and passage of the Voting Rights Act in 1965, the traditional civil rights movement declined fairly precipitously over the next three to four years and was largely moribund by 1970. How did this happen? In reality, this trajectory is not as surprising or as ironic as it might seem at first blush. For starters, the broad contours of the new settlement that would bring the episode to a close were substantially encoded in the central judicial and legal victories achieved by the movement during its heyday. We suspect that this is typically the case in most field crises. Agreements forged at the peak of the conflict contain the seeds of the new settlement that will bring the episode to a close. In achieving their aims, challengers begin morphing into incumbents within reconfigured fields. But we are getting ahead of ourselves. The victories achieved by civil rights forces were but one of four factors that we see as key to an understanding of the decline of the movement, the close of the broader episode of contention, and the institutionalization of the "minority rights revolution" (Skrentny 2002). What were the other three?

In the previous section we attributed the peak period of the civil rights episode to three factors: the international pressures brought to bear on U.S. racial policies by the Cold War, Democratic dominance of presidential politics, and the strength of the internal organization and consensus within the movement strategic action field. In combination with the realization of much of its legislative agenda, the decline of the movement owed to the effective disappearance of each of these three factors.

The Declining Salience of the Cold War Dynamic

The movement's savvy exploitation of the country's Cold War vulnerability on the "Negro question" became much less possible as the decade of the 1960s wore on. This owed to two principal factors. For starters, the perceptible thaw in U.S.–Soviet relations in the late 1960s and 1970s marked not only a lull in the Cold War but also a hiatus in the intense propaganda wars that were so strategically central to the Cold War dynamic characteristic of the movement's heyday. The declining Soviet and, indeed, international attention and pressure on the United States regarding race was also the result of a general perception that the country had, in fact, put its racial house in order, through the legislative civil rights victories and judicial precedents of the 1960s. In a very real sense, however, it probably did not matter that the world was no longer monitoring U.S. race relations quite so closely. The fact of the matter is, with its move to the North, the movement effectively lost the ability to orchestrate the interactive dynamic that had fueled the struggle in the South. The very different character of Northern white resistance deprived the movement, in the late 1960s, of one of the crucial elements in the tactical dynamic that had earlier served as the cutting edge of black insurgency in the South. Without the dramatic instances of overt white oppression characteristic of the Southern struggle, the movement was deprived of both the visible manifestations of racism so valuable as organizing devices and the leverage needed to force federal intervention.

The Revenge of the Dixiecrats and the End of the New Deal Electoral Regime

In popular narrative accounts of the period, the 1968 election is typically represented as a referendum on the war in Vietnam. Without denying the salience of the issue, this account is nonetheless misleading. The contest, and the dramatic restructuring of the field of American electoral politics it signaled, was fundamentally about race. Southern white discontent over the issue had grown exponentially since 1964, as waves of newly registered black voters poured into the Democratic Party in the South. As they did, Southern whites responded by leaving the party in droves, gravitating toward newly minted Republican Party organizations. In one of the great ironies of American history, one of the proudest achievements of the civil rights struggle—the restoration of black voting rights in the South—set the stage for the demise of the New Deal electoral regime, the rise of a Southern-based Republican Party, and the remarginalization of race as an issue in U.S. politics.

But white discontent over the issue was no longer confined to the South. Alarmed by the "urban disorders" of the late 1960s, the specter of "black power," and real and imagined threats to their neighborhoods, schools, and jobs, Northern whites—especially lower middle– and working-class whites—were restive as well. Running in 1968, Richard Nixon sought to exploit this growing white discontent by devising a strategy to play on both the country's deepening racial divide and the traditional association of blacks with the Democratic Party. By reminding voters of the latter, the Republicans hoped to tap the growing undercurrent of white backlash engendered by the changing nature of black insurgency in the late 1960s. Election statistics reveal just how successful the Republican strategy proved to be. From 1964 to 1968 the Democratic share of the popular vote dropped from 61.5 to 42.5 percent. Fully 50 percent of those who voted for Nixon in 1968 had cast ballots for Johnson four years earlier. Most dramatic of all was the racial breakdown of the vote. While African American voters remained deeply loyal to the Democrats, with 97 percent of the black vote going to the Democratic nominee, Hubert Humphrey, only 35 percent of the white electorate voted Democratic (Converse et al. 1969: 1084–85).

The election did more than simply mirror the declining political fortunes of African Americans; it contributed to them as well. With precious little electoral debt to blacks and considerable to civil rights opponents, Nixon's election promised to reduce further the already limited political access and leverage available to civil rights forces. For blacks, however, the negative political consequences of the 1968 election were not confined to the substantive policy outcomes that followed from Nixon's ascension to office. At least as damaging was the effect the election had in restructuring the fields of the two major political parties. In this, the remarkable success enjoyed by George Wallace's third party candidacy in 1968 proved decisive. The significance of the Wallace phenomenon for the future electoral prospects of both parties was clear on the face of the 1968 election returns. With the two major parties evenly dividing roughly 86 percent of the popular vote, the remaining 14 percent who cast their votes for Wallace clearly emerged as a potential balance of power in future elections. For the Republicans, Nixon's narrow victory suggested that the party's future lay not in the 43 percent of the popular vote he captured but in the 57 percent he shared with Wallace. Republican strategists believed this total represented a potentially dominant conservative majority that, if successfully tapped, could well ensure the electoral dominance of the party for years to come. Needless to say, this prediction was to prove remarkably prescient. For us, however, it is the immediate impact of the shift in the parties' electoral fortunes that is key to understanding the decline of the movement. With Democrats no longer in the White House, the access and general policy receptivity that helped fuel contention over race was gone. Or in the language of our perspective, the civil rights coalition that had come to largely control the national field of racial politics for most of the decade had once again been relegated to the status of challengers.

The Rise of Black Power and the Rupture in the Movement Strategic Action Fields

Finally, even if the facilitative political conditions characteristic of the early 1960s had remained intact, trends within the movement would have undercut the ability of black insurgents to hold an increasingly fractious civil rights coalition together in support of an effective challenge to the more complicated forms of racism encountered in the North. The key change involved the stark challenge to the traditional civil rights groups posed by the rise of black power and "black nationalism" in the latter half of the decade. For all the new adherents and radical new perspectives that accompanied the challenge, its effects on the movement strategic action field have to be counted as far more costly than beneficial. Three negative effects are worth mentioning. First, the effective centralization of power and influence in the hands of the big five civil rights groups—so vital to the struggle in the early 1960s—was almost immediately undercut by the black power challenge. Two distinct trends are relevant here. For starters, the most conservative of these organizations—the NAACP and the Urban League—survived the challenge but lost stature and credibility among the younger and more radical activists enamored of black power. In contrast, the more radical of the traditional civil rights groups—the Student Nonviolent Coordinating Committee and the Congress of Racial Equality—retained credibility and influence as they embraced versions of black power/black nationalism, but having grown dependent on liberal white support during the halcyon days of the interracial movement, they slowly collapsed as that funding support was withdrawn. Add to that the Southern Christian Leadership Conference's loss of relevance in the wake of King's assassination, and the latter 1960s witnessed the effective collapse of the entire incumbent structure of the traditional movement strategic action field.

At the heart of this collapse was the shattering of the ideological and tactical consensus that had characterized the field during the Southern civil rights phase of the struggle. This was the second negative effect to follow from the rise of black power and black nationalism. Whatever sympathies one might have with these more radical assessments of the racial ills characteristic of American society, the resulting loss of consensus robbed the movement of the focus and coherence so critical to effective collective action. Finally, the rhetorical embrace (if not actual practice) of violence by black power groups—think only of the Black Panthers—exacerbated white fears, reinforcing all the political trends noted previously while simultaneously encouraging stepped-up repression against all manner of movement groups in the late 1960s/early 1970s (McAdam 1999: chapter 8).

Weakened by these various trends, the movement was largely moribund by the 1970s. And without the driving force of the movement, the broader episode of contention over race wound down as well. In place of the uncertainty and generalized sense of crisis that had made the issue of civil rights, for much of the decade, the modal choice as the "most important problem confronting the country" (Gallup 1972), the broad outlines of a new consensus within the field of racial politics could be glimpsed. The new settlement reflected the following key elements:

- an end to all forms of de jure segregation and the formal legal guarantee of equal rights to African Americans
- a commitment to see the aforementioned principle implemented in all institutional arenas of American life
- opposition to all forms of ongoing black activism that threatened the basic class structure of U.S. society, including calls for compensation for past discrimination (e.g., "reparations"), and the rejection of U.S. sovereignty in favor of an essentialist black nationalism
- a commitment to use social control measures to counter the more violent or threatening forms of "radical" black activism that had developed during the latter half of the 1960s

Obviously, under the terms of the settlement, unrepentant white segregationists were reduced to the status of powerless challengers. Ironically, however, with the Republicans in ascendance after 1968, all but the most conservative or traditional of civil rights groups were also marginalized in the settlement. Federal officials—especially judges and those charged in various federal agencies with overseeing the enforcement or implementation of new civil rights guarantees—emerged as the key incumbents in the reconstituted field of racial politics. It had taken nearly 100 years, but federal officials had essentially reclaimed their

Reconstruction era authority to regulate matters of race and civil rights in the United States.

The Institutionalization of the Civil Rights Movement and Its Impact on Other Strategic Action Fields

While the mass civil rights movement quickly dissipated after 1970, its impact on American society may have actually been greater in the 1970s than it had been during the 1960s. Besides the gradual solidification in the 1970s of the new settlement described above, the decade was marked by two other processes attesting to the longer term impact of the civil rights struggle. The first was the creation of a host of new strategic action fields birthed by the struggle. The second and more important of the two processes involved the movement's destabilizing effect on myriad established fields, with most of these "spin-off" episodes occurring in the 1970s. We take up both of these processes below but only after discussing the general process by which the new civil rights settlement came to be institutionalized.

Among the most popular chronological markers of the death of the civil rights movement is Richard Nixon's election as president in 1968. Not only did the election spell the end of Democratic control of the White House and the political access and influence this control had afforded mainstream civil rights leaders, but it also marked the onset of a period in which Republican presidents owed no real electoral debt to African Americans. Skrentny (1996) shows, however, that this view of Nixon and his effect on civil rights is not nuanced enough. *Affirmative action* was a policy innovation, not of Johnson's Great Society but of the Nixon White House. Nixon's embrace of the policy may, as it has been alleged, represent a preference for what was seen at the time as perhaps the most conservative approach to the problem of employment discrimination or even as a cynical attempt to further alienate the affection of white labor from the Democratic Party (Skrentny 1996). Indeed, we are quite sure that both motives were in play in this instance. Still, it means that the central remedy for redress of past discrimination that liberals have fought so hard to preserve over the past few decades dates to a period that, by all popular accounts, was anathema to movement aims.

At least as important as the embrace of affirmative action by officials in the Nixon administration was the much less visible but far-reaching advocacy of civil rights by a broad array of organizational actors during this period. Skrentny (2002) documents the aggressive efforts of countless federal officials (and by extension government officials at all levels) in the 1970s to extend the legal and legislative gains the civil rights movement achieved for African Americans to a host of new claimants who adopted the rights-based frames of the civil rights struggle. These included Native Americans, Hispanic Americans, women, and those with disabilities. Perhaps more important than the specific legal and legislative gains achieved by the civil rights struggle was the broad institutional legitimacy that came to attach to rights-based discourse during this period.

This legitimacy extended in the 1970s to a host of nonstate organizations and strategic action fields as well. Even as the mass movement was winding down, countless episodes of contention were unfolding in a host of fields as "norm entrepreneurs" sought to actualize movement goals in a wide range of institutional settings. As a result, the pace of civil rights change was arguably higher in the 1970s than it was during the peak of the mass movement in the 1960s. The rate of public school desegregation increased markedly during the period. Following the adoption of the Nixon administration's Philadelphia Plan, equal employment and affirmative action initiatives multiplied as well. This was also the period in which America's colleges and universities finally got serious about increasing the numbers of racial and ethnic minorities on campus. In the 1970s, black (and other minority) faces become much more visible on television and in the movies. Amid fears of legal action, private firms struggled to interpret and implement new practices and organizational forms in response to amorphous legislative and judicial guidelines (Edelman 1992; Edelman, Uggen, and Erlanger 1999). In short, the institutionalized rights revolution of this era extended well beyond the peak period of concerted state action in the 1960s. It also included rights-based challenges to the dominant logic and practices of a host of nonstate organizations and fields.

In addition to its role as an exogenous shock catalyzing episodes of contention in countless established fields, the mass civil rights movement was also the source and inspiration for many new movements and the fields they spawned. McAdam (1988) documents the crucial catalytic effect that the "Freedom Summer" project and the broader civil rights struggle had on the Free Speech Movement, women's liberation, and the antiwar movement. Other authors have argued that the civil rights struggle had a similar effect on a host of other U.S.-based New Left movements including the gay rights movement (Armstrong 2002, 2005; Valocchi 2001), the American Indian movement (Nagel 1995), the disability rights movement (Greene 2007), and the Chicano movement (Acuña 2000). In its later black power/black nationalist incarnation, the movement has also been credited with inspiring a move toward nonstate nationalism in a number of liberation struggles elsewhere in the world (Jenson and Phillips 1996; Johnson 2002).

In addition, every major legislative victory achieved by the movement brought with it new regulatory agencies, compliance regimes, and the fields that developed around these structures. And while virtually all of the scholarly attention has focused on federal regulation, civil rights compliance fields emerged at the state and local levels as well. Finally, as we noted above, a good many nonstate strategic action fields also created compliance units internal to the field to respond to the general challenge posed by the "rights revolution" (Edelman 1992; Edelman, Uggen, and Erlanger 1999). By 1980, the national field of U.S. racial policy had been altered dramatically. The dominant players in the field—elected federal officials (including those from the South), the two political parties, and the federal judiciary—now accepted that formal political and civil rights were to be accorded all citizens. The right to vote, the right to hold office, access to integrated public facilities—issues that had roiled the country just a decade earlier—were now established as consensual policy outcomes. The moderate wing of the civil rights movement had been largely absorbed into the Democratic Party, with a host of former activists going on to become established politicians and officeholders. The number of black elected officials increased rapidly, especially in the states of the former Confederacy. The structure of the government, at all levels, now included state fields and specialized professionals whose job it was to enforce and protect the gains achieved by the movement. For all the movement's limits and the many enduring legacies of institutional racism, there is no gainsaying the dramatic restructuring of the field of racial politics in the United States as a result of the "civil rights revolution."

Summing Up: An Important Postscript

To one who fully appreciates the complexity of the civil rights story, the preceding may well feel like a forced march through nearly a century and a half of American history. To the reader, however, the bigger problem is likely to be the analytic usefulness of the concept of the strategic action field in the context of the civil rights story. What—other than aesthetic clunkiness—does the frequent reference to this or that field bring to the civil rights narrative? To highlight what we see as the important analytic contribution made by the concept and the broader theory on offer here, we close with a stark summary of the case and an important postscript.

Contention over race has been central to the American experience since the country's founding. As a result, a discernible "racial politics field"—or "policy subsystem," if you prefer the language of policy studies (Sabatier 2007)—has been a consistent feature of American politics for most of the country's history. Numerous state- and more local-level racial policy fields have existed in parallel with the national field, but here our attention has been squarely focused on the latter. As we noted above, the field has been dominated for most of its history by elected federal officials—including members of Congress—but from time to time has also included federal jurists (with special emphasis on the Supreme

Court), national interest groups and unions, movement and countermovement groups, and influential journalists. Together, subsets of these actors have comprised what might be thought of as loose pro– and anti–civil rights coalitions. The relative power or influence wielded by these coalitions has determined who the field incumbents and challengers are at any given moment. Only twice in this country's history have the pro–civil rights forces been clearly dominant within the field. The first such period was Reconstruction. The second was the 1960s legislative heyday of the modern civil rights struggle to which we devoted so much attention above.

The aim of the lengthy narrative offered above was to account for the *rupture* of the Jim Crow *settlement* that had structured the field from the end of Reconstruction until Truman's embrace of civil rights reform in the late 1940s. Consistent with the general theory laid out in the book, our argument is that the rupture owed not to developments internal to the field but to destabilizing change processes emanating in proximate fields. Accordingly, much of the narrative was focused on describing the changes that took place in these various fields (e.g., the Democratic Party after 1932, the international system of nation-states after World War II, the field of constitutional law after 1938) and the way in which together these destabilizing pressures altered the balance of power between anti–civil rights incumbents and pro–civil rights challengers in the middle decades of the twentieth century.

None of this is meant to denigrate the crucial contribution that the civil rights movement played in the broader civil rights revolution. Without the social skill of civil rights activists and the pressure they brought to bear on the larger national field of racial politics, we are convinced that the other change pressures noted above would not have been sufficient to undermine the dominant position of the anti–civil rights coalition within the field. In the final analysis, however, this is not fundamentally a movement story but instead a more complicated account of change and stability in the racial policy field, as shaped by developments in a host of proximate state and nonstate fields played out over several decades. Absent the kind of broad lens provided by our theory, standard narrative histories of the civil rights struggle offer an overly simple, truncated account of the revolution.

We end with the promised postscript. Throughout the book we have argued that strategic action turns as much on existential as more narrowly instrumental motivations. You would not know it, however, from the stylized account of the civil rights struggle offered above. In truth, our treatment of the case generally eschewed the issue of motivations, but following convention, it would be easy enough simply to read instrumental aims into the actions of both pro– and anti–civil rights actors. Civil rights forces, from this perspective, were simply advocating changes that would improve the material well-being and broader life chances of African Americans. And in resisting civil rights reforms, white supremacists were merely seeking to safeguard the political and economic benefits conferred by Jim Crow.

End of story? Hardly. The issue of motivation is almost never about material interests alone. Broader issues of meaning and identity shaped the conflict just as surely as did more narrow instrumental ends. Nothing even remotely resembling a full accounting of these existential motivations is possible here, but hopefully a few examples will illustrate their salience in the struggle. To keep things manageable, we confine ourselves to those activists who engaged the grassroots struggle on both sides of the issue. We begin with pro–civil rights activists. And here we use the rational choice perspective to frame our argument. The traditional rational choice theory of collective action holds that it is irrational for any individual to take part in a movement seeking public goods (Olson 1965). Activism must be induced, or so the theory holds, by offering individuals selective material incentives that make it individually rational for them to participate.

There is, however, a flaw in the rational choice argument, an empirical disconnect between the theory and the reality of emergent movements. The theory depicts the challenge to movement organizers as one of inducing outsiders to join an emerging movement. In point of fact, however, most movements develop within established communities (Gould 1991, 1995; McAdam 1999; Morris 1984; Osa 1997; Zhao 1998, 2004). They do so by effectively "appropriating" the shared meanings and identities that bind the community together in the service of the movement. Consider the two key settings that "birthed" the mass civil rights movement. The first were Southern black congregations, in Montgomery, of course, but later in countless other Southern cities as well. It is estimated that something like 90 to 95 percent of black bus riders in Montgomery participated in the boycott there. There is simply no way to account for this level of participation based on the rational choice framework. The key to the success of the boycott was the movement's appropriation of the central sources of meaning and identity in the lives of most black residents of Montgomery. In the language of rational choice, instead of offering selective incentives to "outsiders" to induce participation, the movement—by embedding itself in the central institution of the black community—effectively threatened "insiders" with selective disincentives for nonparticipation. Either way you care to look at it, the decisive motives for participation were clearly more existential than material.

The same was true of the sit-in movement that spread like wildfire through traditional black colleges in the spring of 1960. Just as church membership came to be defined by blacks in Montgomery as including participation in the bus boycott, the normative requirements of being a student at a black college in the early 1960s quickly came to involve active participation in "the move-ment." That is the only conclusion one can draw from the extraordinarily high levels of activism characteristic of black students during this period. Survey data collected by the National Opinion Research Center in 1964 placed the rate of student activism on black college campuses at 69 percent (Orum 1972: 24–25). In view of the fact that some schools in the Deep South—especially Mississippi—experienced little or no protest activity whatsoever, the modal figure at participating schools was probably closer to 80 percent. Needless to say, it is hard to reconcile these numbers with either traditional rational choice theory or with any perspective that focuses exclusively on narrow material motivations for participation. As we saw in Montgomery, black student participation in the movement turned much more on matters of meaning, identity, and community standing, that is, on the existential di-mensions of the social.

Although there is a paucity of systematic data on participation in the segrega-tionist countermovement of the same period, there is no reason to think that issues of meaning, identity, and community membership played any less of a role in grassroots resistance to civil rights as its advocacy. Although Kathleen Blee's extraordinary study of women in the Ku Klux Klan (among other right-wing groups) was conducted in a later period, her research can be seen as a rich body of empirical evidence attesting to the central importance of existential mo-tives in a white supremacist movement (Blee 1996, 2002). The salience of family connections, theological rationales, and broader community ties are recurring themes that run through Blee's account of women's participation in these groups.

More generally, the atavistic zeal with which many disadvantaged white Southerners defended the "Southern way of life" during the civil rights era sim-ply cannot be attributed to material motives alone or even primarily. Indeed, as many observers have noted over the years, in objective terms a case can be made that the material interests of poor white Southerners were closely aligned with those of poor blacks. Both groups suffered disproportionately under the terms of an anachronistic agricultural system that tied them to the land through debt peonage and offered them very little hope of ever escaping the grinding poverty and material deprivation that were endemic to the system. No, the incentives underlying grassroots white supremacist activity have to be accounted as in-volving the same mix of material and broader existential motives as we saw reflected in civil rights activism.

This hardly amounts to the last word on the subject. Indeed, it is barely a be-ginning, but it will have to do for now. In the future, however, we would urge analysts to attend more closely to the issues of meaning, membership, and identity that shape fields but all too often get ignored in favor of conventional accounts stressing only the narrow analytic concepts of power and interests.

The Transformation of the U.S. Mortgage Market, 1969–2011

Housing is at the core of the American economy. But it is more than that: owning a house is the linchpin of the American dream. From the point of view of our theory and its focus on meaning and identity, to make it in America, particularly in the postwar era, has meant to own a house. This goal was the existential bedrock of the middle class. Indeed, it defined being a member of that class. Not surprisingly, public policy in the United States has recognized this as an admirable goal, and governments of all political persuasions have worked to make ownership a reality since at least the 1920s (Quinn 2010). Helping people buy homes brought together both Democrats and Republicans because it resonated with the core values and meanings of the great American middle class (and those who wanted to join!).

This meant that since the 1920s, whenever home ownership was threatened by lack of supply of houses, too little access to mortgages, or mortgage terms that restricted too many people from buying homes, government policy makers innovated new ways to make more home ownership possible. Private business was the principal beneficiary of this tendency of public policy to promote home ownership. Any scheme business constructed that worked toward that goal by making the cost of getting a mortgage lower and more widely available to larger parts of the population got the adoration of not just the state strategic action fields involved in housing but also the president and members of Congress in both political parties. The fields in the state and the private economy that made possible the purchasing of housing were animated by the fact that making this part of the American dream available to everyone who might want it was always considered a good thing.

Our goal is to tell the story of the changing nature of the housing strategic action field by placing that story into the same sequence of elements as our rendition of the Civil Rights movement. Toward that end, we begin by describing the structure of the housing strategic action field as it emerged from the Great Depression and stabilized after the Second World War. In this strategic action field, the dominant players were the local savings and loans banks that, with help from the various federal agencies that provided rules to structure the mortgage industry, created a stable strategic action field for housing mortgages that lasted until the mid-1980s. There were a number of important state strategic action fields that structured the mortgage field: the Federal Housing Administration (FHA), the Veteran's Housing Administration, and the Federal Savings and Loan Insurance Corporation (FSLIC). These strategic action fields basically regulated the terms of mortgages and worked to stabilize the savings and loans banks. In doing so, they created a stable and profitable world for the savings and loans banks. As a result, house ownership rose in the United States from about 25 percent before the Depression to 63 percent in the early 1960s. The industry also contained a set of IGUs, mostly trade associations, that worked hand in hand with government officials to keep housing mostly private and profit in the hands of the banks and construction industry.

Then, we describe the changes that destabilized that regime during the 1970s and 1980s. This created a huge crisis in the strategic action field that took ten years to settle. The new settlement created a whole new set of players in the mortgage markets, both banks and government agencies, and a whole new way to buy and sell mortgages. The largest financial institutions that included mortgage, commercial, and investment banks used the mortgage market to feed their creation of investment products such as mortgage-backed securities (MBSs), credit debt obligations (CDOs), and credit default swaps (CDSs). The federal government has been a key party to this transformation. They pioneered the financial instruments that made this possible and they provided regulation and government-sponsored enterprises (GSEs) to help structure this new strategic action field. It was this newly settled strategic action field that was at the core of the mortgage meltdown from 2007 to 2011. We end by discussing the causes of this meltdown and the impact of this episode on other strategic action fields.

This transformation of the mortgage industry strategic action field entirely reconstructed the identities of the incumbents and challengers. The savings and loan banks that dominated the field from the 1930s until the late 1980s became a bit player. The government, which in 1965 was mainly a regulator to the field, became a player in the market in a central way through its ownership and control of the GSEs. In the 1990s, a whole new kind of financial firm emerged, a vertically integrated bank that worked in all phases of the mortgage market from origination to holding MBSs.

Countrywide Financial, led by Angelo Mozilo, was the firm that acted as the institutional entrepreneur that pioneered the new way of organizing mortgages in the private sector. Its tactics were soon copied by the largest commercial, investment, and savings and loan banks. By 2005, Citibank, Bank of America, Washington Mutual Savings Bank, Wachovia, Merrill Lynch, Bear Stearns, and Lehman Brothers all had operations that spanned the entire market. This transformation changed the nature of the field, the rules governing the field, and the role of the government in the field. The way in which these changes evolved followed the principles laid out in our earlier chapters and had a similar structure to our story about the civil rights movement. An established field experienced a set of exogenous shocks. These shocks undermined the existing order. Just as in the civil rights story, the government played a role in destabilizing the field and, when the savings and loan banks began to fail, provided a new underpinning to the field. But because of the obsessive interest in furthering the American dream by having people own homes, the government was always interested in promoting investment by other financial entities, and it welcomed and indeed enticed the entry of financial firms of all varieties. To begin our story, it is useful to characterize the strategic action field circa 1965 and the strategic action field circa 2005.

The Dominant Strategic Action Fields of the Mortgage Market, 1934–1987

In 1965, the main players in the mortgage market were savings and loan banks. These banks had their origins in the nineteenth century, when they were called "buildings and loans" or sometimes "community banks" (Haveman and Rao 1997). These banks would take deposits from local communities and then make loans to people in those communities that were used to buy or build houses. They would hold on to those loans until they were paid off, either because people sold their homes or, more likely, because they held the loans for the entire term of the loan. A standard line about the industry was that bankers had the "3-6-3" rule. They would borrow money at 3 percent, loan it to homebuyers at 6 percent, and be on the golf course by 3 p.m. From 1935 until the mid-1980s, about 60 percent of mortgage debt was held by savings and loan banks while commercial banks, using the same model, accounted for another 20 percent of the market (Fligstein and Goldstein 2010). The movie *It's a Wonderful Life* portrays the trials of a small town savings and loan bank during the Depression. The model of lending represented in that movie was still dominant as late as 1985.

The government played a number of roles in the formation of this strategic action field. Indeed, without the government, home ownership as a mass phenomenon would have been impossible. It constructed the field, and the strategic action fields of the government constituted the infrastructure of the field. The government set up and supported the privately run mortgage industry. This is a case in which it is the analyst's judgment call in deciding if the state's strategic action fields are outside of the field or are in fact acting as IGUs as part of the field. During the Depression, the government was concerned about home foreclosures and access to mortgages. They passed the National Housing Act of 1934, which created two government agencies, the FHA and the FSLIC. The FHA was authorized to regulate the rate of interest and the terms of mortgages and provide insurance for doing so. The government laid down the conditions for the modern mortgage. It has a fixed interest rate and a fixed term of payment (usually thirty years), and it requires a down payment of 20 percent. This set of innovations put into place and regulated by the government strategic action fields formed what we now call the "prime" or "conventional mortgage market." These new lending practices increased the number of people who could afford a down payment on a house and monthly debt service payments on a mortgage, thereby also increasing the size of the market for single-family homes.

The FSLIC was an institution that administered deposit insurance for savings and loan banks that guaranteed depositor's got their money back if banks went bankrupt. The guarantee on savings accounts meant that small savers were guaranteed to get their money back in case of bankruptcy. This was paid for by creating an insurance pool funded by savings and loans banks. The government regulators acted to stabilize the mortgage market in the aftermath of the Depression. Regulation and depository insurance allowed savings and loan banks to prosper in the postwar era building boom by being able to take in deposits that were guaranteed to account holders and make loans to mortgagees that could be guaranteed by insurance provided by the government. With the return of veterans after World War II, the housing market in the United States exploded and the savings and loan banks with the regulatory backing of the federal agencies grew rich and dominated the market. Later, the FSLIC was merged with the Federal Deposit Insurance Corporation.

The mortgage market circa 2005 bears little resemblance to this relatively simple world. Today, the market contains a number of distinct segments. Borrowers today go to a lending company (frequently a bank, but not exclusively) that now is called an "originator" because it makes the initial loan. Unlike the savings and loan banks, many of these companies do not want to hold on to the mortgages they sell but instead want to have them packaged into bonds, called "mortgage-backed securities," to be sold off to others. If they hold on to the mortgages, then their capital is now spent, they are unable to lend money again, and their ability to generate fees goes away. So, they turn around and sell the mortgages, thereby recapturing their capital and moving back into the market to lend. The mortgages are then gathered together into a financial package called a "special purpose vehicle" by underwriters who are GSEs, investment banks, or commercial banks.

But it is here that government plays a new role. The GSEs are both market makers and market regulators. As such, they are participants in the market but also act as IGUs. We will discuss why the Congress created these organizations and how they came to redefine and re-create the mortgage market in the wake of the collapse of the savings and loan banks in the 1980s. Their complex role in the market is the main way that the government remained directly involved in the mortgage market right up to the 2007 financial crisis. Again, because of the quasi-governmental status of the GSE, it is a judgment call as to whether or not the mortgage strategic action field was really a field of the state.

The special purpose vehicle turns the mortgages into a bond that pays a fixed rate of return based on the interest rates being paid by the people who buy the houses. These bonds are then rated by bond rating agencies in terms of their risk involved and sold to various classes of investors. Bond rating agencies are one of the principal IGUs in the mortgage field. By certifying the riskiness of bonds, they allow bonds to be priced, sold, and bought. Theoretically, buyers of the bonds understand how risky they are by having a single measure of the overall riskiness of the underlying mortgages. Bond rating allowed many long-term financial investors such as pension funds and insurance companies to buy the bonds and hold them for long periods of time. They operated to legitimate MBSs as financial products, expanded the market, and, indeed, made it possible.

These special purpose vehicles divide up the mortgages into what are called "tranches," and the bonds so divided are termed "collateral debt obligations." Here the mortgages are separately rated by bond agencies in terms of their riskiness. In this way, investors can buy riskier bonds that pay a higher rate of return or less risky bonds that pay a lower rate of return. The special purpose vehicles are managed by firms called "servicers" that collect the monthly mortgage payments from the people who actually own the mortgage and disburse them to the bondholder.

Financial firms decide in which of these segments they will do business. From the period 1993–2009, more and more firms decided to participate in multiple segments (Goldstein and Fligstein 2010). We describe the market that emerged as an "industrial model" in which the vertical integration of financial firms across market segments have them making money off of all of the stages of the various transactions. It is in capturing fees from these transactions that financial firms maximize their ability to profit. By participating in many segments of the industry, they can profit from the selling and packaging of mortgages all along the process. Financial firms include the GSE, commercial banks, investment banks, savings and loan banks, and specialists such as GMAC Inc. and GE Capital.

Our imagery is one in which, circa 1975, the strategic action field for mortgages was dominated by local savings and loan and commercial banks that took deposits from their communities, knew the people they loaned money to, and held on to the mortgages over the life of the mortgage. This meant that the business was geographically decentralized in all ways. The strategic action field that collapsed during 2007–2009 displayed a very different pattern. After mortgages were bought, they migrated to a few square miles of Manhattan, where in the offices of the major banks and GSEs they were packaged into special purpose vehicles. They then were redispersed to investors all over the world (although they were serviced from a few locations). The largest investors in these securities were the GSEs that held on to lots of MBSs. But MBSs are held by commercial banks, investment banks, savings and loan associations, mutual fund companies, and private investors here and around the world (Fligstein and Goldstein 2010). The interesting question is how did we move from the strategic action field in which local home buyers went to their local bank to get a loan to a strategic action field in which most of the mortgages in the United States are now packaged into MBSs and sold to a broad national and international market?

Changes That Destabilized the Mortgage Market, 1969–1987

As in our story about the civil rights movement, it was the connections between the mortgage market and related strategic action fields that provided the shocks that eventually undermined the savings and loan bank–dominated strategic action field. There were two main shocks to the savings and loan bank–dominated system of mortgages in the United States. First, the federal government in the 1960s began to worry that the savings and loan banks could not provide enough mortgages for the baby boom generation, and they began to create a set of new policies to expand mortgages and the financial instruments to fund them. The unintended consequence of their actions was to provide an alternative way to finance mortgages to that provided by the savings and loan banks.

Second, and even more important, was the bad economy of the 1970s. As we suggested in chapter 4, deep economic recessions are one of the external causes that undermine the order in a great many strategic action fields. We saw how the depression in agriculture undermined the political system that held African Americans in check. In the case of the savings and loan bank–dominated mortgage strategic action field, the general economic crisis of a different era, this time the 1970s, produced high interest rates that undermined the basic business model of the savings and loan banks. Essentially, the banks found that they could no longer borrow money cheaply. They also found themselves with most of their investments earning very low rates of interest. In order to understand the shocks that undermined the savings and loan banks, it is useful to begin with the role of the federal government in creating the new model of mortgage finance.

It will surprise most readers that the origin of the MBSs and the complex financial structure we just presented was not the financial wizards of Wall Street, but instead the federal government. It is probably even more surprising that this set of inventions dates back to the 1960s. Quinn (2008) shows that the idea to create MBSs began during the administration of President Johnson. The Democratic Congress and president wanted to rapidly increase the housing stock as part of its Great Society programs. They had three goals: to increase the housing stock for the baby boom generation, to increase the rate of home ownership more generally, and to help lower income people afford housing. Why was housing so important for a Democratic administration and a Democratic-controlled Congress? As we have already argued, home ownership was the key to the American dream. The Democrats wanted to make sure that middle-class Americans were helped by government to attain that dream. Quinn (2008) shows that the Johnson administration did not think the fragmented savings and loan industry was in the position to provide enough credit to rapidly expand the housing market. For Johnson, the private sector was too fragmented and did not have enough capital to build and fund enough houses for all who would want them.

But federal officials did not want to directly replace the savings and loan banks as a supplier of mortgages and the ultimate holder of mortgages. Because of the Vietnam War and the Great Society expansion of Medicaid, Medicare, and other social benefits, the government was running large and persistent debts. An expensive housing program in which the government provided funds for mortgages would add to that deficit, because the government would have to borrow money for the mortgages and hold those mortgages for thirty years. The mortgages would count on the government balance sheets as liabilities, not assets, and thereby worsen the indebtedness of the state.

If the government was going to stimulate the housing market, the Johnson administration would need to do it in such a way as to not add to the federal deficit. This caused them to reorganize the Federal National Mortgage Association (now called Fannie Mae) as a quasi-private organization, called a GSE, to lend money and hold mortgages. They also created another GSE, the Federal Home Loan Mortgage Corporation (now called Freddie Mac) to compete with Fannie Mae and a government agency to insure those mortgages against risk of default, the Government National Mortgage Association (now called Ginnie Mae). The idea of the GSEs was that they would not be on the books of the federal government. They would have to raise capital privately and fund loans by creating insurance and loan guarantees. The implication of the existence of the GSEs was the feeling in the industry that the money they were lent would be backed ultimately by the federal government. These GSEs could borrow money at lower rates and afford to sell cheaper mortgages to more people. Not surprisingly, they eventually came to dominate the mortgage market.

But making these mortgage-granting entities private was not the only innovation of the Johnson administration. The government also pioneered the creation of MBSs, thereby making it the collective institutional entrepreneur who invented an entirely new concept of the mortgage strategic action field (Sellon and VanNahmen 1988). The government, even in the GSEs, did not want to be the ultimate holder of the mortgages it helped to sell. In order to do this, it needed to find a buyer for those mortgages. It did so by offering and guaranteeing the first modern MBSs. MBSs were a set of mortgages that were packaged together into a bond created by the GSE. These bonds could then be sold directly to investors by the GSE or through investment banks (Barmat 1990). The GSE would offer tacit guarantees that the bonds would be paid back. Because of their quasi-governmental status, GSEs could borrow money more cheaply to finance mortgages and then turn around and sell those mortgages as bonds. The first MBS was issued on April 24, 1969 by Ginnie Mae (Wall Street Journal 1969).

We note that the GSEs operated as a kind of internal governance structure for the industry. They interacted with government regulators at the Federal Reserve, the Federal Deposit Insurance Corporation, and the FHA. They produced rules for mortgage qualifications that became the standard for the industry. So, for example, the rules that conventional mortgages required a 20 percent down payment and were capped at an amount set by the GSE provided the basic structure to the mortgage market. The GSEs operated to expand the mortgage market and held the market together in times of crisis. They cooperated with mortgage originators, wholesalers, commercial banks, investment banks, and servicers to promote the new market that emerged in the wake of the collapse of the savings and loan banks. Their actions affected every aspect of housing and mortgages.

The market for MBSs barely grew in the 1970s even with government guarantees. There were several issues. The savings and loan industry and commercial banks continued to have control over the bulk of the mortgage market where they took deposits, lent money, and held on to mortgages. But potential buyers of mortgage bonds were skeptical of buying MBSs because of prepayment risk. Almost all mortgages allow mortgagees to pay back the entire mortgage whenever they like with no penalties. This meant that bondholders could get their money back before they made much of a profit. This prospect was made worse by the fact that mortgage holders were more likely to refinance houses when interest rates were falling, thus leaving bondholders with money to invest at interest rates lower than the original mortgages (Kendall 1996).

This problem was ultimately solved through joint cooperation between the GSEs and the investment banks. In particular, Lewis Ranieri, who worked for the investment bank Salomon Brothers, acted as an institutional entrepreneur who played a key role in solving these problems (Lewis 1990; Ranieri 1996). Together, they created the system of "tranching" described above so investors could decide which level of risk of prepayment they wanted (Brendsel 1996). But there were also legal and regulatory issues involved in the packaging of bonds (Quinn 2008; Ranieri 1996). The most important was the problem of turning a mortgage into a security. The issue of a loan originator selling the mortgage into a pool of mortgages required changing the tax laws. The Tax Reform Act of 1986 cleared the way to the expansion of the MBS market. Investment banks and government officials worked together to solve these problems.

By the mid-1980s, the infrastructure to use MBSs as CDOs was in place. The legal problems were solved, and there existed powerful firms that were ready to make the market and IGUs to govern the field. But the mortgage securitization approach to funding mortgages still faced competition from the more traditional savings and loan–dominated strategic action field. This was a case in which we can see that the government was not a unified actor. Some parts of the government continued to support the savings and loan– dominated strategic action field by creating the regulatory conditions that helped those banks. The U.S. Department of Housing and Urban Development and the Federal Deposit Insurance Corporation continued to support the savings and loan banks as the main vehicle for finding mortgages. Not surprising, the Republicans generally favored the business interests of the savings and loans banks.

But at the same time, the government had laid the foundation for an alternative strategic action field. It had created a set of challengers, the GSEs, that had strong supporters in the government who did not think the savings and loans banks were providing enough loans, particularly to low-income people. Given that these were created by Democrats controlling Congress and given that these supporters wanted to expand who could get a mortgage, it is not surprising that these supporters tended to be Democrats. In the late 1970s and the 1980s, the savings and loan industry realized that the GSEs presented a challenge to their control over the mortgage market. They and their friends in government worked hard to prevent the takeover of the mortgage market by the GSEs.

The struggle between incumbents and challengers was eventually resolved in the challengers' favor when the incumbents' model of the field fell apart. The demise of the savings and loan banks was not caused by the challenge of the GSE. Instead, it was caused by the tough economic times of the 1970s, which essentially made the business model of the savings and loan banks untenable. There was a prolonged period of slow economic growth and high inflation in this period that came to be called "stagflation." One outcome of high inflation was very high interest rates for all forms of borrowing.

This struck savings and loan banks very hard. Remember that they relied for most of their funds on individual deposits. The interest rates paid on these deposits were regulated by Regulation Q, which fixed the rate that savings and loan banks could pay on these deposits at a relatively low level. It was the fixing of this rate that allowed savings and loans to make a profit. They borrowed money at, say, 3 percent, loaned it at, say, 6 percent, and made a profit. Since everyone had to offer low fixed interest rates to savers, there was little competition for funds. It also meant there was little competition for borrowers.

Savers began to flee those accounts as they found they could buy treasury bonds, certificates of deposit, money market funds, and other forms of financial instruments that paid higher interest rates. This meant that the savings and loan industry could not raise enough money to make new loans for housing. Moreover, the banks were holding on to a large number of mortgages that were priced at very low interest rates. Congress responded by passing the Garn-St. Germain Act in 1982. This act repealed Regulation Q and allowed the banks to pay whatever interest rate they chose. It also allowed the banks to make riskier investments while still guaranteeing that people would be able to get back their deposits.

The savings and loan banks responded in several ways. First, they began to sell their mortgage holdings at a great loss in order to raise capital to invest in new things. These mortgages were repackaged into MBSs primarily by Salomon Brothers (Lewis 1990). They also began to pay higher interest on government-guaranteed bank accounts in order to attract deposits. They tried to raise their profits by making very risky investments, including many in commercial real estate, which helped create a commercial real estate bubble. These bad investments caused their ultimate demise (Barth 2004). Savings and loan banks around the country began to fail. In the end, the federal government ended up having to take them over and spent $160 billion on a bailout beginning in 1989.

When the savings and loan banks collapsed, their dominance of the field of mortgage lending collapsed. But this did not eliminate the demand for mortgages and the political appeal of home ownership. The question in the late 1980s was who was going to take over dominance of mortgage provision in the United States. Since mortgages were such an important part of government domestic policy and a basic staple of American politics, the Republican regimes of Ronald Reagan and George Bush (who generally favored private over public solutions to economic problems) were looking for a way to have the federal government take up the slack as the provider of mortgage credit. They were quite lucky that the GSEs already existed and that the GSEs had an alternative business model to that of the savings and loans. The GSEs borrowed their money right from the national capital markets on Wall Street and had extensive relationships with the investment banks that dominated those markets. As late as 1980, the GSEs had only issued $200 billion of mortgages, about 13 percent of the total that year. But the collapse of the savings and loan banks caused that share to rise to 63 percent by 1993. Over this same period, the share of the mortgage market controlled by the savings and loan banks, which was 58 percent in 1980, fell to 15 percent by 1993 (Fligstein and Goldstein 2010).

Settlement and the New Strategic Action Field

With the collapse of the savings and loan banks, the mortgage market was quite fragmented. Indeed, if the GSEs had not intervened so quickly and effectively, it would have been impossible to obtain mortgages in America from 1985 until the mid-1990s. Because of the huge role that the GSEs were playing in the market, their tactics and understandings were the main sources of the restructuring of the field. In the wake of the collapse of the savings and loan banks and their business model of "lend and hold," the possibility for a whole new set of players with an entirely new business model emerged. But while the GSEs acted first to structure the mortgage market in the wake of the savings and loan banks' collapse, the model that eventually emerged in that market was one that contained both the GSEs and privately held banks. The GSE idea that mortgages were to be funded through the creation of securities dominated the new market. The GSEs played a big part as actors in that market. But other banks followed what we will call an industrial model to enter and organize the mortgage businesses. Banks such as Countrywide Financial were participating in every segment of the business by the late 1990s. This new settlement persisted and intensified all through the financial crisis of 2007–2011.

Remember that the GSEs were not mortgage originators but operated instead as mortgage aggregators. They would buy mortgages with money they borrowed from the financial markets. They would pay someone to help them package the mortgages into CDOs, and then they would sell the CDOs to banks and other institutional investors. This created opportunities for other kinds of firms both to come into existence and to become part of the large field of mortgage provision.

We argue that this was the social movement phase of the mortgage market. Lots of firms emerged to take advantage of the tremendous number of opportunities to participate in the mortgage market. They saw this huge market, and at the center of it were the GSEs that appeared to offer a government guarantee to the possibility of making profit. Small firms began to come into existence that specialized in finding mortgages for customers. These firms sold off the mortgages to either loan wholesalers or the GSEs directly. Mortgage wholesalers would package mortgages from a number of locations and then sell them to the GSEs. Then, the GSEs would engage investment bankers to help them package mortgages into MBSs and use those same banks to find customers to buy the securities. A whole new class of firms emerged that specialized in servicing loans by taking payments from individual owners and disbursing them to the holders of the bonds. Finally, the bond and stock ratings agencies discovered the new business of rating MBSs. Circa 1993, this market looked quite fragmented, and the players in each part of the market were specialists who tended to stay out of the other parts of the market (Jacobides 2005). There was a kind of "gold rush" here whereby lots of firms rose up to position themselves to make money off of American MBSs.

At the core of this market were the GSEs, which acted as facilitators, funders, regulators, and guarantors of mortgages. By playing all of these parts, they guaranteed that other firms could make money off of the transactions that they would make possible. At the beginning, the private firms in each part of this market were fragmented into smaller pieces, each organized around one of the now necessary parts of the mortgage-providing process. In the end, this model turned out to be transitional. It is useful to consider the rise of the "industrial model" in the mortgage strategic action field.

As the decade of the 1990s went on, the opportunity to make money off of mortgages began to attract banks of all sizes and specializations. Mortgage banks, such as Countrywide Financial, specialized in home loans, and mortgage wholesalers specialized in gathering loans together for sale to those who wanted to create MBSs. Commercial banks had always been involved in the mortgage market, but over the decade of the 1990s became intrigued by entering all phases of the business. Investment banks had historically not been involved in the mortgage market, and it is their aggressive entry into this market that characterizes their dramatic growth during the 1990s.

What attracted all of these banks? The American mortgage market was a trillion dollar market. The repackaging of mortgages as securities attracted the investment banks and anyone on Wall Street whose business it was to buy or sell financial instruments. This meant that banks that could find a place in the market could make large profits in many different ways. What they eventually realized was that all of these activities could be lucrative. As a result, over time, banks began to enter more and more of them. This creation of a new strategic action field for the mortgage market created a financial revolution among banks. It is at this moment that all kinds of the banks became more active in all financial markets related to mortgages. This revolution started with the expansion of securitization but quickly created more complex financial instruments to create new ways to invest and control risk. It is to the story of the past fifteen years that we now turn.

The Rise of the Industrial Model of the MBS Market, 1993–2007

There are several parts to our story. First, the GSEs were interested in expanding the size of the mortgage market and increasing the participation of private banks of all kinds in the market. After they more or less took the market over in the mid-1980s, they worked to attract the participation of commercial and investments banks in the process of securitization. As the IGU of the market, they provided rules, guidelines, and implied guarantees that made doing mortgage business lucrative for all participants. Their "masters" in Congress and the federal government (both Republican and Democratic) all viewed their role in creating the possibility of more homeowners an important goal of social policy. Their ability to borrow money at lower interest rates allowed them to buy mortgages from originators, package them into MBSs, and sell them with implied guarantees back to financial entities such as commercial banks. The GSE remained at the core of the mortgage market through this entire period of growth.

But the industrial model of the industry whereby banks wanted to be in all phases of the business was something that the major banks from different industries hit on from several directions. Commercial banks began in the 1990s to view their business not as based on long-term relationships to customers who would borrow and pay off their debts but instead as fee based (DeYoung and Rice 2004). This meant that commercial banks no longer were interested in making loans to customers and holding the loans but instead were interested in generating fees from various kinds of economic transactions. This was a response to the downturn in their core businesses of lending to longtime customers. Commercial banks began to develop an "industrial" model for their mortgage business (DeYoung and Rice 2004). They realized they could collect fees from selling mortgages, from packaging them into MBSs, from selling MBSs, and from holding on to MBSs when they could earn profits using borrowed money to buy them. Since mortgages that had been turned into MBSs by the GSEs were rated as safe as government bonds, they had the additional advantage of being able to be counted as part of the bank's core capital. This industrial model required the input of more and more mortgages in order to reap the benefits along the entire chain of production and to continue growth and profit. This vertically integrated industrial model was first perfected in the prime mortgage market. It worked spectacularly for financial institutions in the 1990s and the first part of the 2000s.

The pioneer in producing this industrial conception of the market was not a commercial bank but a bank that had specialized in mortgages. Countrywide Financial was founded in 1969 by David Loeb and Angelo Mozilo. During the 1970s, the company almost went bankrupt as it tried to expand its mortgage business across the United States amid the bad economic times of high interest rates and high inflation. But during the 1980s, the firm invested heavily in computer technology in all phases of its business. In the 1980s, the company expanded dramatically across the country and began entering all of the activities of the mortgage industry.

By the mid-1990s, Countrywide Financial had entered into every segment of the mortgage industry. It originated, purchased, securitized, and serviced mortgages. It operated to deal MBSs and other financial products and also invested heavily in mortgage loans and home equity lines. During the mid-1990s, the company began to enter the subprime mortgage market and was a leader in that market for the next ten years. In 2006 Countrywide financed 20 percent of all mortgages in the United States, at a value of about 3.5 percent of U.S. gross domestic product, a proportion greater than any other single mortgage lender.

Its rapid growth and expansion made it one of the most visible and profitable corporations of the past twenty years. Between 1982 and 2003, Countrywide delivered investors a 23,000 percent return on its stock price (Fligstein and Goldstein 2010). Countrywide became the model for a large number of banks and other financial entities such as GMAC and GE Capital. It should not be surprising that Countrywide's model began to be emulated by all of the other major banks in the mortgage strategic action field.

The market for mortgages in the United States increased from $458 billion in 1990 to nearly $4 trillion at its peak in 2003 (Fligstein and Goldstein 2010). Most of these mortgages were packaged into MBSs. Many of these MBSs were sponsored by the GSEs. The GSEs frequently relied on either the commercial or the investment banks to put these packages together and help sell them. This meant that the repackaging of mortgages into bonds became the largest fee generation business for many banks. Those who did this included Lehman Brothers, Bear Stearns, Merrill Lynch, Morgan Stanley, and Goldman Sachs. Of course, commercial banks and bank holding companies such as Bank of America, Wells Fargo, Citibank, and Countrywide Financial were also deeply involved in the selling and packing of mortgages and MBSs. All of these banks aggressively packaged and sold MBSs to insurance companies, pension funds, and banks around the world. They later held on to a large number of these securities, which they financed through short-term borrowing from financial markets.

One of the central features of financial deregulation in the past twenty-five years has been the breaking down of the Glass-Steagall Act. The Glass-Steagall Act was enacted in 1935 during the Depression. One of its main rules was to force banks to choose whether or not they wanted to be investment banks or commercial banks. During the period from 1980 until 1999, policy makers and bankers worked to have this barrier broken down. One reason for this was the MBS business. As that business became larger, commercial banks wanted to be able to sell loans (be originators), package loans (be conduits), and hold on to loans (be investors). As banks such as Bank of America and Citibank saw that fees for putting together these packages ended up with investment banks, they lobbied to have the barrier removed. They got their wish. The Glass-Steagall Act was rescinded in 1999 and banks were allowed to be in any business they chose. The big commercial banks and bank holding companies were then able to fully participate in every part of the market.

The second important change in the industry was more subtle. The new financial services firms, and in particular the commercial banks, began to see their industries as not about giving customers loans but about charging fees for services. DeYoung and Rice (2004) document these changes across the population of commercial banks. They show that these banks' income from fee-related activities increased from 24 percent in 1980, to 31 percent in 1990, to

35 percent in 1995, to 48 percent in 2003. This shows that commercial banks were moving away from loans as the main source of revenue by diversifying their income streams well before the repeal of the Glass-Steagall Act. The largest sources of this fee generation in 2003 were (in order of importance) securitization, servicing mortgage and credit card loans, and investment banking (DeYoung and Rice 2004: 42).

This increased attention to securitization and mortgage servicing was accompanied by a huge increase in real estate loans in financial services firms' loan portfolios. DeYoung and Rice show that banks did not just shift toward a fee-generating strategy but instead shifted the focus of their investments. Instead of directly loaning money to customers, banks would either sell mortgages or package them into MBSs. They would then borrow money to hold on to the MBSs. Commercial banks' real estate loans represented 32 percent of assets in 1986, increasing to 54 percent of assets in 2003. Why did this happen? They did this because holding on to the MBSs was where the money was made. It has been estimated that mortgage origination accounted for 10 percent of the profit on a real estate loan, while holding the MBS accounted for 70 percent and servicing the loan accounted for 20 percent. By 1999, Bank of America, Citibank, Wells Fargo, and JPMorgan Chase, the largest commercial banks, had all shifted their businesses substantially from a customer-based model to a fee-based model in which the end point was for customers' loans to disappear into MBSs. Not surprisingly, all four were among the leaders in businesses located in all parts of the mortgage market.

The deregulation of financial services did not just provide commercial banks with the opportunity to enter into new businesses. It allowed other financial firms to expand their activities as well. While the boundaries between financial industries were clearly eroding from the 1980s on, after 1999 with the repeal of Glass-Steagall, any financial firm could feel free to enter any financial industry. The real estate market was a potentially huge opportunity for all sorts of financial services firms. The potential to earn fees from originating mortgages, securitizing mortgages, selling mortgages, servicing mortgages, and making money off of MBSs was enormous. Countrywide Financial started out as a mortgage broker and Washington Mutual Bank started as a savings and loan bank; both rapidly entered into all parts of the mortgage business during the 1990s. On the investment bank side, Bear Stearns, an investment bank, entered the mortgage origination business by setting up lender and servicer EMC Mortgage Corporation in the early 1990s. Lehman Brothers, another investment bank, bought originators in 1999, 2003, 2005, and 2006. Both GMAC and GE Capital moved after 2004 into the subprime mortgage origination industry and the underwriting of MBSs (Inside Mortgage Finance 2009). During the subprime mortgage boom, Morgan Stanley, Merrill Lynch, and Deustche Bank all bought mortgage originators (Levine 2007).

The vertical integration of production was spurred on by the desire of banking entities to control the mortgages from the point of origination to their ultimate sale. Anthony Tufariello, head of the Securitized Products Group, in a press release distributed when Morgan Stanley bought Saxon Capital suggested, "The addition of Saxon to Morgan Stanley's global mortgage franchise will help us to capture the full economic value inherent in this business. This acquisition facilitates our goal of achieving vertical integration in the residential mortgage business, with ownership and control of the entire value chain, from origination to capital markets execution to active risk management" (Morgan Stanley 2006). Dow Kim, president of Merrill Lynch's Global Markets Investment Banking group, made the very same point in announcing the acquisition of First Franklin, one of the largest subprime originators in 2006: "This transaction accelerates our vertical integration in mortgages, complementing the other three acquisitions we have made in this area and enhancing our ability to drive growth and returns" (Merrill Lynch 2006).

By the turn of the twenty-first century, the MBSs business was increasingly dominated by a smaller and smaller set of players. The largest commercial banks, mortgage banks, and investment banks extended their reach both backward to mortgage origination and forward to underwriting and servicing. Their ability to make money at every stage of the process by capturing fees meant that the three markets were no longer separate. They had been combined into a single market with players vying for opportunities at all parts of the market.

It is useful to document the growth of the business of MBSs since the early 1990s. The American mortgage market was about $500 billion in 1990. It went up to nearly $1 trillion in 1993 and reached around $1.5 trillion in 1998. The real change in the market began in 2001 (the year of the stock market crash). The real estate mortgage market in the United States climbed from about $1 trillion in 2000 to almost $4 trillion in 2003. It then dropped to $3 trillion between 2004 and 2006. Then it dropped in 2007 to about $2 trillion and in the crash in 2008, to $1.5 trillion.

Important factors in the 1990s and 2000s housing booms were the proliferation of mortgage securitization tools and the increased participation of the bigger banks in these processes. The large banks entered these markets with the goal of growing them. They aggressively used securitization tools as a way to raise money for mortgages and a way to sell them. In 1996, the largest players in the mortgage market were mostly either mortgage specialists such as Countrywide and NW Mortgage or regional commercial banks such as Fleet Financial and PNC Financial Services. But by the end of the second bubble, the identities of the largest loan originators had changed. Now the largest mortgage originators were the large national bank holding companies such as Wells Fargo, Citibank, and Bank of America. Countrywide had turned itself into a national bank as had Chase, Wachovia, and Washington Mutual. These large players grew larger as the national market expanded.

One of the least remarked upon features of the mortgage origination market is the degree to which it became concentrated over the period. The market share of the top five originators stood at 16.3 percent in 1996, a remarkably unconcentrated figure. But in 2007, the top five originators accounted for 42 percent of a much larger market. In 1990, the twenty-five largest lenders accounted for less than 30 percent of the mortgage market. This rose steadily during the 1990s, and by 2007 the top twenty-five originators controlled 90 percent of the market. If one looks at the top ten conduits in 2007, the total is 71 percent. So, there was not just a rapid growth in the size of these markets but also a rapid concentration of activities in fewer and fewer banks that were both larger and more nationally oriented (Fligstein and Goldstein 2010).

The housing bubble that began after 2001 had different causes; 2001 will be remembered as the year of the crash in "dotcom" stocks. But 2001 was also the year in which the Federal Reserve, in response to the crash, essentially lowered interest rates to zero. Its actions were met by similar actions in central banks around the world. The Federal Reserve did this to make sure that there was substantial credit in the economy and that lending would continue. But the unintended effect of lowering interest rates so far was that it encouraged the housing bubble in the United States. The rapid rise of that bubble is astonishing.

The bubble was driven along by the availability of low cost loans. The process worked in the following way. Bank originators could use either their own capital or cheap borrowed capital to make loans to homebuyers. Then, they could turn around and turn these loans into MBSs and CDOs. If they used someone else's money (borrowed at, say, 1–2 percent), then they could essentially do the entire transaction with very low cost and relatively high fees. Beginning sometime around 2002, all banks began to realize that they could borrow money for 1–2 percent, create MBSs, and hold on to the MBSs, which might pay as much as 6–7 percent in interest. This allowed them to make a profit using other people's money without risking their own capital.

The low interest rates in the United States and the world encouraged banks of all kinds to make as many loans as they could and to hold on to MBSs because they were earning money on borrowed money. The investment banks increased their holding of MBSs from about $35 billion in 2002 to $175 billion in 2007, a more than 400 percent increase. Commercial banks increased their holding of MBSs from $650 billion in 2002 to $1.1 trillion in 2007. Other private investors (including hedge funds) increased their ownership of MBSs during this period from $25 billion to $700 billion. Finally, mutual fund operators began to buy MBSs as well and went from about $400 billion to nearly $850 billion (Fligstein and Goldstein 2010).

Just as the civil rights movement's strategies and tactics spread to help give other social movements force and create new strategic action fields, so did the invention of securitization create other strategic action fields by being used to organize strategic action fields other than mortgages. The idea that underlying assets could be packaged and sold to investors as bonds that would pay out from the cash flow on these underlying assets caught fire. Markets sprung up in auto loans, credit card loans, equipment leases, home equity loans, mobile home loans, and student loans (Barmat 1990). These markets grew from about $450 billion in 1996 to about $2.3 trillion by 2006. This possibility created a huge expansion in all forms of consumer credit markets. This meant that nearly everyone who wanted to borrow money for nearly everything found a willing creditor to loan them money. These creditors frequently acted as loan originators did in the mortgage markets. They would create debt and then sell off the rights to the cash flow to investment banks, which would package the debt into asset-backed securities (which were then called ABS).

Two sorts of secondary markets also grew up (Barmat 1990). First, the collateralized debt obligation market handles not only mortgages but also any asset products that can be broken up into "tranches" and sold as pieces of "risk" (Enron was one of the firms that expanded the use of these vehicles; see McLean and Elkind 2003). Second, the CDS market allowed firms to insure the risks they held on CDOs and other financial instruments. As the mortgage securitization market has been negatively affected by the collapse of the subprime lending market, this has put pressure on both the CDO market and the CDS market. In the CDS market, losses have been higher than expected. Since many firms bought CDSs to protect themselves against such risks, this has meant that holders of the CDSs have come under pressure to pay off their obligations. One of the largest players in the CDS market was the multinational insurance corporation AIG, and its exposure in this market was the main cause of its takeover by the government.

The Causes of the Crisis

By 2003, investors of all kinds—commercial banks, investment banks, hedge fund traders, insurance companies, and other private investors—had figured out how to use leverage by borrowing money cheaply to buy MBSs and CDOs (sometimes called just CDOs or MBS–CDOs). Investors who actually had cash, such as pensions funds, insurance companies, and governments and banks around the world, were seeking out safe investments that paid more than 1–2 percent, as did government bonds. American mortgages seemed like a good bet. The underlying assets of mortgages were houses, and the MBSs contained mortgages from all over the country, thereby appearing to be diversified geographically. American housing prices had risen steadily for as long as anyone could remember. Finally, MBSs were rated and it was possible to secure AAA rated bonds. This made American mortgages seem like low-risk, high-yield investments.

The real problem that eventually caused the worldwide financial crisis was that the supply of conventional mortgages peaked in 2003 and began a rapid decline thereafter (Fligstein and Goldstein 2010). About $2.6 trillion worth of conventional or prime mortgages were bought in 2003, and this dropped to $1.35 trillion, a drop of almost 50 percent, by 2004. So, while those who had money to buy MBSs were looking for product, those who were originating and packaging MBSs lacked enough to sell them. This meant that there was a huge incentive to increase the number of mortgages. This incentive sent loan originators looking for new markets to expand to feed the securitization machine. This created the subprime market, that is, the market to lend to people with poor credit histories and little in down payments. As noted earlier, the industrial scale of the subprime market was pioneered by Countrywide Financial. But all of the other players in the mortgage business had begun to follow suit in the late 1990s and began to buy up mortgage originators of subprime loans. After 2003, this process became even more pronounced as the search for new mortgage customers intensified.

In 2004, for the first time, the subprime loans exceeded the prime market. In the peak of the mortgage craze in 2006, fully 70 percent of all loans that were made were subprime mortgages. This astounding change in the character of the mortgage market was noticed by regulators and Congress. But the Federal Reserve chose to ignore what was going on. Alan Greenspan famously testified before Congress that he did nothing to stop this rapid growth in subprime mortgages because he did not believe that banks would have made these loans if they thought they were too risky. He is also on record as saying that he clearly was mistaken on this point.

We would argue that the proximate causes of the crisis are twofold. First, the easy credit available to all forms of financial investors after 2001 meant that profits could be made by borrowing money at a low interest rate and then turning around and buying MBSs. This process of leveraging was the core strategy of banks and many other financial institutions. Investors worldwide who were not leveraged were also searching for higher, but safe returns, and American mortgages looked good to them. But the second cause (which is not well understood) is as important as the first. By 2003, there were simply not enough prime or conventional mortgages available in the United States to package into MBSs. This brought about a search for new customers, many of whom had less money to put down or worse credit. It was the dramatic growth of the subprime market that came to replace the prime or conventional market. The aggressive pursuit of that market by banks of all kinds led us to the current situation.

There were two main forces that eroded the positions of banks and the GSEs by 2007. First, the rate of foreclosures on AAA subprime MBS bonds turned out to be higher than was predicted. This in turn led bond rating agencies to downgrade these bonds. As their price dropped, banks that had taken loans to buy the MBSs had to either pay off those loans or put up more collateral to keep them. This was because most of their loans contained covenants that required them to up their capital investment if bond prices fell. Most banks were very highly leveraged and eventually found it impossible to raise enough capital to cover their loans. By mid-2007, it was clear that subprime mortgages were undermining bond prices, and pressure was brought to bear on all of the banks. By spring of 2008, banks such as Bear Stearns began to fail. The entire mortgage securitization industry has undergone reformation as many banks have failed and the government took over Freddie Mac and Fannie Mae.

What prevented an even worse meltdown and 1930s-style depression was the government's takeover of the GSEs and propping up of the rest of the banking system. The strategic action field of the mortgage market is still one characterized by the industrial organization of banks. But now, the government is the prime player. By virtue of its ownership of Freddie Mac and Fannie Mae and its takeover of assets of failed banks, the government now owns half of the mortgages in the United States. Ironically, in the 1960s, the government set up the GSEs and created the MBSs so they could increase home ownership without direct government ownership of mortgages. But their forty-year efforts to create a large private market for mortgages rose spectacularly and failed. Today, they own the largest share of the market.

The Impact of the Strategic Action Field Based on the Industrial Model on Other Strategic Action Fields

In retrospect, we can see a number of important effects of the emergence of the industrial model of mortgages on other strategic action fields. The most important effect was that the strategic action fields of mortgage origination, securitization and bond creation, and investment in assets (particularly in real estate) all became combined into a single strategic action field. This new strategic action field was one of the largest industries in the United States. It also heavily affected nearby strategic action fields such as construction, residential real estate, commercial real estate, furnishings, and all other industries related to housing. These markets rose and fell as the ability for consumers to take out loans against the rising values of their homes greatly affected all forms of consumption. The securitization of mortgages spread to other products as well: student loans, auto loans, credit card debt, and industrial loans.

Indeed, the entire banking industry in the United States was transformed as the barriers between types of banking fell and banks became focused on American mortgages. In the world of 1990, it was possible to identify banks that were in distinct lines of separate businesses. The investment bank business, for example, was relatively small and most focused on the issuance of corporate securities, the sale of treasury securities, and the business of mergers and acquisitions. By the early 2000s, the MBS business and its CDO cousins were the dominant business of investment banks. The MBS and CDO businesses grew so large that they also came to dominate the hedge fund, mutual fund, and securities trading industries. By the time the housing crisis began in 2007, it was difficult to see any financial firms that were not in some way or another connected to the field of mortgages.

The industrial model of the mortgage industry had an even more profound effect on homeowners. First, because of the incessant need to continue to find new mortgages, banks created more and more lenient products that allowed consumers to take out more and more debt. Banks had a very high incentive to make subprime mortgages: they could make more money off of fees, and the higher interest rates required of riskier borrowers implied higher returns as well. Together, this encouraged predatory lending and increased borrowing. In the early 1990s, consumers began to treat the rising value of their homes as cash machines that they could use to refinance and take money out. Banks encouraged these practices because of the fees generated every time a loan was refinanced and the odds that the loan would require a higher interest rate when refinanced. The huge overextension by American consumers on all forms of credit was driven not just by their greed or desire to live beyond their means. It was also propelled by the large, vertically integrated banks, which needed to continue to generate fees from loan transactions and to increase their margins by making riskier and riskier loans.

The importance of the mortgage market for the U.S. economy more generally became apparent when housing prices started to slow their rate of increase. It now seems ironic that regulators missed the close interdependence of banks, traders, the stock market, and the local real estate economy based on the building, sale, and furnishing of homes. They thought that all of these markets were not interdependent fields, but instead separate entities. As late as 2008, Ben Bernanke, the president of the Federal Reserve, viewed the subprime crisis as a small blip in an otherwise healthy economy. What Bernanke did not understand was that the entire banking system was making money off of sale, packaging, and holding of mortgages as investments.

Because in 2008, 70 percent of mortgages were nonconventional, Bernanke missed that the entire financial system and the local economies dependent on residential and commercial real estate were all being driven by house price increases. We can see in retrospect that once those prices slowed down and consumers could no longer refinance their loans, it was obvious that the whole thing would come crashing down. However, we only see that now because we know of the size, importance, and interconnectedness of the strategic action fields.

The complex of strategic action fields that arose as a result of the collapse of the strategic action field of the savings and loan banks has just been sketched out here. Much work remains to be done to show these connections as they evolved over time. What is clear is that the strategic action field approach is useful for understanding the structure of the mortgage market up until the mid-1980s, the crisis that destroyed that structure, and the role of a new set of even more powerful and connected structures. We have documented the central role of the government in all of these processes. We have also shown how the GSEs played the role of internal governance for the market from the mid-1980s onward. In these ways, our story of the changes in the strategic action fields of the mortgage industry parallels the story of the civil rights movement.

Conclusion

The stories of the civil rights movement and the transformation of the U.S. mortgage market obviously concern very different kinds of politics, organizations, ideas, frames, and actors. Yet, if we are right, the underlying logic of both reflects the structure and operation of strategic action fields. In both cases, there was an existing order, one that all of the actors understood and one that had rules, laws, and practices that governed interactions, defined an incumbent-challenger structure, and made it possible to identify who occupied which positions within the field. The "game" in each field was well defined. In the case of the field of U.S. racial politics, local, state, and federal institutions and actors were designed to segregate the African American population by the use of legal and extralegal means. This system proved resistant to change for at least seventy-five years. In the case of the mortgage industry in the United States, the savings and loan banks dominated the field with the help and support of the federal government, which guaranteed deposits and provided terms for mortgages and insurance against their default. This system came into being during the Depression of the 1930s and lasted until the mid-1980s.

The crises for both systems are to be found in their links to other strategic action fields. In the civil rights case, destabilizing changes in the Democratic Party, the field of U.S. constitutional law, and the international nation-state system contributed to undermining incumbent segregationist control over the national field of racial politics. In the case of the mortgage market, the federal government's attempt to increase home ownership pioneered new forms of mortgage finance. They also produced new GSEs to promote those forms. But the real blow to the savings and loan bank–dominated strategic action field was the bad economy of the 1970s, which made it difficult for these banks to get deposits while they had on their books many loans that were not very profitable. The federal government tried to solve these problems by allowing the deregulation of the savings and loan. But that turned out to be a disaster for the banks.

The undermining of the given order in both cases allowed a reorganization of the strategic action fields under new principles. Here, some challenger organizations already existed or came from a nearby field, but a number of them were founded in these eras to pioneer new tactics. In the case of the civil rights movement, the five largest civil rights organizations were able to form a political coalition early on to contest the power of the segregationists at the local, state, and federal levels. Their basic argument, that all citizens were entitled to civil rights, worked to reorganize the field of political race relations in the United States. In the mortgage market, in the wake of the collapse of the savings and loan banks, the federal government through the GSEs began to be the main player in the market. But some banks saw the collapse of the industry as an opportunity and aggressively entered the market. The pioneer in this regard was Countrywide Financial, which invented the industrial conception of the market. Their idea spread across the ranks of all kinds of banks and other financial institutions. This created a vertically integrated industry in which banks made profits at all points in the process.

Both successful strategic action field projects spawned new fields. In the case of civil rights, the language and tactics of movement groups were used by other insurgent groups in the United States and the world. In the case of mortgage securitization, several nearby industries sprung up. One set of industries found new kinds of assets to securitize. Others pioneered new kinds of financial products, for better or for worse, such as subprime loans, CDOs, and CDSs.

Our analyses show the underlying usefulness of the strategic action field approach. The perspective alerts analysts to a finite number of key issues and topics central, in our view, to an understanding of change and stability in strategic action fields. More specifically, it pushes analysts to define the purpose of the field; the key field actors (e.g., incumbents and challengers); the rules that structure relations and action in the strategic action field; the external fields—state and nonstate—that are most important to the reproduction of the strategic action field; and the IGUs that are in place and how they function to stabilize and sustain the field.

These issues are key to understanding field stability. Crisis and change in a field, however, requires attention to a number of additional topics, including the following: the events or processes—typically emanating in one or more proximate fields—that serve to destabilize the field; the specific challengers who come to the fore to exploit the situation; their alternative vision for the field; and the actions taken by all parties to the conflict—incumbents, challengers, external state and nonstate actions—to effect a new settlement. Finally, the analyst will need to be attuned to the terms of the new settlement and how it, among all proposed solutions, came to carry the day. The two cases presented in this chapter were structured around these very issues. In the next chapter, however, we will move beyond specific cases and talk in more generic terms about the methodological implications and requirements of our approach.

6

Methodological Considerations

We devoted chapters 1 through 4 to a systematic sketch of our theoretical perspective. But that sketch remained fairly abstract, leavened only by a few illustrative examples. In an effort to make the theory more concrete we devoted chapter 5 to two extended examples. But examples are not a method; they were employed merely to show how nominally familiar cases could be viewed very differently and profitably through our framework. At heart, though, we are empirical researchers who fashioned the perspective as a way to make sense of the cases we were studying. We are keen to see other researchers employ the framework as well. But to this point, we have said almost nothing about how the perspective might be used to guide research. This chapter is devoted to this issue.

We begin with a logically sequential research template or "roadmap" derived from the perspective. These are the key issues and questions to which the perspective attunes the researcher. We then devote an extended discussion to what we see as four of the trickiest empirical challenges posed by the framework:

- operationally defining and verifying the existence of a field
- differentiating between emergent, stable, and transforming strategic action fields
- assessing the critical relationships between any given field and "external" actors, especially those embedded in various state fields
- credibly accounting for the role of social skill and entrepreneurial action within a field

Having tried to underscore the key empirical challenges posed by our perspective, we then close the chapter with a more general discussion of methodological issues as they apply to the framework. More specifically, we take up four topics. First, we consider how researchers might employ "positivist" or "realist" approaches in the application of the theory. Second, we discuss the ways in which qualitative and quantitative techniques can be employed in the service of the perspective under either a positivist or realist philosophy. Third, we review several exemplary studies that embody our key methodological tenets, while critiquing other attempts to model the formation, reproduction, and transformation of strategic action fields. Finally, we close with a critique of more empiricist approaches to the study of strategic action.

The Roadmap

Insofar as our perspective is geared to understanding the dynamics of strategic action under different field conditions, we have organized our "roadmap" in terms of the three major "states" in which one finds strategic action fields. For us, the first research imperative is that analysts be sensitive to "their" field under conditions of *emergence, reproduction,* and *rupture/crisis/resettlement.* We take up these states in turn, attending to what we see as the major issues or research questions relevant to each condition.

1. *Field Formation or Emergence*—The origins of some fields are well documented. Regulatory fields mandated by legislation, new markets spawned by formal trade agreements, and any strategic action field that is essentially the product of intentional design by public actors would qualify in this regard. We are guessing, however, that most fields arise with much less fanfare and conscious intent and by far more amorphous processes than those mandated by public fiat. In turn, this means that they generally leave far fewer empirical traces in the wake of their origins. Thus, the emergence of a field is often the most challenging of the three states to systematically research. Still, the central research questions pertinent to this state of the field seem clear enough to us. These include the following:

- Who were the key actors who vied for control of the emerging field?
- What alternative conceptions of the strategic action field did these key actors represent?
- What resources—material, political, ideological—did each of the main combatants bring to the founding struggle?
- Who prevailed in this struggle and why?
- What role, if any, did external actors—especially state actors—play in the outcome of the founding episode?
- What were the principal terms of the settlement eventuated at the close of the episode?
- What, if any, internal governance units were established at this time to help routinize and safeguard the settlement?

2. *The Stable Field*—In general, the task of the researcher becomes considerably easier once a field is well established and reasonably stable. That said, the

analysis of field stability and reproduction comes with its own empirical challenges. The key questions guiding field research of stable fields include the following:

- What are the boundaries of the field? Are they formally prescribed or socially constructed?
- Who are the principal incumbents and challengers?
- Does the power structure of the field most closely resemble coalition or hierarchy?
- What are the shared understandings regarding membership, acceptable forms of action, and other rules that structure the everyday life of the field?
- How strong is the consensus with respect to this settlement?
- How do external state and nonstate fields help to stabilize and reproduce the field?
- How do internal governance units serve the same function?
- What are the modal strategies, forms of action, and collective action frames employed by incumbents and challengers in the face of generally stable field relations?

3. Rupture/Crisis/Resettlement—Of the three stylized field states, probably none has drawn more research attention than this last one. Whether the analyst is interested in the general issue of order and change in society or the dynamics of conflict and transformation in the specific field in question, it is hardly surprising that a good many researchers are drawn to those rare moments when the routine structure of social life has dissolved and the possibilities for real change are at their peak. The central goals of such inquiries are threefold. The researcher will want to identify (1) the factors and processes that precipitate the crisis, (2) the actors and events that shape the episode over time, and (3) the interactive dynamics that bring it to a close. These general goals reduce to the following specific research questions:

- What mix of exogenous "shocks" and internal processes precipitate the field crisis?
- What specific social processes mediate between the destabilizing events and the actual mobilization of challengers?
- With what forms of action and collective action frames do incumbents and challengers respond to the developing crisis? How do these change over the life of the episode?
- What role do key external actors/strategic action fields play in precipitating the episode, shaping its trajectory, and ultimately helping to affect a new field settlement?

- What are the terms of the new settlement? And to what extent does it alter the prior power structure of the strategic action field?
- How do the crisis and the new settlement affect proximate fields?

In sketching this roadmap, we want to make clear that we are not arguing that those interested in fields are somehow obliged to embrace the full research agenda defined by these questions. Many analysts will, as we have suggested, be interested primarily in those moments of crisis that portend significant changes in a given strategic action field. Others may be focused on the origin of fields, still others on the means by which fields adapt to changing circumstances in order to reproduce them. In addressing all three major field "states," we have simply tried to provide a list of key questions that have concerned us as researchers and to which we think the theory is responsive. Having tried to sketch an over-time roadmap to the study of field emergence, institutionalization, and change, we turn in the next four sections to what we see as some of the thorniest empirical issues that researchers will need to grapple with if they are to employ the perspective on offer here.

How to Tell If a Strategic Action Field Exists

While observing a field in formation is often difficult, defining the phenomenon is relatively easy. If two or more organizations or groups are attempting to attain ends that are sufficiently similar that they are compelled to take one another's actions into account in their behavior, then we can say that we are observing an attempt at field formation.

A related but more difficult problem is deciding who is and who is not a member of a strategic action field. Some views of fields have been quite expansive. So, for example, Scott and Meyer (1983), who use the term "organizational sector," and DiMaggio and Powell (1983), who use the term "organizational field," have argued that fields consist of not just the participants who are striving for whatever is at stake in the field but also all other participants, including the state and upstream and downstream groups that might be relevant to the field. Other scholars have taken a narrower view of field membership. Laumann and Knoke (1987), who use the term "policy domain," view fields as composed of actors who are orienting themselves to each other but also a defined set of policy goals. Bourdieu and Wacquant (1992) generally conceive of fields as places where there is something at stake. They suggest that all actors who are orienting their actions to one another are members of the field.

In this project, we have embraced the narrower view of fields. So, for us, field membership consists of those groups who *routinely* take each other into account in their actions. This excludes from membership a host of other groups that may be very important to the everyday functioning of the strategic action field. Consider the case of product markets. Producers in a market frequently orient their actions to their competitors (Fligstein 1996, 2001b; White 2004). Producers are obviously dependent for success on their suppliers, but suppliers generally do not command all that much of the producer's attention. Instead, the suppliers comprise a field of their own. In our analysis, at the boundary between the fields, there may be another field that exists that defines the relationship between the two fields.

Defining a field as being concerned with all of the players who have something at stake simplifies doing field analysis by making it clear who the players are and what the relationships are. The advantage of doing this is it focuses the analysts' attention on the players who are jockeying for position for particular purposes. The downside is there might be players on the edges of fields who are pivotal to what happens within the field. If there is a high degree of resource dependence of one field on another, the very nature of the dependent field will be shaped by this dependence. By putting the dependence outside of the field, one might misinterpret what the dynamics of the field are. One way of dealing with this issue is to treat all such players as being outside of the field. But this means that scholars have to be sensitive to how this kind of dependence affects players in the field and what tactics incumbents and challengers use to deal with this dependence.

Two other kinds of groups are constitutive of strategic action fields: internal governance units and states. Typically, the institutionalization of a field will involve the creation of one or more units whose mission will be to implement and routinize some aspect of field operation or otherwise support the maintenance of the status quo. Their specific duties can vary widely. They can collect and disseminate information to field members and/or various outside audiences. They can facilitate field governance. They can certify field membership or adjudicate disputes between members. They can lobby the state on behalf of the strategic action field or otherwise serve as the external public relations "face" of the strategic action field. And these are only the most common internal governance unit functions. Identifying these units and understanding their role in field reproduction is, for us, an important part of the overall analysis of a field.

States often play an important role in the constitution of a nonstate field. For example, government-certified organizations that allow a particular strategic action field to control the credentialing of people in the field operate as a kind of internal governance unit directly sanctioned by the government. To the degree that a particular field depends on the constitution of law or regulations granted by the state, a field may have state input into its very structure and the rules that underlie it. The field—and especially its incumbents—may depend critically on regular infusions of state resources (e.g., grants, subsidies) for support. Understanding the various links that bind nonstate to state fields is another crucial component of the analysis of a field. In some cases, the nature of these linkages may blur the conventional internal/external distinction. For example, are government regulators in the field or outside of it? Government strategic action fields that clearly operate within the bounds of the state, we believe, are distinct from the role of government-sanctioned strategic action fields. In our case study of the mortgage market, many of the state strategic action fields remained under the control of the executive and legislative branches of the federal government. In the case of the government-sponsored enterprises that came to be core players in the mortgage market, one can argue that the market was at least partially constituted as part of the state. Since regulators are not vying for gain in the field, it seems logical to put them outside of the field. On the other hand, to the degree that they are pivotal to adjudicating the relationships in the field, it seems awkward to put them outside of the field. And in the situation in which government organizations are players in the field, they certainly are part of the strategic action field.

This becomes crucial when scholars who focus on a particular field simply ignore pivotal relationships to actors outside of the field. This is one of the reasons we have paid so much attention to the issue of *external* field relations. Typically, field research has focused on the internal workings of a single strategic action field. These dynamics are obviously very important, but as we have tried to make clear, the long-term prospects for stability and change in a field are affected at least as much by threats and opportunities that arise outside of the field—usually in proximate fields or the state—as those within the strategic action field itself. To accurately capture the dynamics of any given field the analyst must, in our view, understand the internal structure and workings of the field *and* the broader set of relationships that tie any given field to a host of other strategic action fields (including various state fields). If the analyst understands the nature of these key linkages, then the issue of field membership is much less important. The key is understanding the crucial relationships that shape the field, rather than neatly differentiating those that are internal and external to the strategic action field. So, analysts' methods are incomplete to the degree that they do not embed their particular strategic action field in its most important contexts.

The issue of the role of government and law in fields helps to underscore the central importance of focusing on both internal field dynamics and external relations. If scholars start out with a narrow view of fields that does not produce a consideration of the impact of law and government, their view of the field will be truncated and inaccurate. Indeed, the problem with many network analyses of fields is that they frequently not only omit any substantive cultural understanding of the field but also ignore important external players (e.g., various state actors) in their internal structuralist mapping of the strategic action field.

Emergence, Stability, and Crisis, Part 1

Empirical analysts must be able to differentiate between three field "states": emergence, stability, and crisis. The differences between these conditions may be more of degree than sharp delineations. Fields may remain inchoate for long periods of time and may drift between being more and less organized. We earlier argued that one way to know whether a field had emerged was by the degree to which four elements of structure existed: a common understanding of what is at stake in the field (Bourdieu and Wacquant 1992), a set of players with known positions in the field, a common understanding of the rules in the field, and a way for actors to interpret the actions of others and frame their own as the "game" is being played.

We expect that actors in a settled strategic action field would share a common view of what is going on. Such a view does not imply that the division of spoils in the field is perceived as legitimate, only that the overall account of the terrain of the field is shared by most field actors. Here, we have in mind that actors occupy a position and they understand who is in what position in the field. One way of thinking about this is that actors know who their friends, their enemies, and their competitors are because they know who occupies those roles in the field. A common understanding about the nature of the "rules" in the field means that actors understand what tactics are possible, legitimate, and interpretable for each of the roles in the field. This is different from knowing what is generally at stake. This is the cultural understanding of which moves make sense as interaction in the field plays out.

While institutionalists are fond of referring to the "taken for granted" understandings that structure fields, the fact of the matter is that the interpretive frames that individual and collective strategic actors employ in a given strategic action field may be quite varied. Here, we consider the degree to which all actors actually share the same perception of what any other actor's actions mean an open question. We expect that actors will tend to see the moves of others from their own perspective in the field. In most fields, we expect that dominant or incumbent actors will have a frame of reference that encapsulates their view of the field, while dominated or challenger actors will have an "oppositional" perspective. The reactions of more and less powerful actors to the actions of others thus reflect their social position in the field, and their interpretation will reflect how someone in their position who perceives the actions of others as directed at "people like them" will react. Their reactions to those actions will be drawn from the repertoire of behaviors that they can mobilize under the rules in reaction to others given their position in the field.

In strategic action fields that are highly conflictual but stable, it is quite likely that challengers and incumbents will have quite different views about the nature of the strategic action field. The difficulty for the analysts is to see through these very different conceptions of the field to understand if there is enough of an underlying order to suggest a common view of the rules in the field. A field that is not yet organized might have multiple groups with quite different conceptions of what is at stake. These groups could differ on means, ends, and/or methods. Such a field will not yield an overriding social structure that defines the positions of actors. Indeed, the nature and relationship between these positions will be central to the conflict. Even in more organized social spaces, there could be substantial differences of opinion about what is going on. This suggests that the difference between organized and unorganized space could be quite subtle.

The problem of telling the exact state of a strategic action field is so difficult precisely because of these differing collective projects that are inherently and continuously contestable. The presence of incumbents and challengers virtually ensures some level of contestation, not just according to the rules that exist and are being enforced but also over the rules themselves. Challengers realize what is going on and often acquiesce, but that does not mean, even in the most stable strategic action fields, that they do not have an alternative conception of the field, including a collective identity that challenges its fundamental meanings and relations. In social space that is emerging or entering crisis, contestation may *not* appear to be more bitter or fundamental than in stable social space. Therefore, the analyst is always confronted by the fact that crisis can seem sudden, and often it is difficult to assess how deep it runs.

Before a single set of rules governing action emerges, one can speak of competing definitions of the situation. These varying cultural conceptions can be viewed as projects that given sets of actors are trying to create and impose on other actors. During the emergence of a strategic action field, there may be much confusion about these projects. It is up to the analyst to try and figure out which cultural conceptions might end up dominating. One of the tasks facing scholars is to figure out at the emergence of a strategic action field what are the realistic projects that might actually happen. In practice, given the nature of what is at stake in any given field, there are usually only two or three such cultural conceptions in any given field that are realistic cultural projects. This makes the analysts' task easier because they are not trying to sift through an infinite amount of information but instead are trying to understand what projects actually appear to have sufficient support and resources to be viable.

Where things are fluid, our approach forces the analyst to consider all of the possible alternatives in that situation. If there are multiple collective projects available, then the analyst must focus on what they are and consider how the actors involved choose to engage in strategic action. While resources available to actors in emergent situations matter a lot, the ability to engage in creative forms of collective action that involve expansion of collective identities can be pivotal. Where strategic action fails, one might even predict the collapse of the social space. Taken together, our view forces the analyst to do more than just tell the story of how the winners were inevitable. Instead, the analyst must carefully specify the players, consider their resource endowments, understand the nature of the collective projects at stake, and study what courses of action were possible and then successful or unsuccessful. This will force the analyst to uncover surprising or subtle results.

This raises another important and difficult problem: that of deciding what a resource is. Access to money is an important resource in many fields. But the kinds of resources that one might expect to be important are quite numerous. Scholars have emphasized how human capital, cultural capital, and social capital (e.g., networks and who you know) might all be pivotal to who wins in a field. Social capital is the vaguest form of capital because it can be any kind of social connection. The idea of social capital does not specify who the important actors are or to whom one must be connected to gain power. Thus, if one does a field analysis and discovers that some social connections seem to matter, one can have a hard time a priori deciding *why* some social connections matter and others do not.

Even more troubling is that these categories do not exhaust all possible resources that can be exploited by groups in the field. So group size, access to government, existing law, knowledge of various organizing technologies, and other external allies all play a role in who in a given strategic action field might be able to gather the resources either to form a political coalition or dominate the field. Indeed, one of the most difficult challenges for a researcher is to identify the key resources that allowed a particular actor/coalition to carry the day. Most field analyses set out to discover this empirically. This is not totally wrongheaded. If one considers strategic action field situations to have three elements—rules, resources, and social skills—one expects that rules and resources will be the most frequent determinant of who is able to organize a strategic action field and how incumbents keep their power once in place. In situations with great resource asymmetries, challengers will generally be too resource poor to compete successfully.

An interesting situation occurs, however, when materially disadvantaged challengers win. If they win, then some set of unknown factors must have come into play. From a logical point of view, challengers may actually have resources that have been underappreciated or misunderstood. The opportunity to create change that comes from a crisis means that such resources all of a sudden might become more important to control the strategic action field. Another source of crisis is a change in the rules that are imposed on a strategic action field. Again, such changes might present opportunities to challengers to shift the balance of power by using resources that were previously held in check or irrelevant. The problem of when social skill becomes pivotal to field formation and transformation is also quite complex. One wants to invoke such a possibility very carefully and with a certain amount of reluctance. Part of what socially skilled actors can do is to appreciate the changed circumstances of a field and then wield new or previously underused resources in a new way. We will return to this issue later in the chapter.

The Problem of the State in Relation to Strategic Action Fields

It is also useful to explicitly consider how one would study the role of the state from our perspective. There are two arenas of action: the relation between the state and the strategic action fields of society and actions within the state strategic action fields themselves. Since most of the quarrel within the state is over tactics with regards to the regulation of strategic action fields, it will often be difficult to separate these issues. But analytically, they remain independent. State actors have their own interests, identities, and institutional missions, which routinely affect nonstate fields. But, of course, the process can work in exactly the opposite fashion: important groups or organizations in established (or emerging) fields can take their grievances to the state and attempt to control the agenda that will regulate relations in their fields. Empirically, it will usually be obvious which case is occurring. Scholars tend to choose to study one end of the process or the other. Of course, if one studies some part of this process historically, what can initially look like the state responding to demands to organize a strategic action field can eventually turn into state agencies setting the subsequent agenda for action in that field.

This introduces two additional ideas. There is likely to be feedback between state and nonstate fields. As situations change on either side, this feedback will have consequences for the boundaries and nature of strategic action fields both in and outside of the government. The result is an iterative stimulus–response "dance" involving state and nonstate actors. Of course, the relationship between what goes on in the strategic action fields of the state and the rest of society can also have unintended consequences. The passage of a law may affect a large number of strategic action fields in intended and unintended ways. Many studies of strategic action fields begin by looking at these kinds of consequences.

One important empirical marker of a strategic action field is formal "certification" by the state (McAdam, Tarrow, and Tilly 2001). If there are legal rules defining the social order of the strategic action field that strongly reinforce the underlying order, then one is almost certainly looking at an organized strategic action field. For example, the delivery of health care is dominated by medical doctors. Doctors and medical boards have gotten the government in the United States to allow them to control the supply and certification of physicians. This gives them a great deal of power and a monopoly over the practice of medicine.

The state may regulate in a large number of ways. Some of the most common forms of regulation include the promulgation of formal property rights, the creation of regulatory bodies, the establishment of legal guidelines for assessing what is fair and unfair economic competition, and the setting of tax rates for the kinds of collective entities that typically comprise fields. The analyst can tell how the balance of power is set up in a strategic action field only by explicitly considering the role of the state in that field. This is one of the fundamental mistakes of organizational theory and sometimes social movement theory; that is, they use the state in an ad hoc fashion and invoke it either as the enemy or as an actor that might occasionally muck things up. However, it is impossible to evaluate any form of strategic action in a field without considering the history of state intervention in that particular arena.

The fervor of regulatory agencies is very much related to the politics of who is running the government, the composition of the membership in that agency, the ideological commitment of those actors, and the current crises in the strategic action fields that these agencies regulate. Sometimes, such agencies can precipitate a crisis in fields and then mobilize to help resolve the crisis through a restructuring of the strategic action field. Other times, those agencies can appear to be captives of the strategic action field they are set up to govern. At still other times, crises in nonstate fields can spill over and destabilize state strategic action fields. One could speculate that crises in the field or more generally in the economy or polity are likely causes of increased action by such agencies and provide actors in those agencies with the relative autonomy for innovative action.

Emergence, Stability, and Crisis, Part 2

As we argued in chapter 2, different forms of strategic action make more sense under different field states (i.e., emergence, stability, and crisis). This carries with it an important methodological implication. One way to make sense of the state of the field is to examine the kinds of actions in which groups are engaged. This will give a clue as to the nature of current conditions (Fligstein 2001a). It is equally important to consider the emergence, stability, and transformation of strategic action fields in specific historical cases. It is here that the theoretical framework sensitizes the analyst to the nature of the events and the possibility for social change in given fields. For instance, one should be able to reconstruct, from historical evidence, the character of strategic action fields at any given point in time. The first step requires that the analyst determine whether a strategic action field exists or, alternatively, whether organizations or groups are struggling to produce one. Next, one needs to decide who the major players are and how they conceive of strategic action. Finally, at the initial point in time, one must establish what, if any, rules the state has produced to guide action and the relation between the state and the strategic action field under consideration. Armed with this knowledge, the analyst ought to be able to suggest what courses of action are possible and impossible.

Even though we argued that unorganized strategic action fields are the most difficult to make predictions about, one can try and gain some analytic leverage on them. It is a good bet that the state will play some role in producing stability for unorganized strategic action fields. While this assertion may not seem very original, it is often the case that scholars, particularly in organizational theory, do not explicitly factor the state into their analysis of field emergence/development. While the state usually does not directly produce the strategic action field, it will often be called upon to certify or enforce some order in that field. Institutional entrepreneurs not only will look to other organizations or groups in the field for support in trying to construct a field that works for them and their partners, but will try to explicitly factor the state into the process as well.

In fields that are in emergence, one would expect a multiplicity of collective identities and a division of resources. One would want to be sensitive to the initial distribution of these resources. In cases where a very large share of resources is concentrated in one group and other groups are fragmented, basic rational choice processes might be operating. Far more interesting are those cases in which no group enjoys a significant resource advantage over other contenders. Here the analyst must be sensitive to a wide variety of factors, including ties to powerful external allies—especially state actors—and variation in social skill.

There are a number of ways for an analyst to measure the degree to which the identities of the various positions in the field and the underlying conception of rules in the field are stable. Survey or field methodologies could be used at multiple points in time to assess these. One would expect that in stable fields, the pecking order of groups and organizations would remain fairly constant and views of appropriate behavior would remain constant and consensually shared. If these methods prove impossible because of the historical nature of the case, it should be possible, using archival methods, to reconstruct the cultural rules of the most important organizations and groups and their emergence and spread to other groups. Similarly, if an innovative tactic was employed successfully, we would expect to see it spread across organizations in the field.

Another approach to the study of stability involves research on the key strategic actors themselves. The leaders of organizations do not just represent themselves but also embody important collective qualities of the groups or organizations they direct. Indeed, one can argue that succession struggles in organizations or groups are a good way for an analyst to identify ascendant groups within organizations or fields as well as the new ideas or action frames that are motivating their actions. For instance, one would expect that in stable strategic action fields, leaders of organizations would be homogeneous in their backgrounds. In newly formed strategic action fields, one would expect that the incumbent groups' or organizations' leadership would provide leverage in challenger organizations for leaders who resemble the dominant group's leadership. We would expect that to the degree that a set of understandings comes to organize a strategic action field, the leadership in all organizations would become more homogeneous.

Perhaps the most critical methodological problem involves measuring the degree to which a strategic action field is in crisis and therefore ripe for transformation. This is both a conceptual and an empirical problem. Conceptually, the notion of crisis is fuzzy and can be read into lots of more routine conflicts within a strategic action field. Here, we have argued that crisis must refer to a situation in which the legitimacy of the principles of the field is being threatened such that they no longer are able to deliver valued ends. One empirical indicator of the crisis in a field is the inability of incumbents to reproduce themselves. When incumbents in the field begin to fail, this is a sign that the underlying principles of the field are not working. One would expect challenger organizations to fail all of the time. But the failure of incumbents means that something is undermining the basic principles of the field.

Unlike more routine conflict processes, a true crisis results in an "episode of contention," by which we mean a temporally bounded period of intense contestation during which the rules and power relations of a given field are very much up for grabs. Such episodes are experienced as clear and distinct ruptures in the social and political fabric and taken for granted routines of the strategic action field. Examples of such episodes are rife in the social movement literature: the occupation of Tiananmen Square by Chinese students in the spring of 1989, the aftermath of the disputed election in Iran in the summer of 2009, the Little Rock school desegregation crisis of September 1957, the Tahir Square protests that led to the ouster of Hosni Mubarak at the height of the 2011 Arab spring—all are canonical examples of movement-initiated episodes of contention. Less well known, but just as memorable for those affected, are the crises that periodically destabilize firms, churches, industries, cities, and other strategic action fields. Examples of these lesser known episodes include the following:

- an attempted hostile takeover of a company
- a prolonged strike
- succession crises within an organization
- the rise of apostate groups within a religious body

Like the better known social movement examples, all of these—and many other types of—contentious episodes are marked by a sharp rupture in the routine institutional understandings and practices of the field.

How is the empirical analyst to recognize the onset of an episode? In the following quote, McAdam touches on two key empirical markers of such crises: "The result is a *generalized sense of uncertainty* within the field and a shared motivation to engage in *innovative contentious action* to advance or protect group interests" (2007: 253; emphasis added). The episode is expected to last "as long as enough parties to the conflict continue to define the situation as one of significant environmental uncertainty requiring sustained mobilization to manage or exploit" (1999: xxvii). There is a clear methodological implication here. Two operational measures of a crisis are a shared sense of uncertainty on the part of members of the field and a rise in innovative, contentious action within the strategic action field. The former might be gleaned through survey or interview data and the latter by observing and coding actions by incumbents and challengers.

We can imagine other measures as well. A time-sensitive accounting of groups in the field is expected to show a sharp rise in foundings and deaths during crises, as new groups arise to take advantage of the situation and others dissolve amid the chaos. Another marker is the actual measurement of whether or not incumbents are able to deliver ends to their members. This, of course, needs to be measured in terms of votes, profits, political change, legal victories, clients served, or whatever unit of measurement makes sense. On the basis of this type of systematic evidence, one should be able to assess how close to crisis a strategic action field is. If the current organizations or groups are attaining ends, then even in a turbulent environment, one would not argue that the field is ripe for transformation.

One final measure of crisis is intervention by outsiders, whether it be state or nonstate actors. In this case, one should be able to measure pre- and post-effects of changes in rules on outcomes of organizations or groups. To the degree that outcomes are disrupted, one can predict that the strategic action field is either in or on the verge of crisis. For example, if the state changes the rules in the field by directly attacking the dominant principles that allow incumbents to dominate or a political coalition to cooperate, then one would predict that this would have a negative effect on the ends of incumbent groups and organizations. To the degree that this proves to be true, a new arrangement will likely emerge that is more in line with those rules. In the case of outside invasion by other organizations, one can compare the performance of outside organizations and groups to those on the inside who continue to stick with what has been working for them. If the outside groups outperform the insiders or if the insiders actually start to fail, then one would predict that in the next period of observation, the insiders will begin to adopt the outsiders' way of doing things.

We close this section with one final methodological suggestion regarding the study of an episode of contention. We have argued that in crises, incumbents will continue—at least for a while—to try and enforce the social order. Therefore, the indication that a crisis is imminent is expected to come from the actions of challengers rather than incumbents. The innovative action that is one of the hallmarks of a contentious episode will come first from challengers, with incumbents continuing to act in conventional ways.

Social Skill, Strategic Action, and the Question of Entrepreneurship

At the core of our theory are our ideas about social action and what we call social skill. We begin with the idea that social life works because at every instant people act. Every day, whether people recognize it or not, they produce social life anew. Our amazing ability to do this and do it with little forethought is part of what is interesting about humans. Now, of course, social life is reproduced along many set paths. The theory of strategic action fields is about how once in place, the mesolevel social orders that structure our lives offer us anchors as to what to do, when to do it, and, of course, how to do it. There exist rules and resources that we draw on (or are victimized by!) as we go through the motions of what we do every day. Those rules and resources constrain *and* enable us.

In order for a strategic action field to be reproduced, however, the people involved have to act. In order to get what they need, people have to interact with others. They must communicate who they are, and they must engage in acts of coordination in order to achieve desired ends. Social skill is the ability to empathetically understand situations and what others need and want and to figure out how to use this information to get what you want. At the level of strategic action fields, the problem is for individual and collective strategic actors to align their actions with those they depend on and to compete with those who want the same things. Social skill is the lubricant that makes social life work. Rules and resources exist and are building blocks. But without the social skill of people who interpret these rules and mobilize these resources, the rules and resources do not matter all that much.

Sociologists have been struggling with the problem of agency for at least the past twenty-five years. With the exception of Mead, classical sociological theorists pretty much take actors out of the equation in their accounts of social life. In Marx's theory, social classes are actors and people who are in such classes are the bearers of such structures. In Weber, the cultural meanings actors share determine what they do. Once we understand those meanings, actors themselves are not important to understanding social action. In Durkheim, the moral order of society largely determines who people are and what they do. People mostly behave in a normative fashion either because they fear social sanction or because they seek out social approval. In all of these theories, social forces compel action, while individuals are largely the passive instruments of these forces.

This tendency to see individuals as products rather than architects of social life plays out in funny ways in contemporary sociology. The problem is that most sociologists are caught in the same trap as classical theory. They believe that everything is the product of social structure and that no matter what anyone thinks, that structure is way more powerful than people. Racism, sexism, classism, ageism, and other forms of discrimination are structurally induced. But if all of the ills of society are determined by social structure and there is little individual agency in social life, then there is no opportunity to actively change society through a critique of these forces. The structures are stronger than ideas or actors who might be in a position to make social change.

This plays out in institutional theory in organizational sociology in a way that profoundly affects contemporary scholarship. The Meyer and Rowan (1977), DiMaggio and Powell (1983), and Jepperson (1991) view of institutional action is that once a set of rules and resources becomes institutionalized, they become "taken for granted." The implication of this perspective for an understanding of how fields work should be clear. Very quickly, fields become powerful systems that automatically reproduce themselves without the need for people to do anything. Institutions take on a life of their own, and people are reduced to automatons who "download scripts" that tell them what to do.

Scholars in this literature have been struggling to reconcile this structural determinist view with grudging recognition that significant piecemeal social changes are ongoing in strategic action fields and more wide scale social change, though rare, does in fact happen. Notwithstanding the empirical fact of social change, the institutionalist argument remains dominant in sociology. Changing existing fields is seen as exceedingly difficult. Besides the coercive force embodied in these systems, people accept them as real and natural. This makes them virtually impossible to change. So, attention has turned instead to the creation of new social fields. Here, absent the force of the "taken for granted," we find a real chance for agency, that is, for individual actors or groups to make a real difference in the organization of social space. There has been an outpouring of scholarship that looks at moments of political, institutional, or cultural entrepreneurship. In these studies, scholars know that some individual or group made a big difference to the outcome in constructing a social space. They become the "hero" of such stories. Frequently, they come from nowhere, invent entirely new forms of action, and then work to institutionalize the resulting field.

This model has a funny view of human agency. For most aspects of human life, people are viewed pretty much as robots, even downloading "scripts" that play the part they have in the fields in which they participate. They do so according to rules that define who they are and what they can do in any given situation. In living day to day they are merely playing out scripts. But every so often, some people or groups acquire agency. They get to act in new or innovative ways. Then, once the new field is institutionalized, they turn back into the role-playing, nonthinking, habitual, script-following creatures of institutional theory.

There are two problems with this story from our perspective. First, the idea that the only time that people have agency is when they are helping to form new social fields is odd to say the least. Our everyday experiences suggest that we exercise at least some degree of agency all of the time. We show up, we do what needs to be done, and if it does not get done, someone suffers the consequences. Agency is everywhere in social life. A theory of action that posits that occasionally some people get to be actors and then they stop is an odd theory.

Second, it ignores the fact that social life is largely played out in fields. Our theory of action stresses that individuals or groups are always acting and they are always looking for an edge. But it is the structuring of those fields that determines which kinds of action make sense. The position we occupy in a field has a huge effect on how we enact our capacity for agency. In settled fields, incumbents will generally work to reproduce their advantage, while challengers can be expected to jockey for position and look for signs of any crack in the system that might reward more innovative forms of action. But make no mistake, agency is on display even in the most settled of times. As we argued in chapter 4, there is always some change going on in strategic action fields. Groups and individuals are confronted with opportunities and constraints all of the time. They are able to try and improve their situation, or they may be the victim of someone else's strategic project. Fields do not stay constant; they constantly change. Scholars who believe that they understand how fields are reproduced are wrong. Field reproduction requires a lot of work by skilled strategic actors in incumbent organizations. Their counterparts in challenger groups need to constantly work to maintain whatever positions they have. This implies a research agenda that is now almost nonexistent (for an exception, see Thelen 2004). Scholars should study how groups in a particular field are able to reproduce themselves on a period to period basis. Their tactics for doing so and their ability to adapt has not been well documented.

To repeat, the organization of the field is what determines what kinds of strategic action make sense. Skilled strategic actors are well aware of the rules and resources and the current state of their fields. Their social skill gives them an understanding of where they stand, what their opportunities are, and what constraints they face. The most skilled actors are able to mobilize others no matter what their current position, either as incumbent or challenger.

From our position, the idea of entrepreneurship misses the fact that the opportunity to be an entrepreneur depends critically on the current state of the field. It should not be a surprise that entrepreneurs appear not in settled social fields but in those that are emerging or those that are on the verge of transformation. Indeed, we are tempted to say that "entrepreneur" is just another name for those skilled actors who come to the fore in emerging or destabilized fields. We do not, however, hold to quite such a determinist view. Entrepreneurs can be found in stable fields as well. It is just that they rarely succeed in such settings.

The position of entrepreneur is not a disposition or a quality of an individual, it is instead a role that is available under certain conditions of social fields. Entrepreneurs can act to bring together other groups in a political coalition in a social movement–like fashion by forging collective identities that allow the structuring of the field. They do so by recognizing what the system gives them. So, they are likely to build a coalition under conditions in which no one group can obviously be dominant. But these same skilled strategic actors may also realize that their group has the most resources and can act to crush or dominate the opposition in a social field. It is this recognition by actors of the structural situation in which they find themselves that gives them the opportunity to help forge new social space.

Having said that, it is easy to overestimate the ability of skilled strategic actors to make a difference even in these fluid situations. This is because they often confront other groups with strategic actors that possess the same skill to organize the field. Even in these fluid situations, resources will matter a lot. The ability to deploy money, connections to the government, connections to other important social actors, and ideas about how to organize and bring together other groups are distributed across socially skilled actors in groups. They will use whatever resources they have to exploit the system for gain.

One of the main ambiguities in such situations is exactly what a resource is. In some ways, actors have to use what they have. They may or may not know if what they have is powerful enough to allow them to organize the field. But they will take what the system gives and use it as a resource. In an emerging field, the value of those resources may not be apparent and the actual resource dependencies may not be clear. Here, again, skilled strategic actors will use what is available to mobilize collective action. So, their position in a given emerging structure will be pivotal to what they can accomplish.

It is useful to consider a case that illustrates some of these points. Rendered in our terms, Ganz (2000, 2009) considers the emergence of the United Farm Workers in California during the late 1960s and early 1970s an example of a field that was organized by actors who appear to have little chance of success. Ganz argues that there were two groups trying to organize farmworkers in this historical period. One was based in the American Federation of Labor and Congress of Industrial Organizations (AFL-CIO). Here, the established, powerful union came to California with a large number of organizers and a lot of money in order to organize farmworkers. Cesar Chavez was a local organizer with few resources. Ganz argues that while Chavez did not have money or organizers on the ground, he did have good social connections to the local communities he was trying to organize. Ganz argues that Chavez overcame the advantages of the larger and better equipped AFL-CIO representatives to create a new field by founding the United Farm Workers of America and making them a force to be reckoned with. Ganz's argument is that Chavez's deeper connections and understanding of the community he sought to organize and his commitment to the struggle afforded him the superior social skill needed to offset the material advantages of the AFL-CIO.

While we would agree that Chavez was a remarkable leader who was unmistakably able to mobilize people with his words, we think that this case shows the difficulty of understanding exactly what a pivotal resource in a particular situation is. Chavez just happened to command a critically important resource for the mobilization of poor communities, that is, knowledge of and embeddedness in that community. This suggests that before one attributes what happens in a particular social field to the charisma or genius of an entrepreneur, one needs to carefully consider how to value the kinds of resources that groups bring to organizing any strategic action field. Having strong local ties and support certainly helped in the United Farm Workers' struggle. It provided community support and allowed Chavez to use many preexisting social channels such as churches, schools, and community organizations to communicate directly with workers. It meant that it was easier to convince farmworkers they should support Chavez because they were more familiar with the people on his side.

This does not mean that Chavez did not have social skill. After all, he did have to recognize that he had the political opportunity to organize an entirely different kind of union. He also realized that he did not have much money to work with and he did not have access to professional organizers. This pushed him to create a more social movement–like structure, one in which people participated because they believed in the cause. He was able to engage these people because they knew him or his principal advisers. He took what the system gave him and recognized that he could mobilize local communities more effectively than the better funded AFL-CIO.

It is interesting to consider a thought experiment about this situation. What if Chavez had worked for the AFL-CIO instead? Would he have successfully founded the union? Would another person with social skill have been able to oppose him by organizing the local communities more effectively? Would we now know that person's name instead of Chavez's? To believe that Chavez made the difference in the situation, one would have to believe that he would have accomplished the formation of the union whichever social position he operated from. One can be sufficiently confident that an equally skilled person who was able to mobilize the community might have defeated Chavez, charisma and all, because in the end the most important resource was the ability to mobilize the community. The genius (or luck) was to figure that out.

Social skill is everywhere, and it is important to the production of social life. Socially skilled actors do see opportunities where others do not. They are able to occasionally take advantage of the system in ways that are novel and unique, and they sometimes build unlikely political coalitions to produce entirely new social fields. But one needs to be careful about delineating such roles and overinterpreting the ability of such actors to be decisive. Actors are everywhere and always acting. But they are also taking advantage of their resources, their positions, their relationships, and the rules. That in emerging social space, they appear to play pivotal roles seems self-evident. But one needs to be careful about giving such actors too much credit and not seeing that what they were able to mobilize was as important as their skill in doing so.

Considering Different Philosophies of Science and Methodological Strategies

Although our framework can be applied across a large number of settings, it does not take into account the wide variety of structural and cultural contexts in which strategic action occurs. The battle over abortion rights in Germany, the competitive struggles in the auto industry, and the emergence of a post-Cold War international order have nothing to do with each other in a structural, cultural, or substantive sense. But in our framework, they have a great deal to do with one another as cases of embedded strategic action. One of the reasons that political sociology, social movements, and organizational theory have grown up more or less ignorant of one another as subfields is that scholars have focused on the substance of action in those fields. So political sociologists care about such things as the determinants of voting, organizational theorists care about such issues as the diffusion of organizational forms, and social movement theorists care about variation in movement outcomes.

If our framework makes sense, it is because we can abstract from the particularities of any given case to the more general factors that are likely to prove decisive for the case. But it remains to the analyst to understand the unique nature of power in the strategic action field under examination in terms of the distribution of rewards, coercion, resources, and culture. Armed with a view toward the strategic action situation in a strategic action field, the analyst can then decide how to think about what is dominating and what is contestable.

We do not want to give up the possibility that many of the deep strategic action field processes in fact are subject to more systematic principles even given what we just said about how knowledge about a particular context matters. The theory of strategic action fields is a flexible set of concepts and relationships that apply across a large number of settings. But its flexibility extends beyond just the number of settings. The concepts in the theory are amenable to use by scholars with radically different philosophies of science. Moreover, both quantitative and qualitative methods have been used with field theory profitably. It is useful to explore how scholars with quite different orientations have used field theory to understand their objects of study. We do not think it is necessary to take a strong philosophical or methodological position on strategic action field theory in this chapter. Indeed, it is quite important to explore how varying conceptions of field theory have been used by different scholars to understand disparate phenomena. Instead, we note how others have used strategic action field theory and celebrate its generality.

Table 6.1 is an attempt to describe the link between various philosophies of science in regards to using the framework and both quantitative and qualitative

Table 6.1 **The theory of fields, philosophy of science, and social science techniques**

	Qualitative Techniques	*Quantitative Techniques*
Philosophy of Science		
Positivist (Theory Testing)	Case studies used to test critical parts of the theory	Large N data set to test propositions in theory
Realist (Concepts Explaining a Particular Case)	Interest in explaining particular phenomena of interest	Focus on particular industry, social movement, or political process in order to understand peculiar dynamics of the case; mechanisms of concepts inform analysis

techniques. Our assertion is that the framework in the earlier chapters can be interpreted differently by very different philosophies of science and is also amenable to being explored through a wide variety of research techniques. Table 6.1 breaks with many contemporary views of sociology that tend to conflate quantitative methods with positivist philosophies of science and qualitative methods with historical or more realist approaches. Instead, we argue that the goals of qualitative and quantitative researchers who use this conceptual framework will differ depending on their philosophy of science. More positivist analysts can use both qualitative and quantitative techniques to test the main propositions of our framework. Scholars who care more about their particular context (those who view the goal of social science as explaining concrete historical phenomena) will use the concepts and either qualitative or quantitative data to illustrate how things worked out in a particular context. It is useful to be explicit about these issues.

From the point of view of more historically oriented scholars, our theory can be seen as a set of orienting concepts that analysts can use to make sense of actions in a particular strategic action field. Here, the analyst is interested in getting the story right and making sense of what happened. This use of the framework produces research that contains a kind of sociological history in which the goal is to use concepts to make sense of how a particular set of actors get organized, stay in power, or perhaps find themselves supplanted by other actors. In this situation, the analyst is interested in the twists and turns of what actually happened in a particular situation. One can view this kind of analysis as realist in its philosophy of science (Keat and Urry 1975). By this we mean analysts believe there is a world out there that can be understood by getting at the underlying structures and mechanisms that produce the actual changes we observe. In this case, the underlying structure is the strategic action field, and the mechanisms revolve around how the field is constructed, who has what resources, what the nature of the settlement is in the field, and the current cultural understanding of the field by actors in the field about the nature of the "game" and their position in the field.

But the framework may be used in a more positivistic fashion as well. Positivism suggests that there is a set of covering laws that apply to many situations (Keat and Urry 1975). If the theory of strategic action fields is correct, we ought to be able to observe similar organizing principles across various kinds of strategic action fields. For example, one of our key assertions is that the relative size of groups at the formation of a strategic action field will determine the structure of a strategic action field. So a strategic action field made up of groups of the same size will tend to form a more cooperative strategic action field that looks like a political coalition. A strategic action field that begins with groups with very different resource endowments will, we believe, tend to develop a more hierarchical structure. This is an empirically testable proposition across a wide variety of fields.

As we suggested above, we are agnostic as to the ultimate ends of sociological research. There are passionate debates about whether or not sociology is a science. Many sociologists are skeptical of the claim that there are general theories of social interaction. The theory of fields, however, includes a highly flexible set of concepts that can be used by scholars of a more positivist bent. But it is equally amenable to scholars who want to understand "local cultures" and particular sets of events. We hope to offer some conceptual clarifications in this chapter that will help analysts who want to use the framework either as a set of orienting concepts or to test the adequacies of its central propositions.

It is useful to try and connect these two general goals to the use of qualitative and quantitative techniques in research on strategic action fields. Our basic argument is that both kinds of data can be used under either philosophy of science. Scholars interested in the historical emergence of particular industries, social movements, or political systems can profitably use both qualitative and quantitative techniques. It is also possible to test the propositions of the theory by using qualitative or quantitative data.

There are many good historical and case studies of the emergence of transformations of fields that rely on archival, interview, or secondary sources. Most of these studies begin by focusing on the way a field ended up being organized. The analyst then tries to reconstruct the origin and development of the strategic action field and the cultural understanding of the settlement in the field around which it came to be structured. Typically there is attention paid to key actors, frame competition, and the forms of organization and action that shaped the development of the field.

While we applaud these analyses, there are several shortcomings. These stem mainly from the failure to consider generic field processes. Many of these analyses do not take into account that at the emergence of a field, there are only a small number of possible outcomes, outcomes that are delimited by the number of players and their relative size. Moreover, by focusing on the actor and group that ultimately wins, the stories we have from these analyses take on a tone of inevitability where other paths could not have been pursued. We will consider such approaches in more detail and offer some suggestions for how to make those studies reveal more about the real strategic action field dynamics in a particular case.

There are a wide variety of quantitative techniques that scholars have used to assess the dynamics of strategic action fields. There have been a great number of studies that use various regression models, network analysis, sequence analysis, Markov models, event history analysis, lattice models, agent-based modeling, and correspondence analysis. From our perspective, these modeling acts have proved useful to understanding many strategic action field dynamics. But we argue that typically these forms of analysis are not rooted in a fundamental understanding of the field they are analyzing or the pivotal relationships that characterize the strategic action field. One of the frustrating aspects of such studies is that they often assume that the technique is isomorphic to the field. That is, the technique in and of itself defines the field. We argue that one needs to have a conceptual understanding of the field before one can apply such techniques. One way to understand this critique is to suggest that there is a lack of linkage between the theoretical arguments one might make about a particular field and the technique one uses to generate a quantitative analysis of that field. It is useful to develop this argument a bit.

Some scholars have tried to link the theory of fields tightly to a particular research technique. For example, Bourdieu (1984) argues that, because of its "relational" focus, field analysis implies the use of the technique called "correspondence analysis." DiMaggio (1986), on the other hand, argues that there is a special affinity between block modeling in network analysis and field theory. Let us be clear; we are fans of both of these techniques (among a host of others). But we reject the idea that field theory favors any particular type of technique or a small subset of quantitative techniques.

There is a complex relationship between the evolution of various quantitative and qualitative research techniques and the theoretical problems for which they are used. We understand the impulse to connect theory and technique together. Hannan and Freeman (1977) have claimed that the "right" way to apply population ecology is through the use of event history analysis. In using these techniques they often try to tightly link the theoretical processes they propose to the data they collect. But even here, they have also used other ecological models, for example, Lottka-Volterra equations, to study such processes as well. The general principles of field theory have generally not been incorporated into the evolution of various data analytic techniques. These techniques frequently do not take into account exactly what field theory implies theoretically. So, to the degree that a field might be organized in a hierarchical fashion, network analysis that focuses on joint ventures will miss the hierarchy in the field. This makes their results difficult to interpret from the perspective of theories of strategic action fields. In essence, the general social scientific techniques we use do not take account of the conceptual framework implied by the theory of fields.

This creates both a set of problems and a set of opportunities. It implies that many techniques might be used to get at the underlying structure of fields. This is certainly a good thing. But there is a tendency by the users of techniques, particularly quantitative techniques, to let the techniques substitute for theory. So, for example, whatever the results are of a particular data analysis, say sequence analysis, they are seen as equivalent to the real structure of the field under observation. This means there is a disjuncture between how fields actually work and the description that is implied by a particular form of data analysis. We will return to this issue and assert that the use of quantitative and qualitative models only makes sense if they are rooted in a fundamental understanding of strategic action fields.

A Positivist Approach to Strategic Action Fields

A positivist approach to the study of strategic action fields would begin by specifying how we would know if a strategic action field exists, what its key features are, and if the basic ideas we have about how it operates can be verified across a wide sample of strategic action fields. This effort is hampered by a number of problems, many of which are empirical. Data requirements for studying strategic action fields are quite high. This is because, theoretically, a field is defined by the relationships between all of the players who view themselves as members of the field. Finding those players and tracking their relationships is a huge challenge to scholars. Understanding the underlying rules of a field requires knowing the views and action of all the key actors in the field. And then there is the recurring issue of emergence, stability, and crisis. To study a single field over time requires multiple observations, sometimes over relatively long historical periods.

Scholars have chosen to deal with these problems in many ways. Most of the time, they restrict the number of potential actors in the field to the most important ones. Often, they observe the field, not continuously, but at intervals. Sometimes, scholars focus only on following the successful project that organized the field. Often, once they believe that they have understood the nature of action in the field, they use that understanding to try and predict what should subsequently happen given how they think the field operates. This means they treat the field as a black box and rely on their knowledge of the field's principles to predict what will happen.

A positivist approach to the study of fields would begin with a set of interrelated propositions that could be tested using various kinds of observational techniques. Table 6.2 presents a list of propositions that were developed in earlier chapters that could be usefully tested using quantitative and/or qualitative data. One of the main problems of field analysis from a positivist point of view is that scholars interested in using the strategic action field conceptual framework have not specified exactly how the underlying social processes might work in enough theoretical detail as to make them testable. Our attempt in this book is to push toward more specific conceptualizations of the structuring of fields to specify the underlying causal mechanisms by which such structures develop. We think it is possible to use the framework presented here to understand the conditions (1) under which fields emerge, (2) under which fields develop a hierarchical or coalitional structure, and (3) that encourage fields' development, stabilization, and transformation. If we are right about how strategic action fields work, then

Table 6.2 **List of propositions that might be tested from a positivist perspective**

Proposition 1: Initial resource allocations affect whether or not strategic action fields become organized hierarchically or cooperatively. The greater the inequality of initial resource distribution, the more likely the field will be hierarchical. Conversely, the existence of a set of groups of roughly equal size will encourage coalition building.

Proposition 2: Unorganized social spaces become organized through a crescive social process akin to a social movement. This means that such orders can coalesce very quickly to produce an incumbent–challenger structure. Strategic action fields are stable when they have role structures and rules governing action that are based on either hierarchical incumbent–challenger structures or political coalitions.

Proposition 3: New strategic action fields are likely to emerge near existing strategic action fields. They are likely to be populated by existing groups who "migrate" or offshoots of existing groups.

Proposition 4: Skilled actors of dominant groups generally defend the status quo even in a crisis. this means that they will make piecemeal institutional adjustments but otherwise seek to reinforce the key features of the prevailing field settlement.

Proposition 5: Strategic action fields are generally destabilized by external shock originating from other strategic action fields, invasion by other groups of organizations, actions of the state, or large-scale crises such as wars or depressions. Changes in external political coalitions or changes in external hierarchies can destabilize the basis of a strategic action field.

Proposition 6: States will be the focus of much action during episodes of contention, as both causes of crises and sites of contention to resolve the conflict. General societal crises are rare, but when they occur, they have the potential to destabilize fields across much of society.

Proposition 7: The more connected a strategic action field is to other strategic action fields, the more stable that strategic action field is likely to be. Similarly, new strategic action fields or those with few connections will be more resource dependent and more likely to be transformed.

Proposition 8: New frames and forms of action within a field will generally originate in invader or challenger groups. Skilled actors in these groups will attempt to use these news frames and/or forms of action to build a new political coalition based on interest or fashion a new set of cultural understandings that reorganizes the interests and identities of field members.

---

their basic features ought to conform to the logic of the interrelated propositions listed in Table 6.2.

It is useful to consider the logic of one proposition in order to explain how the propositions might be tested. Proposition 1 suggests that the initial resource allocations in a field often have a decisive effect on whether the field will have a hierarchical structure (i.e., a challenger–incumbent structure) once it stabilizes or will be more coalitional. Our goal is to suggest how one might go about assessing the veracity of this proposition using either quantitative or qualitative evidence. There are several interesting problems in using quantitative data to test this proposition. First, one needs to define the existence of a strategic action field. Here one needs to know the set of participants who occupy a given field. Then, one needs to define what resources exist in the strategic action field and the relative level of resource allocation across the strategic action field. This is one of the hardest issues to operationalize. So, for example, in commercial fields, having a large market share in a particular new business is one indicator of resources. But there might be others, such as how much capital a firm has, its relationships to important resource suppliers, and its linkages to key government actors. In practice, scholars tend to simplify what they mean by resources (even in this relatively straightforward case) in order to do their analyses. They assume that one measure of resources is enough. (This is an issue to which we return below).

Are there any existing quantitative data that suggest that large amounts of resources concentrated in a few firms at the beginning of a market create a hierarchical incumbent–challenger structure? Because scholars who have studied industry emergence have not chosen to look at the problem this way, they have not tried to model their data to get at this kind of outcome. But we do have several kinds of results that are consistent with this view. First, there is the literature on "first mover advantages" in markets. This literature suggests that those firms that enter the market first take a large amount of market share. As the market expands and new competitors appear, the size and market share advantages of first mover firms tend to reproduce their advantage. So, firms such as Apple, which produced the iPod and iPhone, dominate those markets from the beginning and maintain their advantage over time. From our perspective, this evidence is certainly consistent with the view that groups with more resources at the emergence of a field help create a hierarchical structure. Most of the time, however, this kind of analysis does not end up describing the whole field. In order to really get leverage on our hypothesis, one would have to go back to the data to more carefully scrutinize the relative size advantage of the first movers and to look at the effects of such initial advantages on the actual structure of the field. Reanalyzing such data would provide support for or against the proposition.

Similarly, research in population ecology has repeatedly reported that the size and age of a firm at the opening of a new market increases its odds of survival (for a review, see Carroll and Hannan 2000). This work is generally compatible with our view that, at the opening of a field, large organizations tend to be able to structure the strategic action field to their advantage and, by doing so, promote their longer term survival. But again, these works never look at the overall structure of the field from the perspective of field theory. Therefore an important research project would be to go back to the data gathered in these efforts and look not just at whether or not firms survived but also at whether the largest participants in the market were able to sustain their advantage over time. The existing population ecology data sets would also be quite useful to test whether hierarchical or coalitional structures emerge.

It is also possible to gather qualitative or comparative/historical data to evaluate this hypothesis. If groups have roughly the same size at the beginning of the organization of the field, then one can expect they will form some kind of political coalition. If groups are radically different in size, then the outcome is more likely to be hierarchal. Are there any historical or comparative studies that show this dynamic in action?

The study of early modern states in Europe by Henrik Spruyt (1996) offers an interesting case to test this hypothesis. Spruyt is interested in the emergence of state structures in Europe after 1200. He argues that two sorts of political structures emerged in this historical period, one that was city or region based in which a group of relatively small political entities would form some sort of larger political coalition and another in which hierarchical states eventually came to govern large territories. He presents two cases; the first case is the Hanseatic League and the second is the emergence of the absolutist state in France.

In the case of the Hanseatic League, Spruyt demonstrates that the league was formed by roughly similar sized trading cities. The league mainly emerged to offer military and economic protection to the traders that dominated each city. The cities formed an association to collectively govern their affairs. The emergence of this association was very much based on the fact that the member groups (i.e., the city-states) that joined were roughly of the same size. Instead of forming a hierarchical governing structure, they chose to produce an association based on cooperation in military and economic matters. In the case of France, there were much larger political units at the beginning of the state-building process. The largest of these political units fought a series of wars with the smaller units. In the end, the largest of these units formed the Bourbon monarchy by defeating their prime competitors.

Spruyt never frames his study as a study of the emergence of the political field in the two territories. So, his language is never the language we employ here. But the outcomes he describes in the organization of these fields look a great deal like our two possible outcomes: political coalitions or hierarchies. Consistent with our theory, his central causal mechanism turns out to be the relative size of the political units before unification.

We offer this brief survey of previous work not as definitive support for our propositions but rather as an illustration of how one might go about testing these ideas. Already existing studies may contain enough information that the data can be reinterpreted in terms of the framework presented here. In other cases, the scholars who have analyzed the data might not be working with the field concept. It might be possible to go back to their data and apply the field construct to see if the data do or do not support the propositions. Finally, it is always possible to add to existing case studies or data sets new variables in order to test the proposition.

Realist Approaches to the Study of Strategic Action Fields

Scholars whose work reflects a realist point of view have tended to pursue one of two interesting projects. The first centers on discovering the underlying structures and mechanisms that account for some particular phenomena of interest. By this, we mean that scholars believe the actual causes of something they observe are often not directly observable. These deeper structures can only be uncovered by using theory and surmising how we might either measure the underlying structures or show how their systematic variation causes what we observe. Much of sociology is inherently realist in that scholars begin with the idea that society exists outside and independent of our wills and deeply affects what we think and do.

Indeed, one of the key lessons we teach students in our introductory sociology courses is that their existence is not determined by their will or psychology but that who and what they are is very much the outcome of social structures. Our goal is to convince them that society is the underlying structure that explains the contours of social life and ultimately shapes their life chances. Moreover, their actions always occur in social contexts and therefore are determined by the opportunities and constraints that are presented to them as well as the social influence of others.

The second type of realist project is even more subtle in the context of doing research in sociology. Here, the idea is that while there are common ways in which societies work, the actual structure of mechanisms in a particular situation is the outcome of historical processes. So, for example, while all societies have gender roles, the variation in those roles across societies is the outcome of the history of such roles in each unique society. There is a tension between general theories and the historically determined outcomes favored by realist scholars. This tension sometimes puts the realist at odds with more positivist colleagues who want theories to be general and travel across time and space. Realist scholars frequently embrace the historical and comparative differences between societies and seek not to explain the general but to interrogate the differences between societies (for a spectacular example, see Mann 1986).

Another conflict between realist and positivist scholars concerns the issue of the link between what might be called theories of the midrange and the deeper structuralist understandings that realists prefer. Positivist sociology has created the research subfield structure that currently exists in sociology. Scholars have fashioned their theories at the subfield level (e.g., political sociology, social movements, and organizations). Increasingly, most sociological research is oriented to theories tailored to the specific empirical phenomenon central to a specific subfield. So, for example, scholars who are interested in government are often uninterested in social movements because they believe institutionalized politics requires a fundamentally different theoretical perspective than noninstitutionalized or "contentious politics." Social movement scholars believe that the emergent contentious politics of social movements have different dynamics than the settled politics of political sociology and can be fruitfully studied outside the context of institutional politics.

Our approach is corrosive of these distinctions in several ways. Part of the realist project is to discover deep structures that help explain disparate phenomena. Our main assertion is that there does exist a deeper structure to social, economic, and political life such that collective strategic action has similar roots and dynamics across the otherwise different arenas in which those actions take place. This is a profoundly realist assertion in that a conceptual understanding of these deeper social processes is necessary in order to gain empirical leverage over how these phenomena actually work. We note that, from a realist perspective, having a deeper theory of the structures underlying all forms of collective action does not reduce markets, politics, social movements, and organizations to the same thing. This would be a positivist interpretation of the theory, that is, that all of the things that make these sites different fundamentally do not matter for the outcomes. We note that some theories of collective action such as agency theory, game theory, agent-based modeling, and other versions of rational choice theory do have this as their goal. And a positivist could certainly assert that field theory as a deeper theory of collective action was such a general theory as well.

But a realist view implies that while the elements of the theory provide us with deeper concepts, in order to use the concepts, one needs to incorporate both the general structure of a situation and its unique cultural/historical context into one's analysis. So while the contemporary biotech industry and the collection of sects, churches, and religious orders that comprised Protestantism circa 1550 are both fields governed, we believe, by similar processes, an under-standing of these processes requires a deep knowledge of the historically and culturally contingent meanings that inform the actions and views of these two sets of actors. It is these "historically and culturally contingent meanings" that realist analysts seek to incorporate into their account of whatever field they are studying. Bourdieu's theory of fields is exactly this kind of realist theory (Bourdieu and Wacquant 1992).

Just as in the positivist approach to fields, quantitative and qualitative ap-proaches may be used to study the existence and dynamics of fields from a realist perspective. It is useful to examine both a quantitative and a historical account of two fields in order to explicate how the realist view of fields is used. Dirk Zorn has recently written about changes in the way that top management positions in U.S. corporations evolved from 1970 to 2001 (Zorn 2004). The historical prob-lem Zorn is interested in is how did the position of chief financial officer (CFO) emerge in U.S. corporations and why did it spread so fast across U.S. firms? It is useful to reframe his question in field terms.

The field in question is the field of the largest publicly held corporations. The issue at hand is who gets to claim to manage the largest firms. The largest corpo-rations in the United States have evolved a set of understandings about how they should be governed. These understandings are historical in nature and have shifted dramatically over the course of the past 150 years, as the nature of what large corporations do has shifted (Fligstein 1990). As a result, who has made the claim to power in those organizations has shifted as well (Fligstein 1987). Zorn takes this issue up in a contemporary context. Since 1980, U.S. firms have insti-tutionalized the position of the CFO. Before 1970, large corporations carried out most of their finance functions through a corporate officer called a "trea-surer." These people were not very powerful in corporations. Their main activity was to make sure that bills were paid and accounts were collected. But beginning in the mid-1970s, their role dramatically changed. Corporations upgraded the position and began appointing CFOs. These people engaged in financial engi-neering of balance sheets and became the firm's main liaison to the financial community at large. The CFO slot has now become the position that leads to higher corporate office such as the chief executive officer. Zorn's study is an at-tempt to understand historically what changed in the world of the largest corpo-rations to produce the rise and spread of CFOs.

Zorn uses history to construct his argument about the changing nature of competition among the largest American corporations. He then applies his his-torical analysis to a quantitative data set on the emergence of CFOs across large modern corporations. His historical argument identifies three phenomena that lead to the rise of CFOs. First, large corporations had highly diversified product lines. This meant that they were being managed according to financial criteria.

The person in the firm who had an obvious claim on financial expertise was someone who could be called the CFO. Zorn sees this process as the origin of the first CFOs. He argues that two other historical events encouraged the spread of CFOs. The first is a change in accounting rules in 1979 that forced firms to pay more attention to how they reported earnings. This gave impetus to upgrading the treasurer position and making that person more central to firm decision making. Zorn also argues that the decade of the 1980s, with its focus on maximizing shareholder value, also increased the concern with tools of financial engineering. Zorn's data analysis operationalizes the changes in these factors and shows how they explain the rise of CFOs.

Elizabeth Armstrong's (2002) study of the emergence of the gay and lesbian community in San Francisco between 1950 and 1994 is an exemplar historical study of the organization of a particular field. Armstrong's study tries to understand how San Francisco's gay and lesbian community went from only one or two representative organizations in the 1950s to several hundred times that many four decades later. She sees events in 1966–1968 as catalyzing this process of expansion. She is interested in the cultural frames that produced this change and how the community itself came to be organized. Her study begins with the organization of the gay and lesbian community in San Francisco after World War II. She argues that during this period, the community was not organized at all. Indeed, the idea that people who had sex with each other were in fact a community was not part of the vernacular at that historical moment.

Her study identifies three periods of the organization of the community. In the beginning the community created several organizations whose main purpose was to argue that gays and lesbians were in fact a group that deserved to have rights. In the context of San Francisco politics, she describes this period as characterized by homophile organizations looking to constitute gays and lesbians as an interest group that should be part of the politics of San Francisco. The issues on the table were mostly local and focused on forms of discrimination either by employers or the police.

For Armstrong, the key change comes in the late 1960s as the broader "New Left" splinters largely in response to the separatist turn in the civil rights/black power movement. Instead of interracialism and progressive coalition more generally, the New Left begins to fragment around an escalating "politics of difference." This is reflected in the beginnings of a new discourse in the gay and lesbian community. Instead of seeing homosexuals as an interest group, this perspective argues for "gay liberation" alongside similar projects for blacks, women, and Hispanics. The gay liberation movement provided a fundamental shift in the logic of organizing in the gay and lesbian community that caused people to focus less on politics and more on their right to be different.

Armstrong's most provocative argument is that gay liberation eventually turned into gay cultural identity. Here, the differences between groups within the community became celebrated by all. Any group that had a view of itself as a distinct identity was pushed to form an organization. This resulted in a proliferation of such organizations and the creation of a community organized around complex sexual identities. This has become symbolized by the yearly parade in San Francisco that is called the "Gay, Lesbian, Bisexual, and Transgender Parade." Armstrong's historical study shows how the field of the community was reorganized practically and culturally over time as new waves of people joined in creating new organizations. The organizing logic of the community—as with the New Left more generally—was that all identities were to be respected and represented.

The Zorn and Armstrong projects demonstrate quite clearly how a realist study of the evolution of a field can be carried out. Both ground their studies in a real historical context. But both view that context as a field. In Zorn's case, the existing field of corporations is transformed by the exogenous shock of the government changing accounting rules and by the shift in the largest corporations toward shareholder value as a set of guiding principles. These changes destabilize the field, affording new actors the opportunity to dominate large corporations—actors who can articulate how to be successful in the new order. In his case, these actors are CFOs.

Armstrong's case is the emergence and transformation of a community in a particular time and place. Her community goes through three phases of change. The first is a direct reaction to the repression of gay and lesbian people in San Francisco (an exogenous shock). The attempt to create a united front and a single organization to push for gay and lesbian rights is the dominant motif of this period. In the 1960s, the context of larger political movements profoundly shifts the language and understanding of the community. Instead of just asking for social protection, the gay and lesbian community shifts to celebrating difference and demanding liberation. This demand leads to a proliferation of lifestyles based on the differences among people in terms of their sexual orientation. The community becomes "liberated" by accepting and celebrating its differences. The underlying logic of both cases is decidedly focused on using fields as the basis of collective action. Yet both studies manage to honor the complexity of the historical and cultural context for the changes they observe. In this way, they offer a realist approach to using the theory of strategic action fields.

The Problem of Empiricism

Both positivist and realist approaches to using strategic action field theories start with the premise that one cannot make much sense of the empirical world if one does not have some idea about what drives a given social process. While they have different conceptions of theory and clearly a different theoretical agenda, both view theory as essential to observation. One of the big problems in sociology is a tendency for scholars to be more descriptive and empiricist in their acts of observation. This happens in both qualitative and quantitative research. The result is often a kind of description that is hard to interpret. One of the tenets of the philosophy of science is that all observation is theory laden. This means that even scholars who believe that they are only trying to do dense description are being guided by an implicit social theory.

From our perspective, this is one of the frustrating aspects of trying to create a more synthetic sociology. If scholars believe that the complexity of their case cannot be grappled with by theoretical simplifications, then they are unlikely to investigate the phenomena in such a way as to make it comprehensible to a broader audience. As scholars who work quite closely with graduate students, we frequently find ourselves asking the question, "What is that a case of?" Scholars get interested in some context and then study it in such a way as to make it difficult to generalize.

This danger exists with all observational techniques. Historical or comparative work forces analysts to consider what historical materials are relevant or, in the case of comparative work, exactly what they are comparing. Interviews and observational work can be maddeningly vague, but observers still have to impose some analytic structure on what they observe or ask in a particular situation. This is particularly problematic with quantitative techniques. It is quite possible to model a data set with high-powered data reduction techniques that are supposed to reveal the underlying "structure" of the data. The problem is that the search for those structures should not be left to the computer program, but instead should be consistent with a theoretical view of the underlying social processes. Many of the models people use to look for the structure of fields—network models, sequence analysis, diffusion models, Markov models, lattices, correspondence analysis, and smallest space analysis—are disconnected from any model of the field. So, while such models might in principle be used to detect the emergence of stable challenger–incumbent fields or to capture the shifting connections between groups over time, they rarely are. Most users of these models proceed as if the data will reveal such structures if they exist. But many of the models are not set up to look for core field dynamics. The kind of empiricism they embed will thus not likely lead to a productive partitioning of the field or understanding of its emergence and transformation. Without a view of what such social processes look like, data analysis techniques are generally powerless to reveal field-level dynamics.

Our core argument is that one should begin with the idea that collective action occurs in and around fields. Then one should model the ways in which collective action either does or does not form stable social spaces. The underlying structure of the spaces should mirror the underlying power arrangements in the field. Techniques should be mobilized to look for that structure. Techniques in and of themselves will only reveal incomplete answers about how the relationships between groups in fields might move over time. They do little to explain the positioning of actors in ongoing games and the possibility for the transformation of those games.

Conclusion

We are currently at the beginning of the systematic study of fields in sociology. While the field idea has been around since the 1970s, little progress has been made in systemizing what we mean by fields, how we study them, and how we understand and interrogate the contexts in which they appear. Scholars who study widely disparate phenomena such as firms, organizations, social movements, and religious and political institutions have only recently come to appreciate how their phenomena are related. But this realization has by and large maintained that social movements and firms are really different objects. So while social movements might affect firm behavior (Haveman, Rao, and Paruchuri 2007; King and Soule 2007), the two are in fact different things. Scholars have also tended to put up methodological barriers to one another by using either quantitative or qualitative techniques. They have tended to ignore one another and assume that their techniques in fact revealed the underlying structure of fields. Finally, field analysis has a complex relationship to epistemological issues such as the degree to which the theory of fields can be tested or is in fact a set of orientating concepts that can prove useful to scholars.

In this chapter, we have argued that in order to push field analysis forward, these barriers have to be both better understood and, ultimately, broken down. Most important, we believe that field dynamics are very general across arenas where social actors come to confront one another. When groups begin to organize new social space, it frequently resembles a social movement–like mobilization process because as the space becomes available more groups will try to populate it. Stable strategic action fields appear in the state and in markets, and governance is quite similar. Understanding the generality of field dynamics is the first step to using field ideas more systematically to make sense of the emergence, stability, and transformation of a wide variety of phenomena.

We have argued that both qualitative techniques and quantitative techniques can contribute to our understanding of fields. Quantitative techniques allow us to observe many groups over long historical periods. They allow scholars to observe the emergence of political coalitions and incumbent–challenger structures and observe how these structures can remain stable over time. They also provide for how shocks to such structures can be absorbed or force transformation of the field. Qualitative studies provide us with dense accounts of how individual fields evolve. They provide a grounds for directly observing the role of the state and law, the use of resources and position, and the ability to identify critical actors in the formation of strategic action fields. These techniques operate in a complementary rather than a contradictory fashion. They can be used to buttress arguments about the nature of particular fields.

Finally, we have argued for both a positivist and a realist approach to the empirical use of field theory. Field theory can be tested in a wide variety of settings. It makes predictions about what structure fields will have and how those structures can be stable. It also provides a way to understand how fields are transformed by providing tools to make us think about the role of crisis in the production of fields. But field theory is equally compatible with more realist approaches, approaches that focus on real historical phenomena.

We have clarified the theoretical nature of strategic action fields and proposed ideas about their main dynamics. We have linked them back to more macroprocesses. We have also tried to clarify the role of actors in strategic action fields. In this chapter, we have argued for how to study fields from a variety of perspectives and techniques. There are a great many projects that can be done with field theory. Scholars can reanalyze existing data in order to discover if the basic dynamics of fields can be verified. They can create new studies that employ some of the principles. We are quite sure that the methodological suggestions we have advanced in this chapter are only a beginning—the empirical equivalent of the theory itself. As we have invited other scholars in a range of disciplines and fields to engage creatively with the broader theoretical project, we encourage the same creative, collaborative approach to the systematic study of fields.

Toward a Theory of Strategic Action Fields

We have spent most of the book arguing for and seeking to illustrate a distinctive theory of strategic action fields. That is, the emphasis has been squarely on *our* conception of fields. But we opened the book with an extended acknowledgement of how much our perspective draws on the work of other scholars who have likewise come to see fields as among the central organizing features/templates of contemporary society. In bringing the book to a close, we return to this more collaborative focus and think through what it would take to overcome inter- but especially intra-disciplinary blinders and move toward a more cumulative understanding of fields. We use the chapter to do four things. First, we briefly touch on what we see as the most original aspects of our theory, relative to other perspectives on fields. Second, we discuss the general challenge of accumulating knowledge in sociology and more generally in the social sciences. Third, in light of this general problem, we note a very surprising thing: the discovery of fields is in fact a cross-disciplinary phenomena and, of course, it pervades thinking in many subfields in sociology. This lends support to our view that in spite of the differences in social science, something important is afoot around the theory of fields. Finally, in spite of this exciting collective discovery, there remain many issues that can only be resolved by close scrutiny of scholars working in different disciplines and subfields with different methods. We identify what we see as seven key issues that would need to be resolved in order to arrive at a general theory of strategic action fields. We close with a sketch of, and invitation for, a genuinely collaborative program of research and theory in this area.

So What Is New Here?

We have consistently acknowledged our debt to any number of scholars whose insights have shaped our thinking about strategic action fields, the central importance of meaning and identity in social life, the dynamics of contention, and a host of other topics. We will return to this theme in the next section when we discuss the promise of and challenges to the accumulation of knowledge in the social sciences and, in particular, in theory and research in the study of fields. But before we do so, we want—in this closing chapter—to highlight those aspects of our theory of strategic action fields that are distinctive relative to other perspectives on the topic. In particular, we see seven features of our approach as original.

1. *"The Existential Function of the Social" as Microfoundation*—We count our effort to ground our perspective in a distinctive microfoundation as the first unique feature of our theory. We want to close by being clear about what we see as the important analytic implications of this feature of our argument. It is all too tempting to interpret strategic action in fields as a simple matter of power, interests, and the play of instrumental motivations. But it is hardly the whole of the story, or perhaps even the most important part. What we tried to make clear from our brief foray into the most recent scholarship on human evolution is that we read the cultural "explosion" of roughly 45,000–50,000 years ago as signaling the rise of truly modern humans who suddenly—it would seem—possessed both an unprecedented capacity and *need* for meaning making, or more generally what we have termed the "existential function of the social." No longer was simple survival or the material function of the social the only game in town. Henceforth, the existential and the material would be simultaneously in play. Our point here is similar to Vaisey (2009), who argues that actors have a morality that causes them to view their actions in terms of what is good and bad and right and wrong. It makes no analytic sense to exclude this morality or meaning making in general from our theories of field-based strategic action.

Marx was famous for asserting the primacy of the material in social life. Here we reiterate the rejoinder to Marx that we offered in chapter 2. It is precisely because modern humans need and are relentless in their efforts to fashion shared meanings (like religious beliefs) and identities (like being Christian) to restrain existential doubt that these constructions are available to those (capitalists) who would appropriate and exploit them for their purposes. In short, the material/ instrumental and the existential are inextricably linked. Even as strategic actors are working to advance their interests, they are simultaneously exercising the distinctive human capacity for meaning making and the construction of collective identities. People do what they do both to achieve instrumental advantage *and* to fashion meaningful worlds for themselves and others or, more accurately, in our microfoundational view, because as a species we can do nothing else.

The important implication of this view for our theory is that analysts will need to attend to both power/interests and the existential functions of a field to make sense of its history. Even the most starkly brutal of oppressive regimes derive much of their support and stability from the ideational benefits they confer on their followers. Even as it increasingly retarded the economic development of the American South, the racial worldview embedded in Jim Crow laws retained the fierce loyalty of the great majority of the region's white residents. It simply will not do to dismiss this loyalty as the product of "false consciousness." The struggle to defend the "Southern way of life" against an "inferior" race and an oppressive federal government intent on abridging "states' rights" valorized the lives of generations of otherwise disadvantaged (and plenty of advantaged) white Southerners. And there is simply no denying the powerful meaning and membership benefits conferred on "Aryan" Germans by the Nazi movement. Conversely, we should never make the mistake of assuming that religious or purely cultural fields only reflect the existential function of the social. The Catholic Church, the Shia branch of Islam, the Reunification Church— material interests and naked power shape these fields as much as they do their "secular" counterparts. If in the explication of our theory, we have not always honored the complex mix of material and existential motives that fuel the emergence and development of fields, we do so explicitly here.

2. *Social Skill*—Social skill is the ability to take the role of the other in the service of cooperative behavior. People deploy social skill as part of a collaborative meaning-making project. They do so with a mix of motives. They might materially gain from their actions directly, and this could well be one of their core motives. But collaborating in the creation of a social order is an inherently satisfying endeavor. Having more social skill implies that some actors are better at attaining cooperation than others because some people will be better at "reading" others, at making sense of a particular situation, and at producing shared meanings. All human beings have to be somewhat socially skilled in order to survive, but we all know people who are more socially skilled than others, that is, are better at getting others to cooperate.

Skilled strategic actors in fields that are already structured do not have much choice as to their position in that field, the resources available to them, and the opportunities they have to either reproduce or change their position. This does not, however, mean that social skill will be irrelevant under conditions of field stability. If the actors are in an incumbent group, they will use their skill to keep their group together, to sustain or enhance the group's identity, and, in general, to continue to ensure the realization of the group's instrumental aims. If the actors are in a challenging group, they must convince those who face a more uncertain world that staying the course, using what opportunities they have, and continuing to voice opposition will serve group interests. Social skill may be a property of individuals, but the use of social skill will depend on individuals recognizing their social position, being able to take the perspective of other actors (both those with whom they are trying to cooperate and those with whom they are competing), and settling on a course of action that "makes sense" given their constraints.

Much of sociology wants to either reduce people to positions in social structure (thereby denying them the ability to be self-aware, meaning-making actors) or, alternatively, view them as highly agentic and at every moment creating and re-creating society whether they know it or not. The theory of social skill and its relationship to the theory of fields implies that both the individual skills actors have and the positions they occupy in social space affect their ability to engage in cooperation, competition, and collective action. Action depends on the structural position and the opportunities it affords a given actor as well as her innate ability to read the situation and mobilize others in the service of a strategy tailored to the constraints of the situation. In any given situation, actors' ability to improve their group's situation may be highly or minimally constrained by their position in the structure. But either way, they must use their social skill to recognize and take advantage of whatever opportunities are open to them. They must also continue to motivate their group and provide meaning and continuity to keep their group going.

3. *The Macroenvironment: Fields Embedded in Networks of Fields*—So central is this aspect of the theory that we devoted an entire chapter to it (see chapter 4). What is distinctive about our approach is our insistence that we can only make sense of any given field by embedding it in the broader environment of other fields that powerfully shape its fate over time. By contrast, virtually all prior scholarship on fields basically begins and ends with a focus on the internal dynamics of the strategic action field in question. While sometimes analysts may occasionally gesture to the influence of "the" state or some other external actor on the unique history of "their" field, they do so without reference to any more systematic theory of the relationship between single strategic action fields and the set of proximate state and nonstate fields on which they routinely depend.

In our view, both field stability and crisis/transformation typically owe at least as much to external events and processes as to those internal to the strategic action field. This is especially true, we think, of conflict and change within fields. While fields can, on occasion, descend into crisis as a result of endogenous change processes, most of the time these episodes of contention are set in motion by exogenous shocks of various kinds. These shocks are not, however, disembodied "acts of God." Rather they emanate from significant events or change processes in nearby fields that serve, in turn, to destabilize relations within the field in question and perhaps other fields as well. A precedent-setting legal case roils the waters in a host of fields affected by the ruling. The plant of a key supplier burns to the ground, precipitating a crisis in a host of dependent companies (themselves strategic action fields) and markets.

These cases could be multiplied many times over, but the central point should be clear. Virtually all fields are embedded in a dense network of other fields, some of which they are uniquely dependent on. Some of these dependencies exhibit a unique "Russian doll" character, with a set of fields embedded in one another, to constitute a tightly linked vertical system. But whatever form these dependent linkages take—for example, Russian doll or the more common horizontal latticework structure—given the ubiquity of change in modern society, we assume there is always going to be a certain amount of rolling turbulence flowing through the broader macroenvironment in which fields are embedded. It is only a matter of time before any given field feels the effects of this turbulence. Stability, however, is also partially a product of this very same macroenvironment. The dependent ties to other strategic action fields that render a particular field vulnerable to exogenous shocks in "turbulent times," tend to stabilize the field under ordinary circumstances. Field incumbents cultivate powerful allies in proximate state and nonstate strategic action fields and call on them at the slightest hint of unrest within the field. Besides insulating the field against internal threats, these ties typically serve to maintain the material, political, and ideological advantages of incumbents. The more general point is that absent systematic knowledge of and attention to the links between a given field and that subset of state and nonstate fields on which it routinely depends, analysts cannot hope to understand stability and change in their field.

4. *Coalitions and Hierarchy*—One of the basic issues that one confronts in fashioning a theory of fields is the source of underlying order in the field. In general, we see two ideal-type tendencies in this regard. Some authors see fields as highly conflictual arenas that are largely structured on the basis of absolute differences in the resources and coercive power of those who occupy the field. In this view, the struggle for the valued ends of the field will cause one actor or set of actors to try and dominate others. To the degree that they are successful, the field will have a hierarchical structure. The other perspective tends to stress the role of consensus, coalition, and the legitimacy in the creation and institutionalization of a field. Here, raw power plays a relatively small role, with even the least privileged members of the strategic action field buying into the goals of the field and their place in it.

While acknowledging that virtually all fields contain elements of hierarchy and coalition, our view is that most fields tend toward one or the other of these structural principles and that the conditions at the time of field emergence tend to dictate which structure predominates. More specifically, we believe that the resource endowments of groups and individuals at the moment of field formation will powerfully shape the character of initial interaction within the strategic action field and the way the field tends to get structured. Highly concentrated resources will tend to create hierarchical fields, while groups of individuals with roughly equal resource endowments will be more likely to cooperate in creating a consensual coalition as a way to bring order to the field. This means that the level of consensus in the field is not the real issue nor is the question of social power. Instead, the very organization of the field depends on the relative power of actors to produce either a hierarchical order or one in which they are more dependent on others and cooperate to divide the spoils of the field.

5. *Internal Governance Units*—The final unique feature of our theory is the concept of the internal governance unit. Having devoted considerable attention to the concept elsewhere in the book, we probably do not need to say a whole lot more here. Still, it is worth underscoring the importance we attach to the concept. While acknowledging the usefulness of the incumbent/challenger distinction, too often analysts write as if the stability of a field at any given moment turns on the vigilance and direct application of power by incumbents. Incumbents are, or course, always part of the story of field stability (and crisis for that matter.) But most of the time, at least in established fields of any size, incumbents are spared the burden of zealously safeguarding the stability of the strategic action field by virtue of the presence of a set of internal governance units that serve, through their actions, to routinize and enact key features of the field. Typically founded during moments of field settlement or resettlement, internal governance units are units—credential committees, certifying agencies, lobbying groups, etc.—that are created to help institutionalize and stabilize field practices and understandings. The operation of these units, however, normally does not reflect the well-being of the field as a whole so much as the imprint of incumbent interests. As the dominant actors in the field at the time of a settlement (or resettlement), incumbents are in a position to create internal governance units in their image and interests. This does not mean that these units will slavishly follow the dictates of incumbents forever or that they cannot at some later date be "captured" and used to advance the interests of challengers. Ordinarily, however, we expect the presence of internal governance units to function as a stabilizing, conservative force in most fields. The important empirical implication for us is that to fully understand the history and routine dynamics of any field, the analyst will need to be aware of the presence of any internal governance units and seek to account for their influence within the strategic action field.

6. *Our Conception of Change: Incremental Dynamism and the Occasional Rupture*— To the extent that there is a literature on strategic action fields and social change, it is decidedly schizophrenic. With their emphasis on "dominant logics" and the "taken for grantedness" of everyday routines, institutional theorists stress the stability and routine reproduction of organizational fields. In sharp contrast, social movement scholars have long been attuned to those moments of rupture that set in motion transformative episodes of contention. Taken together, these two literatures suggest that fields conform to something akin to a punctuated equilibrium version of social change. This view stresses the role of actors under uncertain conditions and attributes a heroic role for entrepreneurs and the possibility of entirely new things occurring. Once in place, fields tend toward routine reproduction until such a time

as exogenous shocks render them suddenly vulnerable to periods of convulsive, transformative change.

Our view of conflict and change in fields differs from this stylized image of punctuated equilibrium. First, we argue that actors are always important in fields. This means that social skill is always being deployed in the service of group interests. What is different is how actors operate given the level of organization of the field and their position in it. We subscribe to the idea that episodes of truly transformative contention are rare, arise suddenly, and are generally—though not always—set in motion by exogenous "shocks" to the field. Here what actors do is pivotal to what happens, and genuine surprises can emerge through new ideas and innovative forms of collective action. Our objection centers not on the social movement view of "moments of madness" that decisively reshape fields but rather on the institutionalist characterization of strategic action fields as routinely stable, free of conflict, and geared to something resembling unconscious reproduction. By contrast, we have argued that conflict and piecemeal change are ubiquitous in the life of fields. Challengers are not automatons, lulled by "dominant logics" into unconscious conformity to the "taken for granted" routines of the field. Nor are incumbents normally on cruise control, dominating the field with little or no effort. Socially skilled actors are always working to improve or defend their position.

Incumbents worry about challenges to their advantaged position within the strategic action field; challengers jockey with incumbents and with one another to try to improve their position in the field. Piecemeal change and conflict are more or less constant in fields. Normally, these processes do not undermine the overall distribution of power and resources and the underlying strength of the prevailing consensus within the field. Viewed from a distance, this may look like a form of punctuated equilibrium. Up close there is simply no mistaking the extent to which conflict and change are the stuff of everyday life in strategic action fields.

7. *States as Complex Systems of Fields*—State actors are often featured in empirical accounts of the founding or transformation of particular fields. But to our knowledge, the relationship between states and fields has never been systematically theorized. And certainly no one has conceived of states, as we do, as complex systems of interdependent fields in their own right. State fields, in our view, share all of the characteristics of nonstate fields. So, for example, the following tenets apply as much to state as to nonstate fields:

• State fields can be characterized as emergent, stable, or in crisis, and the interactive dynamics that we argued for in chapter 4 tend to predominate in each of these field states and are as characteristic of state, as nonstate, strategic action fields.

- State fields are embedded in complex networks of fields that render them vulnerable to the "rolling turbulence" characteristic of all field environments.
- By virtue of being embedded in a larger state system, most state fields exhibit the Russian doll structure characteristic of bureaucratic hierarchies. The judicial system in the United States affords a good example of this nested, vertical structure.
- Although we tend to think of state structures—especially in the democratic West—as very stable, perhaps even inertial, we see the operation of state strategic action fields as reflecting the same change principles as articulated in our general theory. So we expect state fields to exhibit both the incremental dynamism we associate with all stable strategic action fields and vulnerability to the rarer, but far more consequential field crises that beset nonstate fields.

There is, however, one very important respect in which state fields are qualitatively different from their nonstate counterparts. In the modern period, state fields have been granted the legitimate authority to set, monitor, and enforce the legal guidelines for the creation and routine operation of most nonstate fields. This grants to state actors/fields disproportionate power to shape the prospects for stability and change in the life of nonstate fields. It may even be that the lion's share of externally generated episodes of contention in the life of most fields stems either directly or indirectly from destabilizing "shocks" set in motion by actors in state fields. At the same time, routinized ties between state and nonstate fields are a powerful source of stability in the life of most fields. Typically, the institutionalization of any new field involves the establishment of strong "certifying," legitimating links between the strategic action field and one or more proximate state field. Once established and routinized, these ties are normally a powerful source for stability and order during times of field crisis, with incumbents appealing to their elite allies in these fields for help in defending the status quo.

This should not, however, be read to suggest that the relationship between state and nonstate fields is always one sided. The dependence runs both ways, even if the claim to sovereign authority enjoyed by state actors means that normally the influence runs from state to nonstate fields. That said, the stability of state fields—and indeed of states more generally—can depend on the support they derive from powerful actors in proximate nonstate fields. We used the example of powerful incumbents in key industries to illustrate this point in our extended discussion of this topic in chapter 4. To reiterate, the critical importance of certain industries to a nation's economy grants to the incumbents in those fields considerable leverage over state actors to whom they are nominally beholden. Indeed, as we noted in chapter 4, entire regimes have succumbed to the withdrawal of the support of these economic elites. Less dramatically, we are guessing that we could probably identify a set of key nonstate actors on whom the stability of most state fields depends.

The Problem of the Accumulation of Knowledge in the Social Sciences

Long ago, Thomas Kuhn (1962) observed that there was little accumulation of knowledge in the social sciences. He attributed this to the fact that the social sciences were in a preparadigmatic phase. This phase was characterized as one in which there was little agreement on theory, method, and, most important of all, the ability to accurately predict various social outcomes.

The problem of the accumulation of knowledge in social science is a difficult one. Many social theorists—most notably, Max Weber—have taken the position that the object of social science is meaning and that the study of meaning is inherently oriented toward understanding rather than explanation. Since meaning was contingent on time and place, the main thing scholars could hope to accomplish was an interpretive understanding of what actors meant by what they were doing. Weber also pointed out that scholars suffered from many problems of gaining intersubjectivity because they had different value systems, were interested in different features of the world, and, thus, tended to see what they wanted to see. Indeed, Weber's assertion that the study of society was fundamentally about the study of meanings is a kind of value judgment that others might not share. He concluded that the only kind of intersubjectivity that was possible in the social sciences was a situation in which scholars shared many assumptions about the nature of society, the importance of particular objects of study, and, of course, a methodology to study that object. It was only when two scholars shared such a perspective that they could hope to settle a theoretical dispute through systematic empirical research (Weber 1949). Weber, not surprisingly, felt that the social sciences would never, in fact, become true sciences. He believed that the social sciences were doomed to be segregated into schools of thought in which like-minded scholars would focus on common research programs that spoke only to the already existing community of believers.

There are at least two more pragmatic reasons that it is so difficult for social scientists to cumulate knowledge. The first centers on the strategic imperatives of the individual academic career. The demands of a successful academic career place an emphasis on a given scholar having a unique empirical and conceptual program of research. This encourages scholars to fashion their own terms for phenomena, ignore similar work by others, and generally engage in conversation only with those in their own theoretical camp. Indeed, journal editors report that such communities populate the subfields of sociology. If you send an article from one of these communities to a member of that community the article will earn praise, but if you send the same article to members of another community working on the problem in a different way, the article will almost certainly be rejected.

To explain the final reason the accumulation of social science knowledge is so hard, we apply our theory to that rather odd class of fields known as academic disciplines. The academy is no less subject to our perspective than any other constructed social order. The social sciences can be seen as a field in its own right, with disciplines competing for overall levels of funding support, total number of faculty positions, and generalized status rewards (e.g., media coverage, public acclaim). But for most academics, the more meaningful competition occurs *within* rather than *between* disciplines. So sociologists compete with other sociologists, economists with other economists, and so on. They compete for specific faculty positions in this or that department, sought after applicants to grad school, scarce grant monies, and a host of other material and status rewards. This internal focus means that most academics attend closely to intellectual trends within their chosen discipline but are only dimly aware, if not entirely ignorant, of new lines of work in other disciplines. Needless to say, this disciplinary myopia represents another significant impediment to the accumulation of knowledge in the social sciences.

All of these factors help us understand why knowledge has become increasingly fragmented and specialized across the social sciences. As the number of social scientists has exploded over the past fifty years and the number of discrete subfields within each discipline has mushroomed as well, the work done by the modal scholar has grown ever narrower and more specialized. Scholars have an interest in trying to grow their career by shutting what they are doing off from what others are doing in order to claim novelty. This applies not only to other disciplines but also to other subfields within their own discipline. Young scholars who enter the field have to confront this and are encouraged to find a niche where they can make some original contribution. It makes sense that they look for company and a side to be on in such debates. It even makes sense that they might want to follow their adviser's lead to join a school of thought or research program. This produces the schools of thought that Weber believed populated social science. As with all strategic action fields, it should be obvious that issues of meaning and identity as well as power and interest are at work here.

The Surprising Discovery of Fields

These various obstacles to knowledge accumulation make it very unlikely that a construct as deep and general as "field" will emerge in a number of different subfields within a single discipline and even less likely that it will emerge across disciplines. All of these centripetal forces make the simultaneous discovery of fields across several social science disciplines and within sociology surprising and substantively interesting. The discovery of fields occurred not just in several subfields within sociology but in economics and political science as well (for an elaborated version of these arguments, see Fligstein 2009; Hall and Taylor 1996). Scholars who were working on a very diverse set of problems began to realize that they were all interested in the construction of mesolevel social orders. Economists were generally concerned with the formation of institutions. One of the main analytical tools employed to interrogate institutions has been game theory, which is centrally concerned with understanding how strategic action is structured in a "game" or field. In political science, two sorts of analyses emerged. One was rational choice theory, which was focused on using game theory in order to understand political action in a defined context. The other was historical institutionalism, which focused on how political domains or institutions came into existence, persisted, or perhaps were transformed or disappeared.

The groups of scholars who fashioned arguments around these particular perspectives were trying to solve analytical problems in their home disciplines and subfields. But eventually many of them became aware of one another and began to attend joint conferences. The Hall and Taylor article (1996) documents the differences of opinion across these various views of mesolevel social orders and typologizes them as rational choice, historical, and sociological institutionalism.

Unfortunately, the promise inherent in the discovery of strategic action fields by scholars from these three disciplines has not been fully realized. We attribute this general lack of progress to the centripetal forces touched on above. Operating from within the logic of this or that perspective, scholars have stayed mostly interested in their empirical problems, their methods, and, most important, their conceptual language. This has meant that there has been little attempt either to bridge differences or to find a common language that would facilitate the discovery of a deeper field of study. Indeed, there has been virtually no attempt to try and seriously understand the real differences of opinion. This verifies Weber's observation that social science tends to lapse into schools of thought and research programs that function independently of one another.

We view this as a lost opportunity. Scholars in different fields looking at very different phenomena had unwittingly discovered something fundamental about how social reality works, yet they resisted the interpretation that they all were trying to solve the same problem. Indeed, the interdisciplinary character of these conversations meant that no one had any interest in keeping them going. The disciplines are divided by an interest in very different empirical problems. Moreover, economists, who have higher prestige in the academy, were wary, it would seem, of being associated with other social scientists unless the latter were willing to simply adopt their perspective. Indeed, this makes perfect sense in the field theory posed here. Economics is the incumbent discipline in the social sciences, and as such economists dictate the rules of the field. This means they can afford to ignore the ideas of challengers and the challengers have two choices: accept the terms of economics or decide to find another game to play. But even if this was not the case, the rewards of each of the disciplines are not tied up with creating a more general social science. Instead, scholars chose to create niches within a discipline where a group of scholars could be seen as making progress on a commonly accepted subfield within the larger disciplines.

But all is not lost. It is in the field of sociology that we see the greatest opportunity for collaboration to push forward the theory of fields. Here, scholars share many disciplinary assumptions. This should allow them to see past their intellectual preferences to the deeper conceptual apparatus at work. We think there are many encouraging signs that this is already happening. But we are also well aware that scholars across subfields have not been keenly interested in acknowledging their agreements and trying to be more systematic about uncovering their real disagreements. Indeed, our main purpose in writing this book was to lay out the case for what a general theory of fields would look like. If we are successful, our hope going forward is that scholars will begin to attend more closely to each others' work and will collaborate to fashion an even more general theory than the one on offer here. This is an issue we consider in our final conclusion. Before we do so, however, we want to briefly review the sociological literatures that have contributed to field theory in the past forty years.

The initial source for the discovery of strategic action fields in sociology comes from organizational theory. During the 1960s, the dominant view of organizations was called "rational adaptation" theory. The basic idea was that the leaders of organizations would search their environment for the current problems and make adaptations in their organizations in order to survive. Beginning in the 1970s, this view came under fire from several quarters. First, some theorists (Hannan and Freeman 1977) questioned whether or not the process of adaptation was really responsible for the fit of organizations to their environments. They argued that actors lacked sufficient foresight to understand the problems of their environment and that the main mechanism by which such fit was achieved was selection.

More relevant for our concerns was the view that the environment itself was a social construction. This meant that environments could be murky and open to interpretation. It also meant that organizational actors could manipulate their external worlds. This view, what became known as the "new institutionalism" in organizational theory was associated with Meyer and Rowan (1977), Meyer and Scott (1983), and DiMaggio and Powell (1983). Both Meyer and Scott and DiMaggio and Powell had a conception of the environment as a socially constructed mesolevel social order. Meyer and Scott described such worlds as organizational sectors while DiMaggio and Powell used the term "organizational field." (We note that the DiMaggio and Powell article does not cite Pierre Bourdieu. There is evidence that DiMaggio was familiar with some of the works of Pierre Bourdieu but mostly those concerned with the idea of cultural capital.) Both had expansive views of field membership. The culmination of this work appeared in a classic volume, *The New Institutionalism in Organizational Analysis*, edited by Powell and DiMaggio (1991).

Zald and Ash (1966), McCarthy and Zald (1973, 1977), Zald and McCarthy (1987) began to apply theories of formal organizations to the study of social movements. We note that Meyer Zald had begun his career studying organizations. McCarthy and Zald began to explore the formation of what they called "social movement industries," essentially fields of formal social movement organizations oriented to the same general social issue (women's rights, the environment, etc). McCarthy and Zald saw a given social movement organization as the "complex, or formal organization which identifies its goals with the preferences of a social movement and attempts to implement these goals" (1977: 1217–18). They argue that, in most cases, social movement organizations will become the carriers of social movements, as informal networks cannot coordinate the complex challenges facing social movements after their emergence. Thus the task of determining the movement's goals and program, strategy and tactics, will tend to be carried out by formal social movement organizations. Later, McAdam (1999) would argue that the civil rights movement could only be understood in the context of the broader political and economic processes ongoing in America. His analysis of the movement focused on the role of crisis, political opportunity, and a processual view of how organizations came over time to innovate new modes of protest.

At the same time, Pierre Bourdieu began to use the idea of field in his study of lifestyles, *Distinction* (1984), and in his later work, *The State Nobility* (1998). Bourdieu was directly affected by Weber's concept of order and saw fields as arenas of action in which actors and their social positions are located. The position of each particular actor in the field is a result of interaction between the specific rules of the field, the actor's habitus, and the actor's capital. In almost all of his empirical study of fields, actors were individuals vying for position in a given order. So, for example, in *Rules of Art* (1996), Bourdieu documents how Flaubert helped form the French literary field in the late 1880s. Bourdieu certainly has a broader view of the relationship between fields in some of his writings (e.g., *The State Nobility* [1998]). He also felt that fields can interact with each other in both a vertical and horizontal fashion.

The sociology of markets has also been built on a field conception. White's (1981) seminal article argued that market participants observed one another's behavior and responded by making a decision to locate their product in terms of a trade-off between price and quality. If stable, this produced what he called, "role structure" (1981: 518). Fligstein (1985, 1987, 1990) advanced another field-based conception of markets by constructing an alternative account of the rise of the large, modern corporation. He emphasized how the largest firms were trying to control competition in their main markets. They evolved, over the course of the late nineteenth and the twentieth century, a set of tactics to maintain their positions as dominant in their fields. He also saw the government as pivotal to this construction of the market.

Other versions of the sociology of markets also focus on the linkages between market participants. Baker (1982) documented that prices were actually less volatile in small trading pits at the Chicago Board of Trade than larger ones. He attributed that to the fact that various participants had more face-to-face interaction and were able to control the market more effectively. Uzzi (1996) shows how being embedded in a network affects the performance of a set of firms involved in the apparel industry in New York City.

We note that these streams of research have remained apart from one another and developed without much awareness of one another's existence until at least 1990. It has really only been in the past twenty years that these three streams of work have come together as scholars working with ideas from organizational theory, social movement theory, and the work of Pierre Bourdieu have seen that they are interested in similar problems.

Unfortunately, even as these scholars have begun to see connections, authors feel compelled to value their intellectual preference for one kind of theory above trying to understand why it is that such common theoretical elements surfaced in the first place. So, for example, Sallaz and Zavisca (2007) have traced the connections between Bourdieu's work and work in American sociology arguing that Bourdieu should be seen as the source of the theoretical legitimation for all of that work. Emirbayer and Johnson (2008) argue pointedly that organizational theory has not taken Bourdieu seriously enough. But neither pair asks the more important question: why did various kinds of sociological studies discover the idea of fields at or around the same time and independently of one another?

The conversation between organizational sociology and social movement theory has gone on for a long time, long enough to yield an important conference volume (Davis et al. 2005) and lots of high quality synthetic work at the intersection of the two fields. But most of the work done in this field and the chapters in the volume continue to see organizations and social movements as distinct phenomena. That is, the underlying field dynamics that undergird both movements and organizations have not been recognized by most scholars working in these two subfields.

John Martin's "What Is Field Theory?" (2003) locates field theory in its broadest context by appealing to both psychology and physics as inspiration for the idea that action takes place in social fields. He argues that field theory has its roots in Kurt Lewin's (1951) attempt to construct a field theory from the point of view of a given actor. This echoes Bourdieu's inspiration for the idea of fields. We note that Lewin saw fields as coconstituted by the organisms that inhabited them and the structural features of the environment. Martin's conception of field differs in one important way from Lewin's view in that he suggests that the idea of field could be thought about as a physicist might, for instance, a gravitational field. The physics view implies that as objects enter the field, what happens to them can only be understood by their positions within the field and not their recognition of the field. Martin's physical metaphor suggests a more structural and a less agentic view of fields.

A large group of scholars loosely associated with network analysis have also tried to map, if not exactly theorize, mesolevel social orders. DiMaggio (1986) was the first to propose modeling fields using the technique known as "block modeling." Powell et al. (2005) use network analysis to map a field over time. This work, while empirically rich, has not confronted the very different notions of field that have been proposed. Instead, it has implicitly argued that the structure of the relationships (whichever ones the analyst chooses to gather data on) is synonymous with the structure of the field. Martin (2009) has tried to create a theory of social structure from very basic assumptions about what minimal network is required to form a group. This work, too, has been inspired by field theory but does not develop that concept at its core.

There has been a virtual explosion of research interested in the formation of new fields and the problems of institutional entrepreneurship and the use of social skill. This research seeks to understand the entrepreneur as a social role and the use of social skill as a way of building coalitions around new frames that create or reorganize fields. These studies have focused on the problem of institutional entrepreneurship and social skill across a wide variety of social contexts, social movements, routine politics, business, and nonprofits (for a review, see Battilana, Leca, and Boxenbaum 2009).

While we are encouraged that many scholars have come to realize that they might be engaged in a common theoretical endeavor, we also see quite clearly that much of the recent discussion of field theory has not tried to make direct sense of the real differences of opinion across the empirical uses of the theory. Our point is that enough scholars working in many different kinds of studies have found the field idea useful empirically. Their research has confirmed the existence of mesolevel social orders everywhere, and their effects have been widely documented.

As a result, we ought to be tuning into what each other is trying to say in order to understand what the differences of opinion really are. Instead of being concerned about who originally constructed the idea or whether or not scholars have sufficiently genuflected to one theorist or another, we all ought to be encouraged by the fact that field theory—as a way to understand all kinds of mesolevel social orders whether of corporations, social movements, political projects, or artistic and literary worlds—seems to be influencing our empirical and theoretical discussions of these phenomena. The discovery of fields or mesolevel social orders by scholars who were and are not committed to finding such a thing in the first place is something we ought to take seriously.

The diversity of cases of field studies implies not that one scholar or another's theory should dominate but instead that many of us are engaged in the clarification of a theoretical construct of great general utility. It is on clarifying the nature of this very general set of concepts that we should be focused. Indeed, it is our contention that the discovery of the theory of fields might just finally allow the accumulation of knowledge in that substantial part of sociology concerned with understanding the organization of social, economic, and political life.

Toward a Collaborative Program of Theory and Research on Fields

So, what are the central issues that, if resolved, would push the theory of fields forward? To make progress in this area, we will need to arrive at provisional answers to the following seven questions:

1. How are we to understand field boundaries and the ways in which they change?
2. What role do power/coercion and more collaborative interpersonal processes play in shaping the structure and dynamics of strategic action fields?
3. What is the nature of individual versus collective action within fields?
4. How are we to understand structure and action—and the relationship between the two—in strategic action fields?
5. What is the nature of social change—both piecemeal and transformative—in fields and how does each get generated?
6. How do fields come to be tied to other fields? And how do these relationships affect stability and change within strategic action fields?
7. How do the dynamics of fields differ across nominally different institutional arenas in society (i.e., economic, political, and cultural)?

1. Field Boundaries—The problem of how we tell who is a member of a field is one of the issues we have struggled with in writing this book. The most expansive views of field theory argue for including all relevant actors to a field, including suppliers, governments, regulators, and, if we are talking about markets, customers or audiences for cultural products. The advantage of such a view of fields is that scholars cannot easily ignore possible participants in the structuring of a field and their effects on a field. But we see two significant problems with this view. It makes it difficult to model mesolevel orders when actors play such different roles in the field. Moreover, drawing the boundaries between fields is nearly impossible if one is prepared to include all relevant groups as part of the field.

In empirical work, scholars have tended toward a narrower view of field participants. They have focused on actors in a field who are vying for whatever is centrally at stake in the field. If a field is an arena of social action where actors come to organize themselves around some outcome, then it makes sense to only focus on the players interested in that outcome. This does not mean that there are no players outside of the arena who affect what goes on inside the arena; it only means that the "game" in the field is being played by those who have something at stake. Our solution to this problem of who is in and out of the field has been to postulate the idea of strategic action fields, that is, linked arenas whereby actors might be playing in multiple arenas simultaneously. So, a given office of a firm has its own internal dynamics, its relationship to its competitors, and its links to its rival divisions in the firm and, of course, outside constituencies such as the state. We postulate that you can study any one of these as a field.

We have tried to clarify this problem by proposing that fields require four sorts of agreements or "institutions": (1) an agreement about what is at stake, (2) an agreement about who the players are and what positions they occupy, (3) a consensus regarding the rules by which the field works, and (4) a shared interpretative frame that allows those in the field to make sense of what other actors are doing in the field in a particular situation. Needless to say, this stress on intersubjective agreements defines fields and field boundaries more narrowly than the expansive perspective alluded to above. But subsequent work will be needed to clarify the matter and adjudicate between these more and less expansive views of field membership.

The problem is partially conceptual, but it is also empirical. It is important to explore different ways of conceiving of field boundaries and membership in order to arrive at the advantages and disadvantages of each. One thought is that the field construct may itself be a kind of ideal type whose advantage is in organizing empirical observation from the point of view of scholars rather than from the point of view of the participants in a field. It may be a handy device to simplify the world in order to understand and less of a causal force than we have suggested. This is a kind of philosophical question that requires us to consider the ontological status of the idea of a field. Martin (2009) argues that a field has to be a realist construct if it is analogous to a gravitational field. That is, if it is going to affect how groups or individuals behave, it must be real. Bourdieu and Wacquant (1992) seem to equivocate on this point. While Martin seems, on the one hand, to want to see field effects as far-reaching, he is prepared to also think that they operate as a shorthand heuristic for guiding analysis.

2. *The Very Nature of Fields*—A related question is what exactly is the nature of a field? We have proposed the view that a field is a set of positions in a field of power relations (similar to the view of Bourdieu). We conceive of it this way since we believe that in every field, something is always at stake. Who gets what and why are the core questions at the heart of the analysis of any field. For us, there are two ideal typical settlements in a field: the one hierarchical and the other coalitional. But both are premised on the idea that the relationships between actors implicitly concern the ultimate distribution of what is valued in the field. One alternative perspective is that the underlying relationships in the field may result from the interpersonal ties that link actors in the field. Much of network analysis has been atheoretical with regard to what relationships should be included in field analysis. Indeed, little time is ever spent justifying why the particular network of interest is the important dimension by which a field is structured. In the article by Powell et al. (2005), the relationships that are measured are ties between biotechnology firms such as joint ventures, funding opportunities, and other forms of cooperation.

In order to push field theory forward, it is important to explore the implications of viewing a field as a system of power versus simply a mesolevel set of social relationships. Obviously, how one thinks about this question determines what one measures in any situation. But it also has implications for how we interpret what is going on in fields. For example, from our perspective, which focuses on understanding the rules of the game and the incumbent–challenger structuring of the field, the fact that a particular industry may be organized with a lot of joint ventures is an outcome of deeper field processes. So, for example, joint ventures in a field may have something to do with the coalitional nature of the field. If one believes this, then the analyst needs to gather data on how and why this is. From the perspective on offer here, understanding why that has happened and if it has resulted in a stable strategic action field is the goal of research.

But many scholars do not accept that the social relationships they model using network analysis need to be linked to a deeper understanding of the nature of the field. Indeed, since scholars have tended toward one or the other interpretation of fields, we have very few studies that measure both kinds of possible effects of fields. It is possible for both kinds of measures to help structure a field, but then this makes our interpretation of action in a field infinitely more complex. This is a place where scholars recognizing their deep difference of opinion might be able to make progress through more systematic study of important cases informed by both points if view.

3. *Individual versus Collective Action*—One of the issues that scholars frequently skirt is whether fields are composed of individuals or groups. Field theory and analysis ought to be able to scale up from individual actions to group actions. But how this happens is another one of those very murky issues. We have argued that through empathetic understanding, socially skilled individuals have the ability to induce cooperation from others. This implies an individualistic starting point that fits to some degree with Bourdieu's tacit view that to understand what actors are doing, we need to know the field, the habitus of individuals, and their forms of capital (resources). For Bourdieu action is explained by the tools the individual actor has, specifically his or her position, habitus, and resources. Our perspective differs from Bourdieu's in that while actors are self-interested in many fields, they are also social creatures. This motivates them to want others to think well of them, to maintain status, and to save face in various situations. It also means that people will cooperate in situations that do not necessarily benefit themselves—that they are capable of acting for the sake of the group as well as their own. They will not see every move as a zero–sum game but instead be willing to make trade-offs in order to safeguard the sources of meaning and identity in their lives. Put more starkly, our stress on the existential function of the social is difficult to reconcile with what we see as Bourdieu's more starkly materialist view. Reconciling these two perspectives will require a lot more collaborative theory and research.

If one moves up a level to a field composed of groups, the question of how orders are established and maintained becomes more salient. One perspective might be to assume that Bourdieu's theory scales up; that is, groups have a position in a field, a habitus, and forms of capital. Perhaps the most jarring idea here is that groups have a habitus. Bourdieu's conception of habitus is very much pitched at the level of the socialization of the individual. But one could argue that groups have collective experiences and that within the practices and culture of the group, there is a shared understanding about who the group is and what its practices are. Nelson and Winter (1982) and others have posited, for example, that the routines and procedures of organizations operate as habits. Standard operating procedures are ways to deal with novel situations. These seem analogous to habitus. In this way, groups experience novel situations in the same way individuals do.

There is certainly some truth to this idea and it should be explored. In the end, however, we are not convinced that groups are simple aggregations of Bourdieusian individuals. One of the problems of doing analysis this way is that scholars have to postulate that groups have something like "group minds" or "collective memory" that transcend the individuals in them in order to imbue them with habitus. While we are not certain this is wrong, it is important that the scaling up of action from an individual to a group or an organization be done explicitly. Again, it is important to understand the implication of doing so.

Our main reservation about this approach is that it tends to remove social skill from the equation. It does so by replacing actors who are constantly working to keep their worlds going with "groups" who are following their standard operating procedures and reacting automatically to threats and opportunities. This raises the important question of how the people who are using these procedures figure out what signals the "world" is giving them. Leaders of groups are generally the ones who are actively framing action. Thus, they interpret the relationships with other groups, they provide reasons for supporting a particular course of action within their group by appealing to who the group is, and they construct courses of action in a self-conscious manner. This process keeps actors at the center of action, something an approach that postulates the automatic response of a group obscures. This also makes it too easy to see groups as fundamentally in less conflict than they might be. Finally, it makes it hard for actors to act creatively, innovate, and improve their collective position over time.

4. *Structure versus Action*—The problem of keeping actors in the model can be framed in another way. Sociologists have typically preferred structural explanations that do not rely on the skill of social actors to affect outcomes. One of the purposes of the DiMaggio and Powell (1983), Meyer and Scott (1983), and Jepperson (1991) conception of actors is to remove them from mattering by making them the passive recipients of scripts from the outside about what "people like them" should or ought to do. This substitutes a cultural kind of structuralism for a more resource-based view of structure. Using a gravity metaphor to understand fields is also a kind of structural determinism, as it provides the individuals or groups who enter into a field with little choice but to obey the forces in the field.

In the Bourdieusian analysis, the way this problem is solved is to emphasize the role of individual actors as having position, capital, and habitus and therefore always having to play the game with their wits. Bourdieu describes this as overcoming the problem of objectivism and subjectivism (Bourdieu and Wacquant 1992). This is true in our social skill formulation of the problem. Actors are always aware and able to respond to challenges. That fields tend to reproduce is a function of the game being played in a skilled way, by incumbents but also by challengers.

5. *The Nature, Forms, and Precipitants of Social Change*—Another fundamental issue for field theory is the problem of change. There are two aspects to this. First, one needs to be clear about what is changing in a field. Since we have argued that a field is shaped by the overall goals, positions, and resources of existing players as well as their understanding of the rules that govern interaction in the field, it follows that all of these can potentially change in any playing of the game. Since one would expect there to be a constant jockeying for advantage in any field, there are likely to be shifts in all of these over time. Deciding how important such changes are is one of the big challenges of field theory and analysis.

So, for example, the academic disciplines have had a relatively stable relationship to one another over the past fifty years. The system of universities, at least in the United States, is also a stable field where the top fifty research universities have maintained their control over huge resources and status for the past half century or so. Yet, within disciplines, we can see big changes in theory, methods, and objects of study. One might even say that the goals of a field can change and the meaning of the moves of players can change, but the relative position and the rules regarding what is high status remain the same. It is important to have ways of distinguishing how much each of these changes alters the field.

The second tricky issue is differentiating between fundamental and more piecemeal changes in a field. At the extremes, this distinction is easy to make. In many instances, however, the extent and significance of change in a field will be much harder to judge. What we can say with some confidence is that truly transformative change will be rare and generally confined to instances of field emergence and deep and prolonged episodes of contention within the field. We have defined "fundamental change" as a reordering of all major aspects of strategic action fields and reserved the term "piecemeal change" for alterations that fall short of that. But it just may be that we have drawn the distinction too sharply here. Put another way, we may want to think about field-level change more as a continuum than as a stark dichotomy. Without more of a sense about how things work generally across fields, it is difficult to decide which view might be more correct.

6. The Relationship between Fields—Probably, the most important issue raised by our perspective concerns the linkages between fields. This is an area that has not been explored empirically very much. The main way in which scholars who study strategic action fields work is to isolate a particular strategic action field, define its relationship to nearby strategic action fields, and then proceed to an account of the formation or transformation of a given strategic action field. Our two cases in chapter 5 follow this kind of logic. But the dynamic linkages between strategic action fields have rarely been explored by scholars.

In our view, this is probably because the data requirements to adequately understand the dynamics of a single field are very high. The ability to gather either qualitative or quantitative data to understand the structuring of even one field is an exhausting activity. But to dynamically track the relationship between a set of fields requires even more data and often study over time. We have argued that the relationship between fields does scale up: they can be hierarchical or interdependent or not have much relationship at all. But having said that, we need to design studies that look at these relationships over time to see how they produce change and stability in the players in strategic action fields. We know almost nothing about these processes.

7. Different Institutional Arenas—Finally, the purpose of this book has been to propose a general view about how strategic action fields are the main way in which to make sense of mesolevel social order in a wide variety of social, economic, and political situations. We have tried to specify the generic process of field formation, the social movement–like quality of such moments, and the social skill of actors to sculpt either a new hierarchy or political coalition, We have also argued that once in place, rules, resources, and skills enable actors to constantly vie for position.

But one could argue that this is a kind of theoretical overreach. The social world, the economy, and the polity might have specific institutional dynamics that would make us alter this general view. It is probably correct to say that over time, new organizing technologies have appeared in all of these arenas of social life. How people take action, how they interact, is often shaped dramatically by previous experience and, of course, the settled strategic action fields that populate various parts of society. In our telling of the story about the civil rights movement and the market for mortgages in the United States, we emphasized the common theoretical elements in the story. But there are also some parts of the story that are uniquely about the events themselves. We are obviously convinced that field theory has great general utility, but we also know that it will take years of careful empirical work to determine the veracity of many of the ideas put forth here and the alternative conceptions that appear in the work of other field theorists.

It is our belief that if we begin to build on the complementarities and reconcile the differences in the various versions of field theory, we can move toward a more comprehensive and truly disciplinary if not interdisciplinary perspective on the topic. It is our hope that this book will encourage scholars to realize that we have the opportunity to capitalize on our collective discovery of how fields organize much of social life. It should encourage us to work more collaboratively to reduce unnecessary disciplinary jargon and to begin to build on the common stock of shared insights that run through the work that has been produced to date. This does not, however, mean that we should suppress our differences. Instead we should be aware that those differences will help shed light on genuinely new aspect of how fields work that need to be incorporated into our general theory. If scholars begin to harmonize the differences across their various perspectives, we might yet see some accumulation of knowledge in the field.

To end, it is useful to consider the promise of the development of a more general field theory. For the first time since the 1960s, scholars have created a set of theoretical concepts that transcend subfield divisions. The prospect of a broad synthetic theory is quite exciting in a discipline that has more or less given up on the idea of a general theory for at least forty years. We are excited to be part of this collective endeavor. We hope that our effort to add to and clarify this discussion pushes the prospects of a more general field theory forward. But for this to happen, we believe that scholars studying all sorts of empirical phenomena from a field perspective must come together and see themselves as involved in a collective endeavor. Only then will we have a chance to realize the promise of an integrated, collaborative theory of fields. We look forward to the conversation.

BIBLIOGRAPHY

Abend, G. 2008. "The Meaning of 'Theory.'" *Sociological Theory* 26(2): 173–199.

Acuña, R. 2000. *Occupied America: A History of Chicanos.* New York: Longman.

Alexander, J., B. Giesen, R. Münch, and N. Smelser, eds. 1987. *The Micro-Macro Link.* Berkeley: University of California Press.

Ansell, C. 2001. *Schism and Solidarity in Social Movements: The Politics of Labor in the French Third Republic.* Cambridge, UK: Cambridge University Press.

Armstrong, E. 2002. *Forging Gay Identities: Organizing Sexuality in San Francisco, 1950–1994.* Chicago: University of Chicago Press.

———. 2005. "From Struggle to Settlement: The Crystallization of a Field of Lesbian/Gay Organizations in San Francisco, 1969–1973." Pp. 161–187 in G. Davis, D. McAdam, W.R. Scott, and M. Zald (eds.), *Social Movements and Organization Theory.* Cambridge, UK: Cambridge University Press.

Arthur, W.B. 1988. "Self-Reinforcing Mechanisms in Economics." Pp. 9–32 in P. Anderson, K. Arrow, and D. Pines (eds.), *The Economy as an Evolving Complex System.* Reading, MA: Addison-Wesley.

———. 1989. "Competing Technologies, Increasing Returns, and Lock-In by Historical Events." *Economic Journal* 99(394): 116–131.

Baker, W. 1982. "The Effects of Trading Networks on the Volatility of Option Prices." Paper presented at the 77th Annual Meeting of the American Sociological Association. San Francisco, CA, September.

——— and R. Faulkner. 1993. "The Social Organization of Conspiracy: Illegal Networks in the Heavy Electrical Equipment Industry." *American Sociological Review* 58(6): 837–860.

Barmat, J. 1990. "Securitization: An Overview." Pp. 3–22 in J. Lederman (ed.), *The Handbook of Asset-Backed Securities.* New York: New York Institute of Finance.

Barnard, C. 1938. *The Functions of the Executive.* Cambridge, MA: Harvard University Press.

Barth, J. 1991. *The Great Savings and Loan Debacle.* Washington, DC: AEI Press.

———. 2004. *The Savings and Loan Crisis.* Amsterdam: Kluwer Press.

Battilana, J., B. Leca, and E. Boxenbaum. 2009. "How Actors Change Institutions: Towards a Theory of Institutional Entrepreneurship." *The Academy of Management Annals* 3(1): 65–107.

Benford, R. and D. Snow. 2000. "Framing Processes and Social Movements: An Overview and Assessment." *Annual Review of Sociology* 26: 611–639.

Berger, P. 1990. *A Rumor of Angels: Modern Society and the Rediscovery of the Supernatural.* New York: Anchor Books.

——— and T. Luckmann. 1967. *The Social Construction of Reality: A Treatise in the Sociology of Knowledge.* Garden City, NY: Doubleday.

Binder, A. 2002. *Contentious Curricula: Afrocentrism and Creationism in American Public Schools.* Princeton, NJ: Princeton University Press.

Blee, K. 1996. "Becoming a Racist." *Gender and Society* 10(6): 680–702.

———. 2002. *Inside Organized Racism: Women in the Hate Movement*. Berkeley: University of California Press.

Boesch, C. and H. Boesch. 1993. "Diversity of Tool Use and Tool-Making in Wild Chimpanzees." Pp. 158–187 in A. Berthelet and J. Chavaillon (eds.), *The Use of Tools by Human and Non-Human Primates*. Oxford: Clarendon Press.

Booth, J. 1982. *The End of the Beginning: The Nicaraguan Revolution*. Boulder, CO: Westview Press.

Bourdieu, P. 1977. *Outline of a Theory of Practice*. Cambridge, UK: Cambridge University Press.

———. 1984. *Distinction: A Social Critique of the Judgement of Taste*. Cambridge, MA: Harvard University Press.

———. 1996. *The Rules of Art: Genesis and Structure of the Literary Field*. Stanford, CA: Stanford University Press.

———. 1998. *The State Nobility: Elite Schools in the Field of Power*. Stanford, CA: Stanford University Press.

——— and L. Wacquant. 1992. *An Invitation to Reflexive Sociology*. Chicago: University of Chicago Press.

Brendsel, L. 1996. "Securitization's Role in Housing Finance: The Special Contributions of Government-Sponsored Enterprises." Pp. 17–30 in L. Kendall and M. Fishman (eds.), *A Primer on Securitization*. Cambridge, MA: MIT Press.

Brown, L. and J. Fox. 1998. "Accountability within Transnational Coalitions." Pp. 439–484 in J. Fox and L. Brown (eds.), *The Struggle for Accountability: The World Bank, NGOs, and Grassroots Movements*. Cambridge, MA: MIT Press.

Burt, R. 1980. "Cooptive Corporate Actor Networks: A Reconsideration of Interlocking Directorates Involving American Manufacturing." *Administrative Science Quarterly* 25(4): 557–582.

———. 1992. *Structural Holes: The Social Structure of Competition*. Cambridge, MA: Harvard University Press.

Campbell, J. 2005. "Where Do We Stand? Common Mechanisms in Organizations and Social Movements Research." Pp. 41–68 in G. Davis, D. McAdam, W.R. Scott, and M. Zald (eds.), *Social Movements and Organization Theory*. Cambridge, UK: Cambridge University Press.

Carroll, G. and M. Hannan. 2000. *The Demography of Corporations and Industries*. Princeton, NJ: Princeton University Press.

Carroll, G. and A. Swaminathan. 2000. "Why the Microbrewery Movement? Organizational Dynamics of Resource Partitioning in the U.S. Brewing Industry." *American Journal of Sociology* 106(3): 715–762.

Clemens, E. 1993. "Organizational Repertoires and Institutional Change: Women's Groups and the Transformation of U.S. Politics, 1890–1920." *American Journal of Sociology* 98(4): 755–798.

———. 1996. "Organizational Form as Frame: Collective Identity and Political Strategy in the American Labor Movement, 1880–1920." Pp. 205–226 in D. McAdam, J.D. McCarthy, and M. Zald (eds.), *Comparative Perspectives on Social Movements: Political Opportunities, Mobilizing Structures, and Cultural Framings*. Cambridge, UK: Cambridge University Press.

———. 1997. *The People's Lobby: Organizational Innovation and the Rise of Interest Group Politics in the United States, 1890–1925*. Chicago: University of Chicago Press.

——— and D. Minkoff. 2004. "Beyond the Iron Law: Rethinking the Place of Organizations in Social Movement Research." Pp. 155–170 in D. Snow, S. Soule, and H. Kriesi (eds.), *The Blackwell Companion to Social Movements*. Malden, MA: Blackwell.

Coleman, J. 1986. "Social Theory, Social Research, and a Theory of Action." *American Journal of Sociology* 91(6): 1309–1335.

Concise Columbia Encyclopedia. 1983. New York: Columbia University Press.

Converse, P., W. Miller, J. Rusk, and A. Wolfe. 1969. "Continuity and Change in American Politics: Parties and Issues in the 1968 Election." *American Political Science Review* 63(4): 1083–1105.

Coser, L. 1956. *The Functions of Social Conflict*. Glencoe, IL: Free Press.

Creed, W.E.D. 2003. "Voice Lessons: Tempered Radicalism and the Use of Voice and Silence." *Journal of Management Studies* 40(6): 1503–1536.

Cress, D. 1997. "Nonprofit Incorporation among Movements of the Poor: Pathways and Consequences for Homeless Social Movement Organizations." *The Sociological Quarterly* 38(2): 343–360.

Dahl, R. 1956. *A Preface to Democratic Theory*. Chicago: University of Chicago Press.

Davis, G., K. Diekmann, and C. Tinsley. 1994. "The Decline and Fall of the Conglomerate Firm in the 1980s: The Deinstitutionalization of an Organizational Form." *American Sociological Review* 59(4): 547–570.

Davis, G. and D. McAdam. 2000. "Corporations, Classes, and Social Movements after Managerialism." *Research in Organizational Behavior* 22: 193–236.

Davis, G., D. McAdam, W.R. Scott, and M. Zald, eds. 2005. *Social Movements and Organization Theory*. Cambridge, UK: Cambridge University Press.

Davis, G. and T. Thompson. 1994. "A Social Movement Perspective on Corporate Control." *Administrative Science Quarterly* 39(2): 141–173.

DeYoung, R. and T. Rice. 2004. "How Do Banks Make Money?" *Economic Perspectives*. 4: 34–51.

DiMaggio, P. 1986. "Structural Analysis of Organizational Fields: A Blockmodel Approach." *Research in Organizational Behavior* 8: 335–370.

———. 1988. "Interest and Agency in Institutional Theory." Pp. 3–21 in L. Zucker (ed.), *Institutional Patterns and Organizations: Culture and Environment*. Cambridge, MA: Ballinger Publishing.

———. 1991. "Constructing an Organizational Field as a Professional Project: US Art Museums, 1920–1940." Pp. 267–292 in W. Powell and P. DiMaggio (eds.), *The New Institutionalism in Organizational Analysis*. Chicago: University of Chicago Press.

——— and W. Powell. 1983. "The Iron Cage Revisited: Institutional Isomorphism and Collective Rationality in Organizational Fields." *American Sociological Review* 48(2): 147–160.

Dix, R. 1984. "Why Revolutions Succeed and Fail." *Polity* 16(3): 423–446.

Dobbin, F. 1994. *Forging Industrial Policy: The United States, Britain, and France in the Railway Age*. Cambridge, UK: Cambridge University Press.

——— and J. Sutton. 1998. "The Strength of a Weak State: The Rights Revolution and the Rise of Human Resources Management Divisions." *American Journal of Sociology* 104(2): 441–476.

Duffy, M., A. Binder, and J. Skrentny. 2010. "Elite Status and Social Change: Using Field Analysis to Explain Policy Formation and Implementation." *Social Problems* 57(1): 49–73.

Durkheim, E. 1995. *The Elementary Forms of Religious Life*. New York: Free Press.

Edelman, L. 1992. "Legal Ambiguity and Symbolic Structures: Organizational Mediation of Civil Rights Law." *American Journal of Sociology* 97(6): 1531–1576.

———, C. Uggen, and H. Erlanger. 1999. "The Endogeneity of Legal Regulation: Grievance Procedures as Rational Myth." *American Journal of Sociology* 105(2): 406–454.

Edwards, B. and J. McCarthy. 2004. "Resources and Social Movement Mobilization." Pp. 116–152 in D. Snow, S. Soule, and H. Kriesi (eds.), *The Blackwell Companion to Social Movements*. Malden, MA: Blackwell.

Elias, N. 1994. *The Civilizing Process*. Oxford: Blackwell.

Emirbayer, M. and V. Johnson. 2008. "Bourdieu and Organizational Analysis." *Theory and Society* 37: 1–44.

Epstein, S. 1987. "Gay Politics, Ethnic Identity: The Limits of Social Constructionism." *Socialist Review* 17: 9–54.

Evans, P. and J. Rauch. 1999. "Bureaucracy and Growth: A Cross-National Analysis of the Effects of 'Weberian' State Structures on Economic Growth." *American Sociological Review* 64(5): 748–765.

Evans, P., D. Rueschemeyer, and T. Skocpol, eds. 1985. *Bringing the State Back In*. Cambridge, UK: Cambridge University Press.

Fligstein, N. 1981. *Going North: Migration of Blacks and Whites from the South, 1900–1950*. New York: Academic Press.

———. 1985. "The Spread of the Multidivisional Form among Large Firms, 1919–1979." *American Sociological Review* 50(3): 377–391.

———. 1987. "The Intraorganizational Power Struggle: Rise of Finance Personnel to Top Leadership in Large Corporations, 1919–1979." *American Sociological Review* 52(1): 44–58.

———. 1990. *The Transformation of Corporate Control.* Cambridge, MA: Harvard University Press.

———. 1996. "Markets as Politics: A Political–Cultural Approach to Market Institutions." *American Sociological Review* 61(4): 656–673.

———. 2001a. "Social Skill and the Theory of Fields." *Sociological Theory* 19(2): 105–125.

———. 2001b. *The Architecture of Markets: An Economic Sociology of Twenty-First-Century Capitalist Societies.* Princeton, NJ: Princeton University Press.

———. 2008. *Euroclash: The EU, European Identity and the Future of Europe.* Oxford: Oxford University Press.

———. 2009. "Fields, Power, and Social Skill: A Critical Analysis of the New Institutionalisms." *International Public Management Review* 9: 227–252.

——— and A. Goldstein. 2010. "The Anatomy of the Mortgage Securitization Crisis." Pp. 29–70 in M. Lounsbury and P. Hirsch (eds.), *Markets on Trial: The Economic Sociology of the U.S. Financial Crisis (Research in the Sociology of Organizations 30).* Bingley, UK: Emerald Publishing.

——— and A. Stone Sweet. 2002. "Constructing Markets and Politics: An Institutionalist Account of European Integration." *American Journal of Sociology* 107(5): 1206–1243.

Fraser, N. 2003. *The Radical Imagination: Between Redistribution and Recognition.* Frankfurt: Springer.

Friedland, R. and R. Alford. 1991. "Bringing Society Back In: Symbols, Practices, and Institutional Contradictions." Pp. 232–263 in W. Powell and P. DiMaggio (eds.), *The New Institutionalism in Organizational Analysis.* Chicago: University of Chicago Press.

Gallup, George H. 1972. *The Gallup Poll: Public Opinion, 1935–1971.* Vol. 3. New York: Random House.

Gamson, W. 1975. *The Strategy of Social Protest.* Homewood, IL: Dorsey Press.

Ganz, M. 2000. "Resources and Resourcefulness: Strategic Capacity in the Unionization of California Agriculture, 1959–1966." *American Journal of Sociology* 105(4): 1003–1062.

———. 2009. *Why David Sometimes Wins: Leadership, Organization, and Strategy in the California Farm Worker Movement.* Oxford: Oxford University Press.

Giddens, A. 1979. *Central Problems in Social Theory: Action, Structure, and Contradiction in Social Analysis.* Berkeley: University of California Press.

———. 1984. *The Constitution of Society: Outline of the Theory of Structuration.* Berkeley: University of California Press.

———. 1990. *The Consequences of Modernity.* Stanford, CA: Stanford University Press.

Goffman, E. 1959. *The Presentation of Self in Everyday Life.* Garden City, NY: Doubleday.

———. 1963. *Stigma: Notes on the Management of Spoiled Identity.* Englewood Cliffs, NJ: Prentice-Hall.

———. 1974. *Frame Analysis: An Essay on the Organization of Experience.* Cambridge, MA: Harvard University Press.

Goldman, H. 1992. *Politics, Death and the Devil: Self and Power in Max Weber and Thomas Mann.* Berkeley: University of California Press.

Goldstein, A. and N. Fligstein. 2010. "The Rise and Fall of the Subprime Mortgage Securitization Industry, 1993–2009." Working Paper. Institute for Research on Labor and Employment. Berkeley, CA.

Goldstone, J. 2004. "More Social Movements or Fewer? Beyond Political Opportunity Structures to Relational Fields." *Theory and Society* 33: 333–365.

Gordon, David M. 1996. *Fat and Mean: The Corporate Squeeze of Working Americans and the Myth of Managerial "Downsizing."* New York: Free Press.

Gordon, Deborah M. 1999. *Ants at Work: How an Insect Society Is Organized.* New York: Free Press.

Gorski, P. 2003. *The Disciplinary Revolution: Calvinism and the Rise of the State in Early Modern Europe.* Chicago: University of Chicago Press.

Gould, R. 1991. "Multiple Networks and Mobilization in the Paris Commune, 1871." *American Sociological Review* 56(6): 716–729.

———. 1993. "Collective Action and Network Structure." *American Sociological Review* 58(2): 182–196.

———. 1995. *Insurgent Identities: Class, Community, and Protest in Paris from 1848 to the Commune.* Chicago: University of Chicago Press.

Granovetter, M. 1973. "The Strength of Weak Ties." *American Journal of Sociology* 78(6): 1360–1380.

Greene, K. 2007. "Understanding Spin-Off Movements: An Examination of the American Disability Rights Movement 1970–1995." Unpublished PhD Dissertation. Department of Sociology, Stanford University.

Greif. A. 2006. *Institutions and the Path to the Modern Economy: Lessons from Medieval Trade.* Cambridge, UK: Cambridge University Press.

Hall, P. and R. Taylor. 1996. "Political Science and the Three New Institutionalisms." *Political Studies* 44: 936–957.

Hannan M. and J. Freeman. 1977. "The Population Ecology of Organizations." *American Journal of Sociology* 82(5): 929–964.

———. 1984. "Structural Inertia and Organizational Change." *American Sociological Review* 49(2): 149–164.

Haveman, H. 1994. "The Ecological Dynamics of Organizational Change: Density and Mass Dependence in Rates of Entry into New Markets." Pp. 152–166 in J. Baum and J. Singh (eds.), *Evolutionary Dynamics of Organizations.* Oxford: Oxford University Press.

——— and H. Rao. 1997. "Structuring a Theory of Moral Sentiments: Institutional and Organizational Coevolution in the Early Thrift Industry." *American Journal of Sociology* 102(6): 1606–1651.

———, H. Rao, and S. Paruchuri. 2007. "The Winds of Change: The Progressive Movement and the Bureaucratization of Thrift." *American Sociological Review* 72(1): 117–142.

Hedman, E. 2006. *In the Name of Civil Society: From Free Election Movements to People Power.* Honolulu: University of Hawaii Press.

Honneth, A. 1995. *The Struggle for Recognition: The Moral Grammar of Social Conflicts.* Cambridge, MA: Polity Press.

Jacobides, M. 2005. "Industry Change through Vertical Disintegration: How and Why Markets Emerged in Mortgage Banking." *Academy of Management Journal* 48(3): 465–498.

Jasper, J. 2004. "A Strategic Approach to Collective Action: Looking for Agency in Social-Movement Choices." *Mobilization* 9(1): 1–16.

———. 2006. *Getting Your Way: Strategic Dilemmas in the Real World.* Chicago: University of Chicago Press.

Jenkins, J.C. and C. Eckert. 1986. "Channeling Black Insurgency: Elite Patronage and Professional Social Movement Organizations in the Development of the Black Movement." *American Sociological Review* 51(6): 812–829.

Jenson, J. and S. Phillips. 1996. "Regime Shift: New Citizenship Practices in Canada." *International Journal of Canadian Studies* 14: 111–135.

Jepperson, R. 1991. "Institutions, Institutional Effects, and Institutionalism." Pp. 143–163 in W. Powell and P. DiMaggio (eds.), *The New Institutionalism in Organizational Analysis.* Chicago: University of Chicago Press.

Joas, H. 1996. *The Creativity of Action.* Chicago: University of Chicago Press.

Johnson, N. 2002. "The Renaissance of Nationalism." Pp. 130–142 in R. Johnston, P. Taylor, and M. Watts (eds.), *Geographies of Global Change: Remapping the World.* Malden, MA: Blackwell.

Keat, R. and J. Urry. 1975. *Social Theory as Science.* London: Routledge and Kegan Paul.

Kendall, L. 1996. "Securitization: A New Era in American Finance." Pp. 1–16 in L. Kendall and M. Fishman (eds.), *A Primer on Securitization.* Cambridge, MA: MIT Press.

King, B. and S. Soule. 2007. "Social Movements as Extra-Institutional Entrepreneurs: The Effect of Protests on Stock Price Returns." *Administrative Science Quarterly* 52(3): 413–432.

Kingdon, J. 1995. *Agendas, Alternatives, and Public Policies.* New York: HarperCollins College Publishers.

Klein, R. 2002. *The Dawn of Human Culture.* New York: Wiley.

Krasner, S. 1988. "Sovereignty: An Institutional Perspective." *Comparative Political Studies* 21: 66–94.

——. 1995. "Compromising Westphalia." *International Security* 20(3): 115–151.

Krugman, P. 1991. "Increasing Returns and Economic Geography." *Journal of Political Economy* 99: 483–499.

Kuhn, T. 1962. *The Structure of Scientific Revolutions.* Chicago: University of Chicago Press.

Kurzman, C. 1998. "Organizational Opportunity and Social Movement Mobilization: A Comparative Analysis of Four Religious Movements." *Mobilization* 3(1): 23–49.

Laumann E. and D. Knoke. 1987. *The Organizational State: Social Choice in National Policy Domains.* Madison: University of Wisconsin Press.

Layton, A.S. 2000. *International Politics and Civil Rights Policies in the United States, 1941–1960.* Cambridge, UK: Cambridge University Press.

Leifer, E. 1988. "Interaction Preludes to Role Setting: Exploratory Local Action." *American Sociological Review* 53(6): 865–878.

——. 1995. *Making the Majors: The Transformation of Team Sports in America.* Cambridge, MA: Harvard University Press.

Lemann, N. 1991. *The Promised Land: The Great Black Migration and How It Changed America.* New York: Knopf.

Leslie, M. 2002. "Suddenly Smarter." *Stanford Magazine.* July/August.

Leuchtenburg, W. 2005. *The White House Looks South: Franklin D. Roosevelt, Harry S. Truman, Lyndon B. Johnson.* Baton Rouge: Louisiana State University Press.

Lévi-Strauss, C. 1966. *The Savage Mind.* Chicago: University of Chicago Press.

Levine, J. 2007. "The Vertical-Integration Strategy." *Mortgage Banking* 67: 58–65.

Lewin, K. 1951. *Field Theory in Social Science: Selected Theoretical Papers.* New York: Harper.

Lewis, M. 1990. *Liar's Poker: Rising through the Wreckage on Wall Street.* New York: Penguin Books.

Lomax, L. 1962. *The Negro Revolt.* New York: Harper and Row.

Lounsbury, M., M. Ventresca, and P. Hirsch. 2003. "Social Movements, Field Frames, and Industry Emergence: A Cultural-Political Perspective on U.S. Recycling." *Socio-Economic Review* 1(1): 71–104.

Lukes, S. 1974. *Power: A Radical View.* London: Macmillan.

Mahoney, J. and K. Thelen, eds. 2009. *Explaining Institutional Change: Ambiguity, Agency, and Power.* Cambridge, UK: Cambridge University Press.

Mann, M. 1986. *The Sources of Social Power, Volume 1: A History of Power from the Beginning to A.D. 1760.* Cambridge, UK: Cambridge University Press.

Marks, G. and D. McAdam. 1996. "Social Movements and the Changing Structure of Political Opportunity in the European Union." *West European Politics* 19: 249–278.

——. 1999. "On the Relationship of Political Opportunities to the Form of Collective Action: The Case of the European Union." Pp. 97–111 in D. della Porta, H. Kriesi, and D. Rucht (eds.), *Social Movements in a Globalizing World.* New York: St. Martin's Press.

Martin, J.L. 2003. "What Is Field Theory?" *American Journal of Sociology* 109(1): 1–49.

——. 2009. *Social Structures.* Princeton, NJ: Princeton University Press.

McAdam, D. 1988. *Freedom Summer.* New York: Oxford University Press.

——. 1995. "'Initiator' and 'Spin-off' Movements: Diffusion Processes in Protest Cycles." Pp. 217–239 in M. Traugott (ed.), *Repertoires and Cycles of Collective Action.* Durham, NC: Duke University Press.

——. 1999. *Political Process and the Development of Black Insurgency, 1930–1970.* 2nd edition. Chicago: University of Chicago Press.

——. 2007. "Legacies of Anti-Americanism: A Sociological Perspective." Pp. 251–269 in P. Katzenstein and R. Keohane (eds.), *Anti-Americanisms in World Politics.* Ithaca, NY: Cornell University Press.

—— and Boudet. 2012. *Putting Movements in Their Place: Explaining Variation in Community Response to the Siting of Energy Projects.* New York: Cambridge University Press.

—— and W.R. Scott. 2005. "Organizations and Movements." Pp. 4–40 in G. Davis, D. McAdam, W.R. Scott, and M. Zald (eds.), *Social Movements and Organization Theory.* Cambridge, UK: Cambridge University Press.

———, S. Tarrow, and C. Tilly. 2001. *Dynamics of Contention*. Cambridge, UK: Cambridge University Press.

McCammon, H. 2001. "Stirring Up Suffrage Sentiment: The Formation of the State Woman Suffrage Organizations, 1866–1914." *Social Forces* 80(2): 449–480.

McCarthy, J.D. and M. Zald. 1973. *The Trend of Social Movements in America: Professionalization and Resource Mobilization*. Morristown, NJ: General Learning Press.

———. 1977. "Resource Mobilization and Social Movements: A Partial Theory." *American Journal of Sociology* 82(6): 1212–1241.

McCullough, D. 1992. *Truman*. New York: Simon and Schuster.

McGrew, W.C. 1994. "Tools Compared: The Material of Culture." Pp. 25–39 in R. Wrangham, W.C. McGrew, F. de Waal, and P. Heltne (eds.), *Chimpanzee Cultures*. Cambridge, MA: Harvard University Press.

McLean, B. and P. Elkind. 2003. *The Smartest Guys in the Room: The Amazing Rise and Scandalous Fall of Enron*. New York: Portfolio.

Mead, G.H. 1934. *Mind, Self, and Society*. Chicago: University of Chicago Press.

Merrill Lynch. 2006. "Merrill Lynch Announces Agreement to Acquire First Franklin from National City Corporation." *Press Release*, September 5.

Meyer, D. and N. Whittier. 1994. "Social Movement Spillover." *Social Problems* 41: 277–298.

Meyer, J. and B. Rowan. 1977. "Institutionalized Organizations: Formal Structure as Myth and Ceremony." *American Journal of Sociology* 83(2): 340–363.

Meyer, J. and W.R. Scott. 1983. *Organizational Environments: Ritual and Rationality*. Beverly Hills, CA: Sage.

Meyer, J., W.R. Scott, and T. Deal. 1981. "Institutional and Technical Sources of Organizational Structure: Explaining the Structure of Educational Organizations." Pp. 151–179 in H. Stein (ed.), *Organization and the Human Services: Cross-Disciplinary Reflections*. Philadelphia: Temple University Press.

Midlarsky, M. and K. Roberts. 1985. "Class, State, and Revolution in Central America: Nicaragua and El Salvador Compared." *Journal of Conflict Resolution* 29(2): 163–193.

Minkoff, D. 1995. *Organizing for Equality: The Evolution of Women's and Racial-Ethnic Organizations in America, 1955–1985*. New Brunswick, NJ: Rutgers University Press.

Morgan Stanley. 2006. "Morgan Stanley to Acquire Residential Mortgage Servicer and Originator Saxon Capital for $706 million." *Press Release*, August 9, 2006.

Moore, K. and N. Hala. 2002. "Organizing Identity: The Creation of Science for the People." Pp. 309–335 in M. Lounsbury and M.J. Ventresca (eds.), *Social Structure and Organizations Revisited* (Research in the Sociology of Organizations 8). Bradford, UK: Emerald Group.

Morrill, C., M. Zald, and H. Rao. 2003. "Covert Political Conflict in Organizations: Challenges from Below." *Annual Review of Sociology* 29: 391–415.

Morris, A. 1984. *The Origins of the Civil Rights Movement: Black Communities Organizing for Change*. New York: Free Press.

Myrdal, G. 1970. "America Again at the Crossroads." Pp. 13–46 in R. Young (ed.), *Roots of Rebellion: The Evolution of Black Politics and Protest Since World War II*. New York: Harper and Row.

Nagel, J. 1995. "American Indian Ethnic Renewal: Politics and the Resurgence of Identity." *American Sociological Review* 60(6): 947–965.

Nagel, T. 1986. *The View from Nowhere*. Oxford: Oxford University Press.

Nee, V. and P. Ingram. 1998. "Embeddedness and Beyond: Institutions, Exchange, and Social Structure." Pp. 19–45 in M. Brinton and V. Nee (eds.), *The New Institutionalism in Sociology*. New York: Russell Sage.

Nelson, R. and S. Winter. 1982. *An Evolutionary Theory of Economic Change*. Cambridge, MA: Belknap Press of Harvard University.

Nietzsche, Friedrich. 1988. *Kritische Studienausgabe*. Edited by Giorgio Colli and Mazzino Montinari. Munich: Deutscher Taschenbuch Verlag.

Nyberg, D. 1993. *The Varnished Truth: Truth Telling and Deceiving in Ordinary Life*. Chicago: University of Chicago Press.

Olson, M. 1965. *The Logic of Collective Action: Public Goods and the Theory of Groups*. Cambridge, MA: Harvard University Press.

Orum, A. 1972. *Black Students in Protest: A Study of the Origins of the Black Student Movement*. Washington, DC: American Sociological Association.

Osa, M. 1997. "Creating Solidarity: The Religious Foundations of the Polish Social Movement." *East European Politics and Societies* 11: 339–365.

Padgett, J. and C. Ansell. 1993. "Robust Action and the Rise of the Medici, 1400–1434." *American Journal of Sociology* 98(6): 1259–1319.

Passy, F. 2003. "Social Networks Matter. But How?" Pp. 21–48 in M. Diani and D. McAdam (eds.), *Social Movements and Networks: Relational Approaches to Collective Action*. Oxford: Oxford University Press.

———. 2000. "Increasing Returns, Path Dependence, and the Study of Politics." *American Political Science Review* 94(2): 251–267.

———. 2004. *Politics in Time: History, Institutions, and Social Analysis*. Princeton, NJ: Princeton University Press.

Powell, W. 1991. "Expanding the Scope of Institutional Analysis." Pp. 183–203 in W. Powell and P. DiMaggio (eds.), *The New Institutionalism in Organizational Analysis*. Chicago: University of Chicago Press.

——— and P. DiMaggio, eds. 1991. *The New Institutionalism in Organizational Analysis*. Chicago: University of Chicago Press.

———, D. White, K. Koput, and J. Owen-Smith. 2005. "Network Dynamics and Field Evolution: The Growth of Interorganizational Collaboration in the Life Sciences." *American Journal of Sociology* 110(4): 1132–1205.

Quinn, S. 2008. "Securitization and the State." Paper presented at the 103rd Annual Meeting of the American Sociological Association. Boston, MA, August.

———. 2010. "Government Policy, Housing, and the Origins of Securitization, 1780–1968." Unpublished PhD Dissertation. Department of Sociology, University of California, Berkeley.

Ranieri, L. 1996. "The Origins of Securitization, Sources of Its Growth, and Its Future Potential." Pp. 31–44 in L. Kendall and M. Fishman (eds.), *A Primer on Securitization*. Cambridge, MA: MIT Press.

Rao, H. 2009. *Market Rebels: How Activists Make or Break Radical Innovations*. Princeton, NJ: Princeton University Press.

———, P. Monin, and R. Durand. 2003. "Institutional Change in Toque Ville: Nouvelle Cuisine as an Identity Movement in French Gastronomy." *American Journal of Sociology* 108(4): 795–843.

———, C. Morrill, and M. Zald. 2000. "Power Plays: How Social Movements and Collective Action Create New Organizational Forms." *Research in Organizational Behavior* 22: 237–281.

Rosenberg, H. 1958. *Bureaucracy, Aristocracy, and Autocracy: The Prussian Experience, 1660–1815*. Cambridge, MA: Harvard University Press.

Sabatier, P., ed. 2007. *Theories of the Policy Process*. Boulder, CO: Westview Press.

Sallaz, J. and J. Zavisca. 2007. "Bourdieu in American Sociology, 1980–2004." *Annual Review of Sociology* 33: 21–41.

Scharpf, F. 1997. *Games Real Actors Play: Actor-Centered Institutionalism in Policy Research*. Boulder, CO: Westview Press.

Schattschneider, E. 1960. *The Semisovereign People: A Realist's View of Democracy in America*. New York: Holt, Rinehart and Winston.

Schneiberg, M. and S. Soule. 2005. "Institutionalization as a Contested, Multilevel Process: The Case of Rate Regulation in American Fire Insurance." Pp. 122–160 in G. Davis, D. McAdam, W.R. Scott, and M. Zald (eds.), *Social Movements and Organization Theory*. Cambridge, UK: Cambridge University Press.

Scott, J. 1985. *Weapons of the Weak: Everyday Forms of Peasant Resistance*. New Haven, CT: Yale University Press.

———. 1990. *Domination and the Arts of Resistance: Hidden Transcripts*. New Haven, CT: Yale University Press.

Scott, W.R. 2001. *Institutions and Organizations*. 2nd edition. Thousand Oaks, CA: Sage.

—— and J. Meyer. 1983. "The Organization of Societal Sectors." Pp. 129–153 in J. Meyer and W.R. Scott (eds.), *Organizational Environments: Ritual and Rationality*. Beverly Hills, CA: Sage.

——, M. Ruef, P. Mendel, and C. Caronna. 2000. *Institutional Change and Healthcare Organizations: From Professional Dominance to Managed Care*. Chicago: University of Chicago Press.

Selbin, Eric. 1993. *Modern Latin American Revolutions*. Boulder, CO: Westview Press.

Sellon, G, Jr. and D. VanNahmen. 1988. "The Securitization of Housing Finance." *Economic Review* 73(7): 3–20.

Sewell, W. 1992. "A Theory of Structure: Duality, Agency, and Transformation." *American Journal of Sociology* 98(1): 1–29.

Simmel, G. 1955. *Conflict and the Web of Group-Affiliations*. New York: Free Press.

Sitkoff, H. 1978. *A New Deal for Blacks: The Emergence of Civil Rights as a National Issue*. New York: Oxford University Press.

Skocpol, T. 1979. *States and Social Revolutions: A Comparative Analysis of France, Russia, and China*. Cambridge, UK: Cambridge University Press.

Skrentny, J.D. 1996. *The Ironies of Affirmative Action: Politics, Culture, and Justice in America*. Chicago: University of Chicago Press.

——. 2002. *The Minority Rights Revolution*. Cambridge, MA: Belknap Press of Harvard University.

Snow, D. and R. Benford. 1988. "Ideology, Frame Resonance, and Participant Mobilization." Pp. 197–218 in B. Klandermans, H. Kriesi, and S. Tarrow (eds.), *From Structure to Action: Comparing Social Movement Research Across Cultures (International Social Movement Research, Volume 1)*. Greenwich, CT: JAI Press.

Snow, D., E.B. Rochford, S. Worden, and R. Benford. 1986. "Frame Alignment Processes, Micromobilization, and Movement Participation." *American Sociological Review* 51(4): 464–481.

Smith, J. 2002. "Bridging Global Divides? Strategic Framing and Solidarity in Transnational Social Movement Organizations." *International Sociology* 17(4): 505–528.

Spruyt, H. 1996. *The Sovereign State and Its Competitors: An Analysis of Systems Change*. Princeton, NJ: Princeton University Press.

Starr, P. 1982. *The Social Transformation of American Medicine: The Rise of a Sovereign Profession and the Making of a Vast Industry*. New York: Basic Books.

Steinmo, S., K. Thelen, and F. Longstreth, eds. 1992. *Structuring Politics: Historical Institutionalism in Comparative Analysis*. Cambridge, UK: Cambridge University Press.

Strang, D. and S. Soule. 1998. "Diffusion in Organizations and Social Movements: From Hybrid Corn to Poison Pills." *Annual Review of Sociology* 24: 265–290.

Stryker, R. 1994. "Rules, Resources, and Legitimacy Processes: Some Implications for Social Conflict, Order, and Change." *American Journal of Sociology* 99(4): 847–910.

Swaminathan, A. and J. Wade. 2001. "Social Movement Theory and the Evolution of New Organizational Forms." Pp. 286–313 in C.B. Schoonhoven and E. Romanelli (eds.), *The Entrepreneurship Dynamic: Origins of Entrepreneurship and the Evolution of Industries*. Stanford, CA: Stanford University Press.

Tarrow, S. 2011. *Power in Movement: Social Movements and Contentious Politics*. 3rd edition. Cambridge, UK: Cambridge University Press.

Tattersall, I. 1998. *Becoming Human: Evolution and Human Uniqueness*. New York: Harcourt Brace.

Thelen, K. 2004. *How Institutions Evolve: The Political Economy of Skills in Germany, Britain, the United States, and Japan*. Cambridge, UK: Cambridge University Press.

Tilly, C., ed. 1975. *The Formation of National States in Western Europe*. Princeton, NJ: Princeton University Press.

——. 1978. *From Mobilization to Revolution*. Reading, MA: Addison-Wesley.

Uzzi, B. 1996. "The Sources and Consequences of Embeddedness for the Economic Performance of Organizations: The Network Effect." *American Sociological Review* 61(4): 674–698.

Vaisey, S. 2009. "Motivation and Justification: A Dual-Process Model of Culture in Action." *American Journal of Sociology* 114(6): 1675–1715.

Valocchi, S. 2001. "Individual Identities, Collective Identities, and Organizational Structure: The Relationship of the Political Left and Gay Liberation in the United States." *Sociological Perspectives* 44(4): 445–467.

Wagner-Pacifici, R. 2000. *Theorizing the Standoff: Contingency in Action.* Cambridge, UK: Cambridge University Press.

Walder, A. 2009a. *Fractured Rebellion: The Beijing Red Guard Movement.* Cambridge, MA: Harvard University Press.

———. 2009b. "Political Sociology and Social Movements." *Annual Review of Sociology* 35: 393–412.

Wall Street Journal. 1969. "Ginnie Mae Offers First Mortgage Backed Bond." April 24.

Weber, K., H. Rao, and L.G. Thomas. 2009. "From Streets to Suites: How the Anti-Biotech Movement Affected German Pharmaceutical Firms." *American Sociological Review* 74(1): 106–127.

Weber, M. 1949. *The Methodology of the Social Sciences.* Glencoe, IL: Free Press.

Weber, M. 1978. *Economy and Society: An Outline of Interpretive Sociology.* Berkeley: University of California Press.

White, H. 1981. "Where Do Markets Come From?" *American Journal of Sociology* 87(3): 517–547.

———. 1992. *Identity and Control: A Structural Theory of Social Action.* Princeton, NJ: Princeton University Press.

———. 2004. *Markets from Networks: Socioeconomic Models of Production.* Princeton, NJ: Princeton University Press.

Wickham-Crowley, T. 1989. "Understanding Failed Revolution in El Salvador: A Comparative Analysis of Regime Types and Social Structures." *Politics and Society* 17: 511–530.

———. 1992. *Guerrillas and Revolution in Latin America: A Comparative Study of Insurgents and Regimes since 1956.* Princeton, NJ: Princeton University Press.

Wrong, D. 1961. "The Oversocialized Conception of Man in Modern Sociology." *American Sociological Review* 26(2): 183–193.

Yearbook of the Mortgage Market. 2009. Bethesda, MD: Inside Mortgage Finance Publications.

Zald, M. and R. Ash. 1966. "Social Movement Organizations: Growth, Decay and Change." *Social Forces* 44(3): 327–340.

Zald, M. and J. McCarthy, eds. 1987. *Social Movements in an Organizational Society: Collected Essays.* New Brunswick, NJ: Transaction Books.

Zhao, S. 1998. "A State-Led Nationalism: The Patriotic Education Campaign in Post-Tiananmen China." *Communist and Post-Communist Studies* 31(3): 287–302.

———. 2004. *A Nation-State by Construction: Dynamics of Modern Chinese Nationalism.* Stanford, CA: Stanford University Press.

Zorn, D. 2004. "Here a Chief, There a Chief: The Rise of the CFO in the American Firm." *American Sociological Review* 69(3): 345–364.

INDEX